Spotlight on First

Exam Booster Workbook

Second Edition

Alastair Lane

NATIONAL GEOGRAPHIC LEARNING | CENGAGE Learning

Australia • Brazil • Japan • Korea • Mexico • Singapore • Spain • United Kingdom • United States

NATIONAL GEOGRAPHIC LEARNING | **CENGAGE Learning**

**Spotlight on First Exam Booster Workbook
With Key (2nd Edition)**

Alastair Lane

Publisher: Gavin McLean

Publishing Consultant: Karen Spiller

Freelance Editor: Jess Rackham

Marketing Manager: Charlotte Ellis

Content Project Manager: Tom Relf

Manufacturing Buyer: Eyvett Davis

Head of Production: Alissa McWhinnie

Cover design: Oliver Hutton

Original page design: Oxford Designers & Illustrators/
   MPS Limited

Compositor: MPS Limited

National Geographic Liaison:
   Wesley Della Volla

Practice Test: Helen Chilton

Audio production: Tom Dick and Debbie Productions

ISBN: 978-1-285-84950-8

National Geographic Learning
Cheriton House, North Way, Andover, Hampshire, SP10 5BE
United Kingdom

Cengage Learning is a leading provider of customized learning solutions with office locations around the globe, including Singapore, the United Kingdom, Australia, Mexico, Brazil and Japan. Locate your local office at:
international.cengage.com/region

Cengage Learning products are represented in Canada by Nelson Education, Ltd.

Visit National Geographic Learning online at **ngl.cengage.com**
Visit our corporate website at **www.cengage.com**

Credits

Although every effort has been made to contact copyright holders before publication, this has not always been possible. If contacted, the publisher will undertake to rectify errors or omissions at the earliest opportunity.

Cover photo: Andrew Watson/Getty Images.

Inside photos: pp 7 tl (Aletia/Shutterstock), 7 ct (Solominviktor/Shutterstock), 7 cb (Andrew Lever/Shutterstock), 7 bl (Sergey Peterman/Shutterstock), 8 (imagebroker/Alamy), 10 (Alexander Raths/Shutterstock), 11 (Minerva Studio/Shutterstock), 12 (Hiya Images/Corbis), 13 (Martin Heitner/Alamy), 15 (hassedesign.com/Elliot Hasse), 16 (Farmpix/Alamy), 20 (Ocean/Corbis UK Ltd), 23 (Urban Myth/Alamy), 24 (Sport Fotos Magdeburg), 28 (ZUMA Press, Inc./Alamy), 29 t (Alfred Abad/Age Fotostock/Alamy), 29 b (Joel Saget/AFP/Getty Images), 31 (John Foxx Images/Imagestate/NGSP), 34 (Steve Davey Photography/Alamy), 37 t (David De Lossy/Photodisc/Getty Images), 37 b (Adie Bush/Cultura/Getty Images), 39 (Image Asset Management Ltd./Alamy), 40 (Scott Macmillan/Alamy), 43 (JH Photo/Alamy), 45 (Monkey Business Images/Shutterstock), 47 (Asaf Eliason/Shutterstock), 48 (P Phillips/Shutterstock), 51 (fStop/Alamy), 52 (Alex Segre/Alamy), 55 (Stephane de Sakutin/AFP/Getty Images), 56 (Bournemouth News/Rex Features), 58 (Masatoshi Okauchi/Rex Features), 60 (Moviestore Collection Ltd/Alamy), 63 (Melanie Stetson Freeman/The Christian Science Monitor/Getty Images), 67 (Alex Segre/Alamy), 69, 5b (Hero Images/Getty Images), 71 (Glasgow University Library, Scotland/Bridgeman Art Library), 72 (Blend Images LLC/Corbis UK Ltd), 74 (Felix Man/Getty Images), 77 (Stockbroker/Alamy), 79 (dpa picture alliance/Alamy), 80 (Alex Segre/Alamy), 83 (Anton Gvozdikov/Shutterstock), 85 t (dotshock/Shutterstock), 85 b (Digital Vision/Photodisc/Getty Images), 87 (Tyler Olson/Shutterstock), 88 (Paul Maguire/Fotolia), 89 r (Dima Sobko/Shutterstock), 90 (Tino Soriano/Getty Images), 92 (Chris Rout/Alamy), 93 l, 5 tl (John Lund/Blend Images/Getty Images), 93 r, 5 tr (Julie Edwards/Alamy), 95 (M. Timothy O'Keefe/Alamy), 97 (World Foto/Alamy), 98 (Gary Weber/AFP/Getty Images), 99 (John T. Barr/Hulton Archive/Getty Images), 100 (Paul Doyle/Alamy), 101 t (Geoffrey Welsh/Alamy), 101 b (Phil Dent/Red Ferns/Getty Images), 103 (David J. Green - lifestyle themes/Alamy), 104 (Viktoria/Shutterstock), 106 (vichie81/Shutterstock), 109 (Tony Hutchings/The Image Bank/Getty Images), 111 (micro10x/Shutterstock), 112 (Andreas Rentz/Getty Images), 116 l (Fine Art/Corbis), 116 r (Corey Ford/Stocktrek Images/Getty Images), 119 (Barry Lewis/Alamy), 122 (George Blonsky/Alamy), 124 (Johannes Simon/Getty Images News/Getty Images), 125 l (Iain Crockart/Photodisc/Getty Images), 125 r (Bill Bachman/Alamy), 145 tl (VIEW Pictures Ltd/Alamy), 145 tr (Roger Bamber/Alamy), 145 bl (charistoone-travel/Alamy), 145 br (Tom Ferguson/Alamy).

Illustrations: 9 (Mark Draisey), 17 (Piet Luthi), 21 (Paul Cemmick), 26 a_d (Kathrin Jacobsen), 32 (Paul Cemmick), 41 a_f (Mark Draisey), 44 (Marco Shaaf/NB Illustration), 48 (Piet Luthi), 50 a_f (Kathrin Jacobsen), 59 a_f (Adrian Braclay/Beehive Illustration), 64 (Mark Draisey), 89 l (Mark Draisey), 96 (Piet Luthi), 107 (Mark Draisey), 112 t (Cengage Learning), 113 (Mark Draisey), 121 (Mark Draisey).

Text: Wright's Media for material adapted from '13 Recruiters Share The Weirdest Job Applications They've Ever Received' by Aimee Groth, 6 February 2012 and '12 Of The Coolest, Most Creative Resumes We've Seen' by Melissa Stanger and Vivian Giang, 28 September 2012: http://www.businessinsider.com. Copyrighted 2014. Business Insider, Inc. 107488:114DS; Telegraph Media Group Ltd for extracts adapted from 'My great escape from the jaws of a big saltie' by Nick Squires, The Telegraph, 10 January 2007; 'It felt like being trapped in a dark cave, says diver "swallowed" by a great white shark' by Nick Squires, The Telegraph, 25 January 2007; '£60,000 a year, and all you've got to do is zap the bad guys' by Nic Fleming, The Telegraph, 3 July 2006; 'How handbags became a girl's best friend' by David Derbyshire, 17 March 2006; and 'Genghis Khan, law giver, free trader and diplomat, is back with a new image' by Richard Spencer, The Telegraph, 11 July 2006, copyright © Telegraph Media Group Limited 2006, 2007.

Printed in China by RR Donnelley
Print Number: 02   Print Year: 2014

Contents

Overview of the exam

The *Cambridge English: First* (FCE) examination is an exam at B2 level of the Common European Framework. It consists of four papers. Grades A, B and C represent a pass grade. Grades D and E are a fail. It is not necessary to achieve a satisfactory grade in all four papers in order to receive a final passing grade.

PAPER 1 (1 HOUR 15 MINUTES)

Reading and Use of English

- Seven parts (a variety of texts and comprehension tasks).
- You must answer all seven parts.
- 52 questions in total. (You have 1 hour 15 minutes.)
- You receive one mark for each correct answer in Parts 1, 2 and 3, up to two marks for each correct answer in Part 4, two marks for each answer in Parts 5 and 6, and one mark for each correct answer in Part 7.

Use of English

Part 1: Multiple-choice cloze
This is a cloze test with eight gaps and four possible options for each one.

Part 2: Open cloze
This is a cloze test with eight gaps. You complete each gap with one word.

Part 3: Word formation
You read a text with eight gaps. There is a word-stem after each gap. You must change the form of the word and complete the gap.

Part 4: Key-word transformations
There are six questions. Each question has a lead-in sentence. Then a key word is given. You must use this word in a second gapped sentence so that it has the same meaning as the first.

Reading

Part 5: Multiple choice
You read a text and answer six multiple choice questions. Each question has four possible answers (A, B, C or D).

Part 6: Gapped text
You complete a text with six missing sentences. There is one extra sentence which you should not use.

Part 7: Multiple matching
You read one or more texts (often four shorter texts) and match prompts to parts of the whole text. There are ten prompts.

PAPER 1

See the following pages for Paper 1 exam tasks:

Part 1 19, 33, 43, 67, 83, 91, 99, 107

Part 2 11, 43, 51, 67, 76, 99, 107

Part 3 11, 19, 27, 36, 59, 91, 115, 123

Part 4 27, 51, 61, 76, 83, 115, 123

Part 5 14, 38, 86, 102, 110

Part 6 22, 54, 70, 94, 118

Part 7 6, 30, 46, 62, 78

PAPER 2 (1 HOUR 20 MINUTES)

Writing

- Two parts.
- You must answer both parts.
- Two questions to answer in total. (You have 1 hour 20 minutes.)
- You receive equal marks for each question.

Part 1: An essay
This part has one question and you must answer it. You read an essay title and respond, using notes, with an essay giving your opinion. Your answer must be 140–190 words (or 120–180 words in the Cambridge English: First (FCE) for Schools exam).

Part 2: An article, an email or letter, a report, a review or a story
This part has three or four possible questions and you answer one only with 140–190 words (or 120–180 words in the Cambridge English: First (FCE) for Schools exam).
Questions 2–4 can ask you to write an article, an informal letter or email, a report or a review. You read about a situation and then write a response using the correct type of text.
In the Cambridge English: First (FCE) for Schools exam, students may also be given the option to write a story in Part 2, or answer a question based upon the set reading text (optional).

PAPER 2

See the following pages for Paper 2 exam tasks:

Part 1 12, 20, 34, 84, 100

Part 2 28, 44, 52, 60, 68, 74, 92, 108, 116, 124

PAPER 3 (APPROXIMATELY 40 MINUTES)

Listening

- Four parts.
- You must answer all four parts.
- 30 questions in total (approximately 40 minutes).
- You receive one mark for each correct answer in all four parts.
- Text types: you hear four different sets of recordings (*monologues* or *interacting speakers*).

Monologues could include answerphone messages, radio broadcasts and features, public announcements, news, lectures, reports, speeches, advertisements and stories. *Interacting speakers* could include conversations, radio plays, interviews and discussions. After you listen, you have five minutes to write your answers onto the answer sheet.

Part 1: Multiple choice
You listen to eight short unconnected recordings. Each one is about 30 seconds long. For each recording you answer a question with three answers to choose from.

Part 2: Sentence completion
You listen to a monologue. It lasts about three to four minutes. You have to complete ten sentences with words you hear on the recording.

Part 3: Multiple matching
There are five short recordings and you match five questions to the correct option. There are eight possible options.

Part 4: Multiple choice
You listen to a longer text with two speakers. You have seven questions and each one has three options to choose from.

PAPER 3

See the following pages for Paper 3 exam tasks:

Part 1 10, 18, 50, 82, 114

Part 2 26, 58, 90, 106

Part 3 35, 66, 75, 122

Part 4 42, 98

PAPER 4 (APPROXIMATELY 14 MINUTES)

Speaking

- Four parts.
- You must answer all four parts.
- You take the Speaking test with another candidate. In certain circumstances, you may take the Speaking test in a group of three.
- The interlocutor (examiner talking to you) asks you questions and gives you prompts (pictures and words) which you may have to talk about or discuss with the other person.
- You are assessed on your performance throughout.

Part 1: Conversation between interlocutor and each candidate (asking and answering)
This is general interactional and social language – a conversation between the interlocutor and each candidate. You will answer questions on topics such as home, family and personal interests. This part will last approximately two minutes.

Part 2: An individual 'long turn' for each candidate with a short response from the second candidate
You look at two photographs and the interlocutor asks you to talk about them (describing, comparing and giving an opinion). The other candidate listens, then has to respond at the end of your talk. Each candidate's turn should last approximately one minute, with a further 20 seconds given for the other candidate to respond and comment on what you have said. This part will last approximately four minutes.

Part 3: A two-way conversation between the candidates, with a decision-making task
Both candidates are given spoken instructions with written stimuli. You work together in a collaborative task (exchanging ideas, expressing opinions, agreeing and/or disagreeing, speculating, suggesting, evaluating, reaching a decision through negotiation). Your discussion should last two minutes followed by a one-minute decision making task. This part will last approximately four minutes in total.

Part 4: A discussion on topics related to the collaborative (Part 3) task
The interlocutor now joins in the discussion (from Part 3) and asks further questions to each candidate so that it is a three-way conversation lasting four minutes. The focus here is expressing and justifying opinions, and agreeing and/or disagreeing.

PAPER 4

See the following pages for Paper 4 exam tasks:

Part 1 13

Part 2 29, 36, 85, 93, 125

Part 3 21, 45, 53, 61, 69, 77, 101

Part 4 109, 114

1 Friends and family

☐ I know words to describe family, page 8.

☐ I know some phrasal verbs for describing relationships, page 8.

☐ I know how to use the present simple and present continuous, page 9.

☐ I know how to use the present perfect simple and present perfect continuous, page 9.

☐ I know how to change -ic adjectives to adverbs, page 10.

☐ I know how to use intonation in questions, page 13.

EXAM CHECKLIST

☐ I have practised the multiple matching question from the Reading and Use of English paper, page 6.

☐ I have practised the multiple choice question from the Listening paper, page 10.

☐ I have practised the word formation question from the Reading and Use of English paper, page 11.

☐ I have practised the open cloze question from the Reading and Use of English paper, page 11.

☐ I have practised the essay from the Writing paper, page 12.

☐ I have practised the opening conversation from the Speaking paper, page 13.

Reading and Use of English

MULTIPLE MATCHING: PAPER 1, PART 7

1 **You are going to read an article about a family choosing a name for a baby. For questions 1–10 choose from the people (A–D). The people may be chosen more than once.**

Which person

1 does not like their name? ___

2 is not concerned about other people's opinion of the name? ___

3 wants to make a change from tradition? ___

4 had trouble because of their name? ___

5 is happy to give the baby a name which doesn't come from their own country? ___

6 doesn't suggest a name for the baby? ___

7 says their name is not very modern? ___

8 wants the baby to have the first name of another family member? ___

9 has changed their opinion of the name because of a recent decision? ___

10 has a name which is not understood in other countries? ___

2 **Now read the text again and find words that mean the following:**

1 pregnant (introductory paragraph) _____

2 a difficult decision (introductory paragraph) _____

3 the history and culture of a nation or people (paragraph A)

   _____

4 very pleased or excited (paragraph A) _____

5 to other countries (paragraph B) _____

6 when people attack or laugh at someone in an unkind way (paragraph C)

   _____

7 almost (paragraph D) _____

8 become an adult (paragraph D) _____

The Name Game

Steven and Maria have been married for two years and now Maria is expecting their first child. They know the baby will be a boy, but now they have a dilemma which is very familiar to couples who come from different countries. Steven is from Scotland and Maria from Greece, and they have to decide whether to give their baby a British or a Greek name. We spoke to Steven's family in Inverness and Maria's family in Thessaloniki.

A Dimitra, Maria's mother

Of course I'm just happy that I'll be a grandmother! Maria is my only child. My husband was from a different generation and his parents were very proud of our Greek heritage, so they gave him the name Aristotélos. He was a wonderful man and I've been a widow for ten years now, so I'd be thrilled if they named the baby after his grandfather. It would be a bit unusual though because, here in Greece, we normally give the first-born baby a name from the father's side of the family.

B Hamish, Steven's brother

Steven and Maria said that they think the baby needs to have a name that works in both countries, something very international. I personally don't think that should be a big issue. Take my name: it's very common here in Scotland, but when I go overseas, people don't understand it because they've never heard it before. But that's only a problem when you meet people. I'm Scottish and I'm proud I have a Scottish name. I think they should just choose a name that's interesting.

C Hilary, Steven's uncle

It's always a problem naming a baby and everyone has an opinion. But I can only give my personal experience. My parents gave me a name that's quite old-fashioned and could be a man or a woman's name, and I've never been fond of it. I had a lot of bullying when I was at school because of it. So that's what they have to be most careful about. What's wrong with James or John? They're common names.

D Maria

Everybody keeps asking me what name I'm going to give my baby and I just don't know what to do. Practically everyone I know has suggested a name to me, except Steven! He's as worried as I am. Originally, I was worried because our plan was to live in Britain and I was worried that the baby wouldn't know about his own culture. Luckily, Steven has just found a job in Athens and I now know our child will grow up here in Greece. So, I think it would be fine for him to have a British name, if we can think of a nice one. I have told Steven though that we must give the baby Aristotélos as a middle name. That's very important for my family.

Vocabulary

FAMILY

1 Complete the crossword.

Across

2 This is someone you are going to marry.

5 Your _ _ _ _ -brother or _ _ _ _ -sister shares one parent with you.

7 This is a formal word for the person you are married to: it could be a man or a woman.

9 These are all the members of your family: grandparents, uncles, aunts, etc.

10 Two children born on the same day to the same mother.

11 The son or daughter of your uncle and aunt.

Down

1 If you have no brothers or sisters, you are an only _____.

3 When you talk about your family, including all the grandparents, uncles, aunts, etc. that do not live with you, you talk about your _____ family.

4 A formal word for children.

6 Your brothers and sisters.

7 If a woman is married to your father, but she is not your real mother, she is your _ _ _ _ -mother.

8 Your son is married to your daughter-in- _ _ _ .

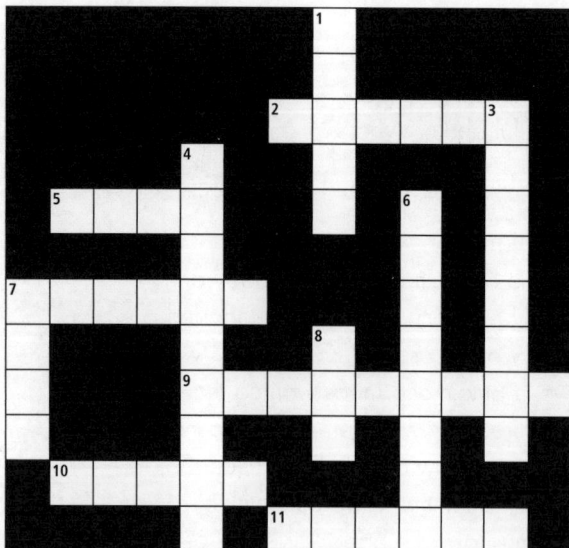

DESCRIBING RELATIONSHIPS

2 Complete the phrasal verbs in the blog with the words from the box.

after   back   by   down   into   on   out   up   with

Crisis on the Skeleton Coast

What a week! It started in disaster but in the end everything was OK, thanks to my friend Naomi.

I work for a company which run tours in Namibia. We fly over the Skeleton Coast. Unfortunately, this month, the airline company let us [1]_____.

The company is run by a couple, Fritz and Susan, and it has not been a success. Well, they fell [2]_____ over the bills. They had a huge argument and Susan decided to break up [3]_____ Fritz. When their relationship ended, Susan left the business and that was bad news for me. They are our two pilots!

We needed two planes but now we could only provide one. We were looking [4]_____ a large group of tourists and they would be extremely angry. They pay a lot of money for these tours and they would not put [5]_____ with such bad service.

I didn't know what to do, and then I ran [6]_____ Naomi in a restaurant. She works for a rival company but she and I get [7]_____ really well. We started in the same company about ten years ago. In the beginning, I had lots of problems, but Naomi always stood [8]_____ me. So I asked her for help . . . and she said 'yes'! Isn't 'yes' the best word in the English language?

Naomi arranged for her company's planes to run one of the tours. She saved the day! In fact, I think that now she and I may start our own company. Susan and Fritz will not get [9]_____ together, so I think my present company does not have a future. What do you think? Maybe it's time for a change?

Grammar

PRESENT TENSES

1 <u>Underline</u> the correct form of the verb.

1 Our children *grow up / are growing up* really fast.

2 On Sundays the whole family *eats / is eating* lunch together.

3 The situation *changes / is changing* dramatically at the moment.

4 My son-in-law *speaks / is speaking* English, French and German.

5 *Do you usually send / Are you usually sending* your grandmother a present on Mother's Day?

6 Andrea isn't here because *she plays / she is playing* with her nieces in the garden.

7 Statistically, families *get / are getting* smaller.

2 Complete the sentences with the verb in brackets. Decide if the verb is being used as a state or a dynamic verb.

1 My aunt _____ a house in London and another in the South of France. (own)

2 We _____ of sending the children to a language school this summer. (think)

3 She _____ that you know the answer. (not / believe)

4 You can't use the bathroom because Denise _____ a shower. (have)

5 I _____ Francesco's new girlfriend. (like)

6 I love your lemon cheesecake. It _____ great! (taste)

SPOTLIGHT ON STUDY TECHNIQUES

A learner's dictionary such as the Collins Cobuild will give you a lot of information about verbs. It can tell you if the verb is transitive or intransitive, and it can also tell you if the verb is a state verb. State verbs are usually identified with an instruction such as 'not used in the progressive tenses'.

State verbs tend to be verbs of the mind or thinking: *think, know, remember, forget.*

They also cover possession: *have, own, possess.*

Verbs of the senses are also typically state verbs: *taste, smell, sound,* etc.

PRESENT PERFECT SIMPLE AND PRESENT PERFECT CONTINUOUS

3 Look at the pictures of Rachel. They show recent activities. Write sentences using the words in brackets and the present perfect or present perfect continuous.

1 _____ (write / five letters)

2 _____ (jog)

3 _____ (clean / house)

4 _____ (break / a plate)

5 _____ (make / cake)

6 _____ (work /computer)

Spelling

Changing -ic adjectives to adverbs
When an adjective ends in -ic, you make the adverb by adding -ally to the ending. Note that the adverb is spelt -ll-.
Example: dramatic ➡ dramatically

1 **Complete the sentences by changing the adjectives in the box into adverbs.**

economic genetic logic periodic
sympathetic tragic

1 My uncle doesn't visit all the time, but he comes here
_____.

2 _____, my grandfather died of malaria when he was just 38.

3 If x + 7 = 20, _____ x must be 13.

4 _____, the country looks good: unemployment is low and there are lots of jobs.

5 Many people buy organic vegetables because they are worried about _____ modified food.

6 If you are a doctor, you need to listen
_____ to your patients' problems.

Listening: friends and family

MULTIPLE CHOICE: PAPER 3, PART 1

1 🎧 1.1 **You will hear eight people talking about their family and friends. For questions 1–8, choose the best answer (A, B, or C). Remember to listen to the recording twice.**

1 You hear two friends meeting. Where are they?
  A in a restaurant
  B in a shop
  C at the cinema

2 You hear a girl talking about her evening. Who is she looking after?
  A her brothers and sisters
  B her cousins
  C the children of her friends

3 You hear a man talking about a friend. Why did he argue with his friend?
  A His friend was laughing at him.
  B His friend broke his sunglasses.
  C His friend never phones him.

4 You hear a woman talking about her marriage plans. Who is she marrying?
  A a soldier
  B an accountant
  C a doctor

5 You hear a woman talking to her neighbour. What is the problem?
  A He has lost some money.
  B He is worried about work.
  C He can't get into his house.

6 You hear a woman talking about her family. What does she say about her brother?
  A He is very good looking.
  B He looks different from everyone else in the family.
  C He is the only person in the family who has lived abroad.

7 You hear a boy talking about his brothers. What does he say about them?
  A They have a different mother from him.
  B They are twins.
  C They are younger than him.

8 You hear a man talking about his wife. Where did he meet her?
  A at school
  B at work
  C at a party

Reading and Use of English

1 **Read the text below. Use the word given in capitals at the end of some of the lines to form a word that fits in the gap in the same line. There is an example at the beginning (0).**

I used to think that jogging was a form of **(0)** .... _madness_	**MAD**
I was never interested in **(1)**	**FIT**
But last year I was working with a **(2)** .... sports agency	**PROFESSION**
in my job. My company provided **(3)** .... for a lot of	**SPONSOR**
their athletes and as a present they gave me and my family free	
(4) .... of my local	**MEMBER**
gym. My life was transformed! I went two or three times a week and	
(5) .... I was going	**EVENTUAL**
every day. I've also hired a **(6)** .... trainer to help	**PERSON**
me. He's been great. We've agreed that thirty minutes is the perfect	
(7) .... for our	**LONG**
sessions. I don't have the **(8)** .... to exercise for	**STRONG**
more than half an hour at a time.	

2 **Read the text below and think of the word which best fits each gap. Use only one word in each gap. There is an example at the beginning (0).**

In Britain **(0)** .... _everybody_ .... knows a mother-in-law joke. Comedians love laughing about them. Well I'm very happy to say that I am really good friends with my mother-in-law. We got on fantastically well from the first moment we met and we **(1)** .... never fallen out.

Her name is Tracy, and she and my father-in-law, Don, have been like second parents to me. My wife and I go round to their house for lunch every Sunday and they normally visit us **(2)** .... least once a week. We get on so well because we have the same sense of humour. There are always loads **(3)** .... jokes and funny stories whenever we meet.

At the moment, my wife **(4)** .... expecting our first child. Don and Tracy are very excited about their first grandchild. Every time they visit, they bring a new present **(5)** .... the baby and want to hear all the latest news.

As **(6)** .... as my wife, Don and Tracy also have a son: my brother-in-law, Peter. He works overseas, so we don't see him very often. He works as **(7)** .... chef on a cruise ship and his cooking is amazing. **(8)** .... he is in the country, he always stays with us. We have become good friends. So you see, I am very happy with my in-laws.

SPOTLIGHT ON STUDY TECHNIQUES

Many of the answers in the open cloze are part of set phrases such as:
He _works as_ an engineer.
We go there _at least once a week_.
As well as ice cream, we have chocolate cake and strawberries.

Make a list of these phrases as you study for the exam, and try to use them in your own writing and homework so that you become familiar with them.

Writing: organising your ideas

COMPULSORY TASK: PAPER 2, PART 1

1 When taking the Writing test, it is essential to answer the question correctly. Look at the exam question below and decide which of the subjects (1–6) you must include in your answer.

1 How people use text messages.

2 The best smart phone to buy.

3 The price of smart phones.

4 The size of the modern family.

5 Your personal experience of smart phones.

6 Your own feelings about the question.

You **must** answer this question. Write your answer in 140–190 words in an appropriate style **on the separate answer sheet**.

In your English class, you have been talking about mobile phones and smart phones. Your English teacher has asked you to write an essay for homework.

You will see the essay title and some notes you have written below. Now write your essay using the notes and give reasons for your point of view.

Essay title

Mobile phones and smart phones are destroying family life. Do you agree?

Notes

Write about:

1. how people use smart phones
2. instant messaging
3. your own family life

Write your **essay**. You must use grammatically correct sentences with accurate spelling and punctuation in a style appropriate for the situation.

---

2 Before you start writing, it is important to organise your ideas and plan your answer. You have to write between 140 and 190 words in Part 1 of the Writing test. So you need to write about four to five paragraphs. Look at Zdeněk's answer to the exam question. Match the paragraphs (1–5) to their contents (a–e).

a Conclusion: my opinion. ___

b The bad things about mobile phones. ___

c Family life before mobile phones. ___

d Introduction. ___

e The good things about mobile phones. ___

3 Zdeněk's teacher marked his essay. Read the teacher's comment. Then look again at the question. What did Zdeněk forget?

....

Zdeněk, this is a great answer, but you have failed! To pass the writing exam, you must include all the information in the question. You have forgotten one thing. Always check you include everything from the question.

Everyone has a mobile phone these days. Younger people usually have a smart phone too, and it's often their most precious possession. Unfortunately, smart phones are destroying family life.

People think they have to answer instant messages like Whatsapp all the time. When lots of their friends are sending messages at the same time, people spend hours writing replies. At a family dinner, some people don't talk, they just look at their smart phone screen.

It is true that mobile phones are important. Elderly relatives need them to call for help. They are essential for parents too. If they are worried about their children, they can phone them and check that everything is OK.

In the old days, parents could not call their children when they were worried. On the other hand, people spoke to their family more. Real face-to-face communication was much more important. At dinner, families talked about their lives and school. Now people eat with their smart phone next to their plate.

To sum up, mobile phones are destroying family life. Parents and children don't talk together any more. People just want to send messages and chat online. Personally, I think that is very sad.

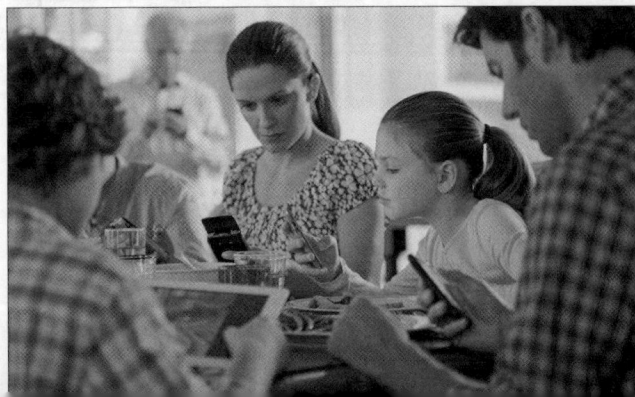

4 Now write your own answer to the exam question in exercise 1.

....

....

....

....

....

....

....

....

....

....

....

....

....

....

Speaking: answering questions

OPENING CONVERSATION: PAPER 4, PART 1

1 🎧 1.2 **At the start of the Speaking test, the interlocutor asks some general questions. Often these questions will be about your family. Listen to two students, Julieta and Philippe, in the first part of the Speaking test. What answers do they give to the following questions?**

1 Do you live alone or do you live with your family?

2 Do you come from a large family or a small family?

3 What do your parents do?

2 **Julieta and Philippe made the following mistakes in the interview. Correct the mistakes in these sentences.**

1 We are four in my family.

2 I have one older sister, Ana, who has 24 years.

3 I don't have some brothers and sisters.

4 My father is teacher and my mother works as doctor.

3 **If you are working with a partner, look at listening script 1.2 on page 148. Role-play the interview, with one person being the interlocutor and the other the student. Ask and answer questions. Then swap roles and repeat the role-play.**

Pronunciation

1 **Work in pairs. Ask and answer the questions.**

1 What do you enjoy doing in the evening?

2 Where are you planning to go this evening?

3 Do you like surfing the Net?

4 Which sites on the World Wide Web do you recommend visiting?

5 What TV programmes do you like watching?

2 🎧 1.3 **Listen to the questions in exercise 1. Which question has a different intonation? Why?**

SPOTLIGHT ON PRONUNCIATION

Intonation in questions

Remember that in questions with a question word (*who, what, when, why*, etc.), intonation falls at the end of the question. In questions with no question word (*Do you like . . . ? Have you got . . . ?*, etc.), intonation rises at the end.

---

3 **Look at the questions (1–7). Decide if the intonation falls or rises at the end of the question.**

1 Are you good at learning languages?

2 Where do you go when you have to study?

3 Do you think you'll pass the exam?

4 Which do you think is hardest: listening in English, speaking or writing?

5 Have you got a lot of work to do at the moment?

6 Will you be working this weekend?

7 What book are you reading at the moment?

4 🎧 1.4 **Listen and check your answers.**

5 **If you are working with a partner, ask and answer the questions in exercise 3.**

2 Jobs and work

LANGUAGE CHECKLIST

☐ I know words to describe jobs and work, page 16.

☐ I know some phrasal verbs with *off*, page 17.

☐ I know phrases for making comparisons, page 17.

☐ I know how to pronounce words with the schwa /ə/, page 18.

EXAM CHECKLIST

☐ I have practised the multiple choice question from the Reading and Use of English paper, page 14.

☐ I have practised the Part 1 extracts + multiple choice question from the Listening paper, page 18.

☐ I have practised the word formation question from the Reading and Use of English paper, page 19.

☐ I have practised the multiple-choice cloze question from the Reading and Use of English paper, page 19.

☐ I have practised how to expand points in the Writing paper, page 20.

☐ I have practised the collaborative task from the Speaking paper, page 21.

Reading and Use of English

MULTIPLE CHOICE: PAPER 1, PART 5

1   You are going to read a blog post. For questions 1–6, choose the answer (A, B, C or D) which you think fits best according to the text.

1 This blog has been written to

A criticise people.   C shock people.

B entertain people.   D train people.

2 When did the applicant with the pizza apply for the job?

A When he brought the pizza to the company.

B When he saw the job advertisement online.

C When he received the order for the pizza.

D When they had eaten the whole pizza.

3 Kelly Weihs got her inspiration from

A adverts.   C history.

B books.   D paintings.

4 The video idea may not be successful because

A it was the riskiest idea.

B it showed the person wanted a different job.

C nobody watched it.

D people were shocked by the loud music and the dancing.

5 What does the writer mean by 'out of the blue' in line 52?

A At the wrong time.   C When you are feeling tired.

B In the beginning.   D Without warning.

6 From the text, we understand that the author's favourite CV idea was

A the chocolate bar.   C the video with singing.

B the pizza box.   D the Wanted poster.

2   Find these words and phrases (1–8) in the text. Then match the definitions (a–h) to the words and phrases.

1 face to face ___   a look different (especially in a large group)

2 toppings ___   b got a reward, was a success

3 show off ___   c personal assistant (a type of secretary)

4 PA ___   d in person, not by email or phone

5 a break ___   e a time when you stop working for a short time

6 wrapper ___   f paper packaging, especially for food

7 paid off ___   g demonstrate something to impress people

8 stand out ___   h extra flavours that you add to foods like pizza or ice cream

The world's most unusual job applications ... ever!

Job hunting is one of the most stressful times in your life. You can spend hours perfecting a CV or filling in online application forms. For many people, the
5 result is the same: a polite 'no thank you'. You know you have the personal qualities to do the job, but you can only show them when you meet your employer face to face. So how can you get that elusive
10 interview? Here are some of the most surprising ways, and they're all real.

One of the very best was the job applicant who arrived at a company with a takeaway pizza, with his CV printed on
15 the box. The interview took place while they ate and the applicant got the job before they had finished. In this case, it's important to pick the right toppings.

Crime was the inspiration for Kelly Weihs
20 of Baltimore, USA. Looking for a job as a designer, she decided to show off her design work with her own CV. She used a series of old fonts and interesting colours to make her CV look like a nineteenth-century Wanted
25 poster from the Wild West. Her imaginative approach worked and she got the job.

However, it can be risky to make a CV like this. Kelly's poster idea was perfect because she was looking for a job in
30 design. Other people make less intelligent CV decisions.

For example, some job candidates record a video of themselves singing for their new potential employers, even if they are only
35 applying for a position as a PA. This is never going to work. It's too obvious that the candidate wants to be in the more exciting world of the music business, not answering the phones all day in an accountant's offices.
40 America seems to be the home of the creative CV, no doubt because it has one of the world's largest populations and thousands of people are competing for every job. Think about the poor managers
45 who have to read through hundreds and hundreds of applications in a day. It's

one of the most boring jobs in the world. Anyone might start thinking about more interesting things, like a break for coffee. So imagine what happens when you
50 get a free chocolate bar, completely out of the blue, with a CV wrapped around it. That's was Nick Begley's big idea.

Nick printed his CV on a chocolate wrapper with his skills in the ingredients
55 section. He then placed it around a Nestlé Crunch bar and he sent it in. It paid off immediately because Begley got two job offers and ended up working in ... you guessed it, marketing.
60 So if you want to stand out from the crowd, try one of these ideas for yourself. Just remember that if you apply for a job at my company, I hate anchovies and black olives.
65

HI MY NAME IS
ELLIOT HASSE.

WORK ★ play

I AM A **GRAPHIC DESIGNER.**
WE SHOULD WORK TOGETHER.

a. Elliot Hasse was born at 4:15 AM on December 15, 1985.

b. After graduating from Lindbergh High School in Saint Louis, Elliot decided to attend the University of Missouri-Columbia otherwise known as Mizzou. It is here that he began to pursue his love of design.

c. As a Sophomore at Mizzou, Elliot began interning as a Graphic Designer at N.H. Scheppers, an Anheuser Busch beer distributor. This internship soon turned into a job and ever since Elliot has been working with the sales and marketing team to create a point of sale vision. Elliot has been there since February of 2007.

d. During his Junior year Elliot came across an opportunity to work with Adobe software. This was a year long position that involved selling and marketing the Adobe brand.

e. During his first Senior year at Mizzou, Elliot applied to be an Apple Campus Representative. After landing the job Elliot was again working a year long contract selling, promoting, and creating Apple awareness across the Mizzou campus.

f. In 2009 Elliot and a few friends founded RADTANKTOPS.COM. Elliot not only founded Rad Tanks, but also managed the company and did most of the designing. Rad Tanks provides to be a successful and reliable service for students to order custom apparel. The company is still up and running today.

g. In May of 2011 Elliot will officially graduate from the University of Missouri with an honors degree in Graphic Design and a minor in Business.

h. This is where you come into play. If you have received this poster Elliot would love the opportunity to work with you and share his creative and somewhat crazy ideas.

a. 1985 — I'm an 80's Baby.
b. 2005 — I'm a college kid.
c. 2007 — Mmmmmm Beer.
d. 2008 — No alternative.
e. 2009 — I'm a Mac Genius.
f. 2009 — Tank tops are totally rad.
g. 2011 — College is so over.
h. TBD — I want to join your team.

Vocabulary

JOBS AND WORK

1 Complete the puzzle. What is the word in grey?

1 Personal characteristics, such as patience.

2 An employer makes you _____ by giving you some money and asking you to leave the company.

3 The money that you receive by week or by hour in your job.

4 This is the money you receive when you get the same money every month or year.

5 When you work more than your usual hours and you get paid some more money.

6 A system where workers can choose when they start and finish work.

7 When your company gives you more money (two words: 3, 4).

8 A document that gives the history of your education and your working life.

9 When a company asks an employee to leave, perhaps because they have done something wrong.

10 To find and give a job to a new employee.

11 To tell your employer that you will leave your job.

12 When you decide to leave your job, you have to give this to your employer.

13 New employees learn about their job on a _____ programme.

14 Extra benefits you get from your job.

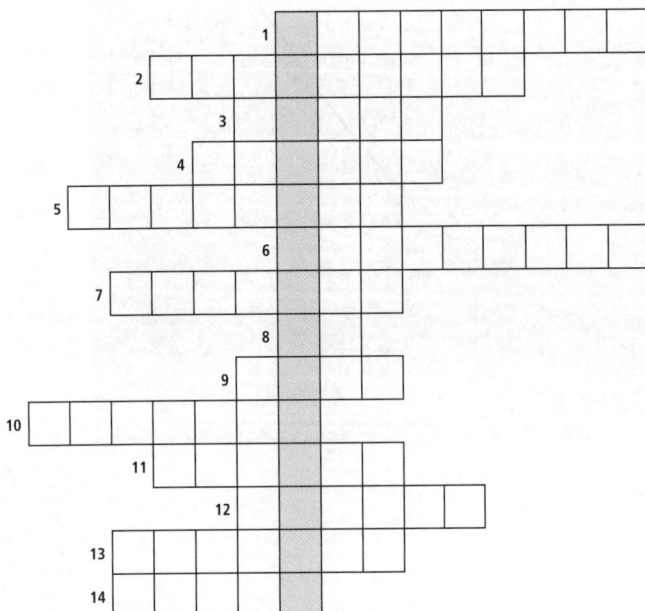

2 Complete the online chat with the words from the box.

deal fill find lay look send take turn write

» Anita
Tom! Help! I'm trying to ^{1}_____ for a summer job but I can't find one anywhere.

» Tom92
Have you spoken to the Deer Agency in the town centre? They help lots of people to find work.

» Anita
I'm doing an application form for them now, but there are so many stupid boxes to ^{2}_____ in. Anyway, I don't feel optimistic. Deer only ^{3}_____ with large companies. They all want experience and I haven't got any. How do you get experience if you haven't got a job?

» Tom92
It's the same for me. I decided to ^{4}_____ my CV out to hundreds of companies but I haven't had a single reply. I just want someone to ^{5}_____ back to me now.

» Anita
I know. It's so unfair!

» Tom92
Oh, I just remembered something. Last summer, my brother lost his job. His company had to ^{6}_____ off hundreds of workers. He was desperate, so he got a job at a garlic farm for the summer.

» Anita
A garlic farm? That's going to smell horrible!

» Tom92
A job's a job. They always ^{7}_____ on lots of new workers every year. Maybe we could get a summer job there?

» Anita
How much do they pay?

» Tom92
I don't know. I'll phone my brother now to ^{8}_____ out what the wages were like. We should apply for the jobs anyway.

» Anita
I'm not sure. If the wages are poor, I'm going to ^{9}_____ the job down. I don't want to smell of garlic all summer!

EXTENSION: PHRASAL VERBS WITH *OFF*

3 *Off* has many different meanings in phrasal verbs. Look at the phrasal verbs in **bold** in the sentences (1–6) below. Then match the pictures (a–f) to the sentences.

1 They worked really hard and eventually the project **came off!** ___

2 There was a problem in Alaska, so we **sent** Julia **off** to fix it. ___

3 I **took** the day **off** because there wasn't much to do in the office. ___

4 The company is **laying off** six hundred staff because there isn't enough work. ___

5 We realised that they were never going to pay the money, so we **wrote** the debt **off**. ___

6 He had a very stressful year, but his hard work **paid off** when they asked him to be the new boss. ___

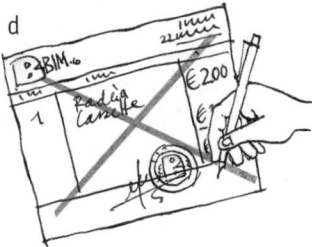

a

b

c

d

e

f

4 Look again at the sentences in exercise 3. In which sentence(s) does *off* mean the following?

a had a successful result ___ ___

b to another place ___

c to cancel/remove ___ ___

d not at work ___

Grammar

MAKING COMPARISONS

1 Complete the sentences with the comparative or superlative form of the word in brackets.

1 It's a lot _____ (sunny) today than yesterday.

2 This is the _____ (bad) CV that I've ever seen. It's terrible!

3 Filling in forms is the _____ (boring) part of my job.

4 When we offer extra perks to our employees, extra holiday time is always _____ (popular) than free training courses.

5 The bus station is _____ (far) from our office than the railway station.

6 Nick and I do the same job, but his salary is _____ (big) than mine.

2 Look at the sentences below. Four of them contain a mistake. Find and correct the mistakes.

1 The harder you work, the quick you get promotion.

2 My new job isn't as interesting than my old one.

3 People in London are much more highly paid than people in the rest of Britain.

4 We're more busier this year than last year.

5 London is the expensive city in Europe.

6 I think that writing reports is the least interesting part of my job.

3 Put the words from the box into the sentences below. Add one word to each sentence.

| a almost any as bit far like |

1 The new program is a more complicated than the software we were using before.

2 The new office is as good the old one.

3 I have to do lot more overtime in my new job than in my old one.

4 My job is too easy. I want a job with more responsibility.

5 The job in Berlin pays €30,000 and the one in Madrid pays €29,000. So the money is the same.

6 My new project is easy. It isn't anything the project that I've just finished. That one was a nightmare!

7 I don't think working as a journalist is more difficult than working as an editor.

Listening: Do you like your job?

EXTRACTS + MULTIPLE CHOICE: PAPER 3, PART 1

1 ⌒ 2.1 **You will hear eight people talking about their jobs. For questions 1–8, choose the best answer (A, B or C).**

1 You hear a man complaining about his job. Where is he?
   A in the staff canteen
   B at his desk
   C at home

2 You hear a woman talking about her new job. How does she feel?
   A worried
   B delighted
   C disappointed

3 You hear two people complaining about their boss. What do they complain about?
   A his qualifications
   B the amount of work he gives to people
   C the way he speaks to people

4 You hear a man talking on the telephone. Who is he speaking to?
   A his boss
   B his secretary
   C his business partner

5 You hear two people speaking in a café. What do they want to do?
   A take a career break
   B quit their jobs
   C go back to study at university

6 You hear a woman talking about her job. What is she describing?
   A her working conditions
   B who she works with
   C where she works

7 You hear a woman describing her day at work. What did she like about it?
   A It was a lot of fun.
   B She did something very important.
   C Her boss congratulated her.

8 You hear a man talking about something he has been working on. What is it?
   A a job application
   B secretarial work
   C an advertising campaign

Pronunciation

SPOTLIGHT ON PRONUNCIATION

The schwa (1)
The most important sound in English is also the smallest sound: the schwa /ə/. In English words, syllables that are unstressed are often pronounced /ə/.

Sometimes the schwa appears more than once in the same word.
Example: position /pəzɪʃən/

1 ⌒ 2.2 **Listen to the words below. The stress in each word is underlined. The sound in *italics* is the schwa /ə/.**

d<u>oc</u>tor   <u>big</u>ger   <u>app</u>l<u>y</u>

2 ⌒ 2.3 **Look at the words below. <u>Underline</u> the stress. Which syllables are pronounced with the schwa /ə/? Listen and check your answers.**

organisation	qualification
possessions	powerful
international	certificate
information	computer

SPOTLIGHT ON PRONUNCIATION

The schwa (2)
Small words like articles (*the, a*), prepositions (*of, to, from*), auxiliary verbs (*do, can*), and conjunctions (*and, but*) have two pronunciations. The pronunciation with the schwa /ə/ is called the weak form. We use the weak form in everyday speech and the strong form when we need to stress the word.

3 ⌒ 2.4 **Listen to two versions of each sentence below. In which sentence (a or b) is the word in *italics* pronounced with the schwa /ə/?**

1 I need to speak to you *and* Gary. ___

2 Karen is *the* best manager I have worked with. ___

3 I *can* help you if you like. ___

4 You *should* get a letter from her boss. ___

4 ⌒ 2.4 **Listen again to the sentences in exercise 3. Which other words are pronounced with the schwa /ə/?**

5 ⌒ 2.4 **Listen again to the first sentence in each pair in exercise 3. Listen to the stronger form of the words in *italics*.**

6 **If you are working with a partner, practise together reading the sentences in exercise 3, using both pronunciations.**

Reading and Use of English

WORD FORMATION: PAPER 1, PART 3

1 Use the word given in capitals at the end of each sentence to form a word that fits in the gap. The word in each pair of sentences is formed the same way. There is an example at the beginning (0).

0 a I have been working for this _organisation_ for ten years. **ORGANISE**

  b Companies in this country have an _obligation_ to give training to their employees. **OBLIGE**

1 a Can you make an .... of the security situation in the company? **ASSESS**

  b The new artwork and furniture has made a big .... to the appearance of the offices. **IMPROVE**

2 a Have you got an .... form for the job? **APPLY**

  b We do most of our .... by email. **COMMUNICATE**

3 a The new advertising campaign has been extremely .... **SUCCESS**

  b It's .... that Richard will be at the meeting tomorrow. He's got so much work to do. **DOUBT**

4 a When you apply for a new job, you should provide a .... from your previous employer. **REFER**

  b I don't believe in the .... of life on other planets. **EXIST**

5 a We need to recruit someone with the .... to speak French and German. **ABLE**

  b There is no .... between our company and your company. **SIMILAR**

MULTIPLE-CHOICE CLOZE: PAPER 1, PART 1

2 Read the text below and decide which answer (A, B, C or D) best fits each gap. There is an example at the beginning (0).

They say that if you want to **(0)** ....C........ a lot of money, you should **(1)** .... to be a plumber. However, the reality is that plumbers actually only command an annual **(2)** .... of £25,000. Nevertheless, more women are currently **(3)** .... from their office jobs and entering the profession.

Why? Well, there is a skills shortage in the UK at the moment across the construction **(4)** .... and employers are turning to women to fill the gap. A number of schemes have also started to help women make the career change. For example, a college in Wales is offering a **(5)** .... in plumbing which is only for female students.

Women do often still need determination to enter a male-dominated world. Some employers won't accept female employees at all. In **(6)** .... to fighting against this prejudice, some women plumbers also complain that people try to take advantage of them by not paying. Twenty-eight-year-old Pauline Brown, who has starred in a government advertising campaign to encourage women to **(7)** .... up plumbing, takes a no-nonsense approach. She says, 'I have a policy of same-day payment – if **(8)** .... try to avoid paying, I'll rip the work out and take my materials away.'

---

0 A win	B collect	<u>C earn</u>	D pay
1 A train	B educate	C instruct	D practise
2 A payment	B wages	C cash	D salary
3 A resigning	B sacking	C quitting	D leaving
4 A manufacturing	B factories	C industry	D working
5 A document	B paper	C profession	D qualification
6 A addition	B combination	C development	D excess
7 A put	B take	C begin	D make
8 A buyers	B purchasers	C shoppers	D clients

Writing: expanding points

COMPULSORY TASK: PAPER 2, PART 2

1 In Part 2 of the Writing test, it is important to give extra information to develop each of your points. Look at the exam question below. Match the three points (A–C) from the exam question to the sentences with extra information (1–6).

You have seen this advertisement in a newspaper.

Tour guides wanted

We are looking for people to work as tour guides around the city castle and museum. Applicants should be available to work throughout the summer (July to August) and be aged 21–65.

In addition, the ideal applicant will:

- have an interest in history Ⓐ
- have good communication skills Ⓑ
- be able to speak at least one foreign language Ⓒ

Please write requesting an information pack to Julian Hinchcliffe at the address below.

---

1 I often speak in front of groups as I act in a local theatre club. ___

2 On my course, I have visited very many castles and learnt about how they worked. ___

3 In addition to which, I presented a student radio programme when I was at High School. ___

4 I am a native speaker of Japanese and I have been working in English for the last year as an au pair in London. ___

5 As well as studying this subject, I also enjoy reading books about this period. ___

6 I have also completed a German course at B1 level. ___

2 Now look at the student's answer to the exam question in exercise 1. Place the sentences (1–6) from exercise 1 into the gaps (a–f) in the letter.

Dear Mr Hinchcliffe

I am writing to you to request an information pack for a Tour guide position.

I am currently studying Archaeology at the University of London. ª_____ b _____

You mentioned that you were looking for candidates with good communication skills. c _____ d _____

I am also able to speak three languages. e _____ f _____

I look forward to your reply.

Yours sincerely,

Mineko Kamimura

---

3 Now write your own answer to the exam question in exercise 1.

....
....
....
....
....
....
....
....
....
....
....
....
....
....
....
....
....
....

Speaking

COLLABORATIVE TASK: PAPER 4, PART 3

1 If you are working with a partner, look at the diagram. Imagine that you are going to take a part-time job while you are studying at university. Decide together which job is the best one. When you are speaking, use the phrases below and tick (✔) each one after you have used it.

___ Working as X is (much) better than working as Y …

___ This seems like a better / the best (idea)

___ I don't think it's anything like as (good) as …

___ It looks fairly similar to …

___ How do you think it compares to …?

___ Is it much different from …?

2 🎧 2.5 Listen to two students doing Part 3 of the Speaking test, Bastien and Victoria. Which of the jobs in exercise 1 do they forget to talk about?

3 🎧 2.5 Listen again. Complete the phrases that Bastien and Victoria use to ask for each other's opinion.

1 Which one should we _____ with?

2 What do you think about _____?

3 Do you think _____?

4 So how does the office job _____ to the lifeguard?

5 Why do you _____ that?

6 Which job would you go _____?

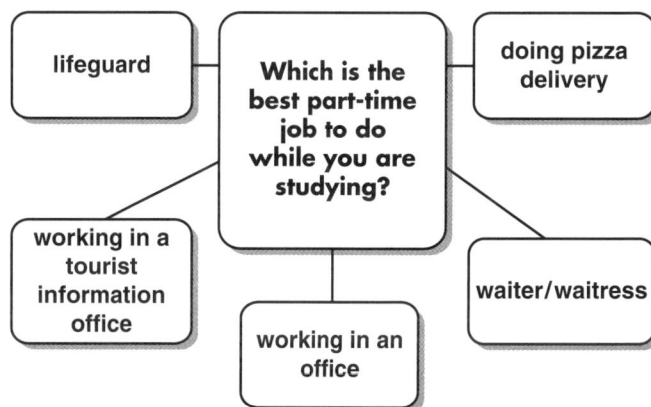

lifeguard

Which is the best part-time job to do while you are studying?

doing pizza delivery

working in a tourist information office

working in an office

waiter/waitress

3 Sport and free time

LANGUAGE CHECKLIST

- [ ] I know words to describe sport and free time, page 24.
- [ ] I know how to talk about obligation and necessity, page 25.
- [ ] I know how to spell adjectives ending in -*ful*, page 25.
- [ ] I know how to pronounce /v/, /w/ and /b/, page 26.
- [ ] I know how to pronounce words ending in -*age*, page 29.

EXAM CHECKLIST

- [ ] I have practised the gapped text question from the Reading and Use of English paper, page 22.
- [ ] I have practised the sentence completion question from the Listening paper, page 26.
- [ ] I have practised the key word transformation question from the Reading and Use of English paper, page 27.
- [ ] I have practised the word formation question from the Reading and Use of English paper, page 27.
- [ ] I have practised writing an article from the Writing paper, page 28.
- [ ] I have practised the individual 'long turn' from the Speaking paper, page 29.

Reading and Use of English

GAPPED TEXT: PAPER 1, PART 6

1   **You are going to read an article about the Japanese sport of sumo. Six sentences have been removed from the article. Choose from the sentences (A–G) the one which fits each gap (1–6). There is one extra sentence which you do not need to use.**

A   One popular souvenir is a print of the wrestler's hand.

B   Once you have control of this, it is easy to move the other wrestler around the ring.

C   This will reflect the history of the sport.

D   The typical retirement age for a professional wrestler is thirty.

E   The largest wrestler ever pushed the scales at over 270 kilos, although most weigh around 160.

F   Nowadays, the athletes come from many different countries.

G   Alternatively, a fighter can win by forcing their opponent to touch the ring itself.

2   **Now match the words in bold in the text to the definitions (1–10) below.**

   1   very difficult _____

   2   an object that gives you good luck _____

   3   a fight between two wrestlers or boxers _____

   4   easy to win, without real competition _____

   5   make your body larger (fatter or more muscular) _____

   6   a kind of thick soup _____

   7   the bottom part of your feet _____

   8   a very strong hold on something _____

   9   of religious importance, holy _____

   10 find evidence in history _____

A beginner's guide to SUMO
Japan's national sport

Two huge men stare across a 4.5 metre ring. The spectators fall silent. Suddenly, there is an enormous clash as the wrestlers

5　jump up and start to fight. The **bout** might last seconds or almost a minute. This is a true contest of champions. This is the Japanese sport of sumo wrestling.

10　　The rules are simple. The objective is to push your opponent outside the circle. **(1)** _____ They must not come into contact with this with any

15　part of their body except for the **soles** of their feet.

There are around seventy different winning moves. Most involve getting a **grip** on the

20　opponent's belt. **(2)** _____ Many sumo fights are **one-sided** and they end as soon as they begin. However, when two grandmasters face each other, the fights are longer, and more exciting.

That excitement explains why sumo is one of the world's oldest sporting contests. Experts can **trace** its origins **back** 1,500 years. Despite its roots in the distant past, the sport remains enormously popular across Japan. Fans follow the wrestlers just like the baseball or basketball

25　stars. **(3)** _____ Known as a _tegata_, these are made in red ink and then autographed.

Not all of these stars are Japanese. **(4)** _____ The last three grandmasters of the sport (_yokozuna_), the highest sumo rank, have all been from Mongolia. Perhaps most surprising of all is Kotooshu Katsunori from Bulgaria. He was the first European to win a major sumo trophy, amazing fans across the country.

30　Like all sumo wrestlers, Kotooshu had to take a fighting name. **(5)** _____ It also works as a kind of **talisman**, giving good luck throughout the fighter's career.

These names are not chosen by the fighter alone. They are supposed to be chosen with the help of the head of the fighter's 'stable'. This is the place where wrestlers live and train. All sumo fighters begin their career in these stables and the life is very hard.

35　Young wrestlers train from 5 to 11 a.m. each day before stopping for breakfast. Fortunately, the life of more experienced wrestlers is slightly less **demanding**. For example, they don't have to get up as early as the apprentices.

When they are not fighting, sumo wrestlers spend their time eating and sleeping. **(6)** _____ To get to that size, they need to eat a lot. The main meal of the day is a rich **stew**. This provides

40　the wrestlers with enough calories to **bulk up** and reach a fighting size.

Interestingly, there is also a religious element to the sport. For instance, the ring where it takes place is a **sacred** area which nobody must enter except for the referee and the combatants. This mixture of tradition, action, history and religion is what keeps bringing new fans to one of the world's most exciting sporting contests.

Vocabulary

SPORT AND FREE TIME

1 **Cross out the word that doesn't work in each sentence, as in the example.**

0 To be honest, I don't know how to play *badminton / mah-jong / ~~windsurfing~~*.

1 Why don't you join an after-school club where you can play *chess / computer games / karate*?

2 We usually go *running / sailing / wrestling* at the weekend.

3 When we were on holiday, we did *archery / backgammon / karate* for the first time.

4 Do you know a good place to go *bowling / cycling / golf*?

5 I want to play *backgammon / bowling / tennis*, but I don't know anyone who wants to play with me.

2 **Read the descriptions and decide which sports they describe.**

1 You fire arrows from your bow and you try to hit the target. _____

2 You can play this sport on an indoor court or on the beach and you try to hit a ball over a net with your hands. _____

3 This is a bit like dancing. You do this with other people in a swimming pool and you all try to move at the same time to music. _____

4 You hit a little white ball over a net using bats.

   _____

5 You play this on a court where you hit a ball over a net using rackets. You can play it indoors, on a grass court or a clay court. _____

6 This is a sport where you hit a shuttlecock over a net with a racket. _____

7 This is where you throw a very hard ball at ten wooden objects, which you try to knock down.

   _____

8 You do this in the mountains. It's a bit like skateboarding except that your board doesn't have any wheels. _____

3 **Complete the words in the news article.**

It's this way!

When it comes to soccer, German teams are often the strongest in the world, and they are used to holding the [1] tr _ _ h _ at the end of a tournament. That is except for FC Magdeburg. After they failed to score for five successive games, Magdeburg's loyal [2] f _ _ s decided to help them out in their next game against BAK '07. The [3] sp _ c _ _ _ _ _ s all carried enormous arrows in their hands which they used to point at the goal. They then followed the players around the [4] p _ _ c _ to show them where to score. Unfortunately, their goalkeeper [5] le _ in a goal at the start of the match, but then the new strategy started to work. An FC Magdeburg striker put the ball in the net after eighty minutes to make the score 1–1. Unfortunately, BAK '07 scored again in the last minute and Magdeburg [6] l _ _ t 1–2. Nevertheless, the club's [7] s _ p _ _ _ t _ _ s had made a big impression – and the news story went all around the world.

4 **Look at the sentences below. Six of them contain a mistake. Find and correct the mistakes.**

1 I like table games like chess and backgammon.

2 There's a gym in the city centre where people play boxing.

3 We played tennis on a grass park. It was really different to playing on clay.

4 We played golf yesterday and Sarah won me!

5 Gareth Bale used to play by Tottenham Hotspur.

6 We lost the game 5–1.

7 We played a game of football at our local stadium, but the court was terrible.

8 The goalkeeper let in three goals! She was useless!

Grammar

OBLIGATION AND NECESSITY

1 Read the sentence beginnings (1–6). Match the endings (a–f) to the beginnings to make complete sentences.

1 You'd better book a squash court now ___

2 You're supposed to wear proper tennis shoes, ___

3 You mustn't buy tickets from the ticket touts waiting outside the stadium ___

4 You don't have to buy tickets before the game ___

5 You needn't buy a baseball bat ___

6 I needn't have bought my tennis racket on holiday ___

a because I've got one you can borrow.

b because it's illegal.

c because lots of people want to play on Saturday.

d because nobody wanted to play with me.

e because you can buy them on the day.

f but most people don't.

2 Put the words from the box into the sentences below. Add one word to each sentence.

are	better	didn't	don't	has	have

1 Roger to go running at 5 a.m. every morning to train for his triathlon.

2 When we got to the slopes, we discovered that we needn't brought our skis.

3 You need to be a member of the tennis club to use the courts. Anyone can play here.

4 You supposed to wear special shoes when you play golf.

5 I have to buy my own bowling ball, but I bought one because I really wanted it.

6 You had start training if you want to run the marathon in July.

3 Complete the sentences with the correct form of the verbs in brackets.

1 She only had twenty minutes, but she _____ (manage/pack) her bags and get to the match on time.

2 I'm sorry I _____ (able/come) to training yesterday – I was ill.

3 The company _____ (succeed/develop) new lightweight swimwear.

4 He broke his leg and so he _____ (could/drive) for two months.

5 The team played well but they _____ (succeed/make) the final.

6 After three years at college, he _____ (able/speak) Japanese!

Spelling

Adjectives ending in -ful
Adjectives do not end -full except for the word full itself. This is a very common spelling mistake.
Example: careful ~~carefull~~

1 Find twelve adjectives ending -ful in the wordsearch. Words can be found vertically, horizontally and diagonally.

a	d	e	l	i	g	h	t	f	u	l	l	c
g	k	r	o	d	k	t	l	h	p	w	f	o
o	e	t	e	u	p	m	v	o	a	g	o	l
l	x	w	a	a	w	e	p	f	y	r	o	l
b	w	c	m	o	d	i	w	e	i	j	g	u
e	g	o	n	h	z	f	b	f	b	b	e	r
a	r	e	n	c	t	u	u	u	e	t	f	l
u	a	i	f	d	v	b	n	l	h	l	f	u
t	t	y	a	o	e	v	e	n	t	f	u	l
i	e	w	s	s	r	r	p	a	n	r	l	x
f	f	p	o	w	e	r	f	u	l	l	l	a
u	u	o	z	r	e	u	j	u	b	y	d	n
l	l	g	r	a	c	e	f	u	l	l	m	r

Listening: footvolley

SENTENCE COMPLETION: PAPER 3, PART 2

1 In Part 2 of the Listening test, you will need to complete some sentences or notes. You can anticipate some of the answers. Look at the notepad below. Which answers do you think will be:

a a number?   c an adjective?

b a place?   d something else?

You will hear a woman called Vera Silva, a footvolley player from Brazil, talking about her sport.
For questions 1–10 complete the sentences with a word or a short phrase.

There are **(1)** .... players on a footvolley team.

Each team can only kick the ball
(2) .... times before it goes over the net.

You lose a point if the ball goes out of the
(3) ....

Footvolley comes from **(4)** ....

Footvolley was originally a
(5) .... for football games.

Vera has coached the sport in
(6) ....

They held the Birmingham tournament indoors because Birmingham doesn't have a
(7) ....

Vera showed her **(8)** ....
in São Paulo.

Vera thinks one day footvolley will be in
(9) ....

Vera likes footvolley because games are
(10) .... , but they also have a good atmosphere.

---

2 🎧 3.1 **Now you will hear Vera talking about the sport of footvolley. For questions 1–10, complete the sentences. You will need to write a word or a short phrase in each gap.**

Pronunciation

1 🎧 3.2 **Listen and number the pictures 1–4.**

2 **Work with a partner. Read the sentences to each other.**

1 Vincent will visit Valerie in Vienna.

2 We worked very well this week.

3 We will wait with the van.

SPOTLIGHT ON PRONUNCIATION

/v/, /w/ and /b/
To make a /v/ sound, press your front teeth on your bottom lip. To make a /b/ sound, press your lips together. Your teeth should not touch your lips.

---

3 **Now practise /v/ and /b/.**

1 Bob's brother Vivian brought a box of vegetables.

2 Valerie borrowed that valuable bracelet.

3 Did Vanessa buy vanilla or blackberry ice cream?

4 🎧 3.3 **Listen and circle the words you hear.**

---

vote boat **vase bars**
vending *bending* very berry
vest best *via* buyer

Reading and Use of English

KEY WORD TRANSFORMATIONS: PAPER 1, PART 4

1 Complete the second sentence so that it has a similar meaning to the first sentence, using the word given. Do not change the word given. You must use between two and five words, including the word given. There is an example at the beginning (0).

0 You won't be able to win the competition.
   CHANCE
   You have ..*no chance of winning*.. the competition.

1 You're not allowed to go on the court if you're not wearing the right shoes.
   MUST

   You .... on the court if you're not wearing the right shoes.

2 Diana plays the guitar really well.
   AT

   Diana .... playing the guitar.

3 It's very important to tell the coach that you can't play tomorrow.
   HAD

   You .... the coach that you can't play tomorrow.

4 You shouldn't use the swimming pool if there isn't a lifeguard on duty.
   SUPPOSED

   You .... use the swimming pool if there isn't a lifeguard on duty.

5 It's not necessary to watch the game tomorrow if you don't want to.
   HAVE

   You .... watch the game tomorrow if you don't want to.

6 Jake always beats me at tennis.
   KEEPS

   Jake .... me at tennis.

7 We play cricket sometimes.
   FROM

   We play cricket ....

8 We worked on the report for ages.
   LONG

   We .... working on the report.

WORD FORMATION: PAPER 1, PART 3

2 Read the text below. Use the words given in capitals at the end of some of the lines to form a word that fits in the gap in the same line. There is an example at the beginning (0).

After a lot of campaigning, last year the city council agreed to hold a local swimming **(0)** ..*championship*.. .	**CHAMPION**
They did however demand that all **(1)** .... in the competition should come from the local area. Unfortunately, there were not enough local people who wanted to take part. It does not take a lot of	**CONTEST**
(2) .... to realise that the more people who compete, the more money the competition will raise. So, as they had received a lot of	**INTELLIGENT**
(3) .... from people in other towns who wanted to take part, the organisers decided that anyone resident in the state could compete. Eventually, they had over a thousand	**CORRESPOND**
(4) .... I was one of the organisers, so I was delighted that the competition was taking place as arranging it had taken a lot of	**ENTER**
(5) .... from all of us. The swimming clubs spent a lot of money too. Although it was	**PATIENT**
(6) .... , we decorated the pool for the competition. It was worth doing this as the decorations looked really	**EXPENSE**
(7) .... In the end, the swimming races went well and all our swimmers were	**IMPRESS**
(8) .... , even if we didn't win any of the gold medals. Nevertheless, in my opinion we should hold the tournament again next year.	**COMPETE**

Writing: an article

OPTIONAL TASK: PAPER 2, PART 2

1 Look at the exam question below. Then choose the correct options to complete the student's answer to the exam question.

You see this announcement on an English-language website.

Sports and hobbies around the world

We are running a series of articles on sports and hobbies around the world.

What is your favourite sport or hobby? Why did you start doing it? Why do you enjoy it?

Write us an article answering these questions. We will publish the best articles on our website.

Write your **article**. Write your answer in 140–190 words in an appropriate style.

---

2 Look again at the article. Write the answers to the questions in the exam question.

1 What is your favourite sport or hobby?

....

2 Why did you start doing it?

....

3 Why do you enjoy it?

....

3 Now write your own answer to the exam question in exercise 1.

SPOTLIGHT ON STUDY TECHNIQUES

When you write an article in the exam, you should include your own opinion or a comment. You could include this in your final paragraph, for example. *It's just a great hobby that anyone can do.*

My hobby is a bit unusual. It's a new activity from the USA: upside-down yoga.

In upside-down yoga, you do yoga in a hammock. The hammock hangs from the ceiling so you are above the floor. It looks [1]**frightened / frightening**, but it's easy. I go to a class once a week and afterwards I feel completely [2]**relaxed / relaxing**.

I started upside-down yoga because I had terrible back pain. I felt [3]**frustrated / frustrating** because everything hurt my back. My doctor suggested going to the gym, but I think sports are [4]**bored / boring**. Then my sister told me about upside-down yoga. I had done yoga in the past because I am [5]**fascinated / fascinating** by Indian culture. Upside-down yoga sounded [6]**interested / interesting** and when I tried it, I loved it!

The first time you do upside-down yoga, it's [7]**excited / exciting** because you think you will fall. However, you soon get used to it. I never worry about falling now. I just close my eyes and relax.

Personally, I really recommend upside-down yoga. I love it because it's fun, it's active and it's unusual. I was also [8]**amazed / amazing** because it has completely cured my back pain. It's just a great hobby that anyone can do.

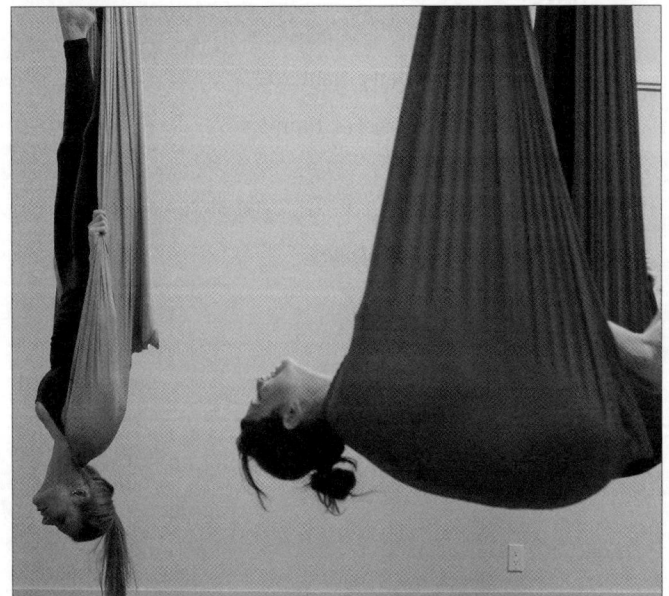

Speaking

INDIVIDUAL 'LONG TURN': PAPER 4, PART 2

1 🎧 3.4 **In Part 2 of the Speaking test, you have to describe and contrast a pair of photographs for about a minute. Listen to two students doing the individual 'long turn' and talking about the photographs below. Which student does not answer the interlocutor's question? (Note that in the exam you and your partner will always have different pairs of photographs to talk about.)**

2 🎧 3.4 **Listen again and complete the sentences with useful words for comparing photographs.**

1 So the first picture is indoors _____ the second picture is outdoors.

2 _____ I like chess, I prefer the second activity.

3 Both pictures _____ people in competitions.

4 In each picture there's a different _____ of competition.

5 So cycling _____ harder, but I think chess is the most difficult activity.

3 **If you are working with a partner, ask and answer the interlocutor's question for the photographs. The question is in listening script 3.4 on page 150.**

Pronunciation

> **SPOTLIGHT ON PRONUNCIATION**
>
> **Words ending in -age**
> Words ending in -age are usually pronounced /ɪdʒ/ not /eɪdʒ/.
> Example: marriage ➜ /mærɪdʒ/
> There are some exceptions however. One-syllable words are usually pronounced /eɪdʒ/.
> Example: page ➜ /peɪdʒ/
> Some verbs that begin en- are also pronounced /eɪdʒ/.
> Example: engage ➜ /ɪngeɪdʒ/
> Some words are pronounced /ɑːʒ/. These words originally come from French.
> Example: sabotage ➜ /sæbətɑːʒ/

1 **Complete the table with the words from the box. Note that garage has two possible pronunciations.**

> age   average   cage   camouflage   collage   cottage
> courage   damage   encourage   enrage   espionage
> garage (UK English)   garage (US English)   heritage
> image   manage   massage   message   stage   village

/ɑːʒ/	/eɪdʒ/	/ɪdʒ/
	age	average

2 🎧 3.5 **Now listen and check your answers.**

3 **If you are working with a partner, read all the -age words to each other.**

LANGUAGE CHECKLIST

☐ I know words to describe nature and animals, page 32.

☐ I know how to use adjectives and prepositions, page 32.

☐ I know the spelling of some words with double letters, page 32.

☐ I know the grammar of phrasal verbs, page 33.

☐ I know how to pronounce linking sounds, page 35.

☐ I know how to pronounce /r/, /w/ and /l/, page 37.

EXAM CHECKLIST

☐ I have practised the multiple matching question from the Reading and Use of English paper, page 30.

☐ I have practised the multiple-choice cloze question from the Reading and Use of English paper, page 33.

☐ I have practised the essay from the Writing paper, page 34.

☐ I have practised the multiple matching question from the Listening paper, page 35.

☐ I have practised the word formation question from the Reading and Use of English paper, page 36.

☐ I have practised the individual 'long turn' from the Speaking paper page 36.

Reading and Use of English

MULTIPLE MATCHING: PAPER 1, PART 7

1   **You are going to read an article about four encounters between people and animals. For questions 1–10, choose from the animals (A–D). The animals may be chosen more than once.**

Which animal

1   was hit by its human victim? ___

2   lost interest in its victim? ___

3   was hunting in an urban area? ___

4   thought its prey was a different animal? ___

5   travelled across two continents? ___

6   can chase its victims for a long way? ___

7   is now very difficult to find in the wild? ___

8   is creating panic in the media? ___

9   watched its victim after the attack? ___

10 kills its victims by preventing them from breathing? ___

2   **Find these words and phrases (1–10) in the text. Then match the definitions (a–j) to the words and phrases.**

1   exceptional ___   a went into the wrong place by accident

2   a spate ___   b a place where birds and reptiles keep their eggs

3   strayed ___   c a large group of flying insects

4   a swarm ___   d the part of the mouth that moves up and down

5   hives ___   e very unusual

6   seized ___   f places where bees live

7   drown ___   g a series of bad/unfortunate events

8   a nest ___   h die in water when you cannot breathe

9   jaws ___   i a tool often used with a hammer to cut stone

10 a chisel ___   j taken strongly and quickly

ANIMAL ATTACK!

As the spread of humanity gets wider and natural habitats are destroyed, more and more people are coming in contact with wild animals. The vast majority of these encounters pass peacefully, but in exceptional circumstances some unfortunate people have been attacked. We investigate four such encounters.

A Leopards, India

There have been a spate of leopard attacks on people in the Indian state of Maharashtra. In January this year, three men were attacked by a leopard which had strayed into their town in search of food. The newspapers have been talking of a 'leopard storm' in this region as more attacks of this type take place. The leopards themselves have had to abandon their secretive lives in the depths of the forests because their habitats are being destroyed. Woodland is being cut down to make room for more bungalows, and the big cats are being forced out of the parks in which they live.

B Killer bees, the USA

In a scene from a Hollywood movie come suddenly to life, an elderly woman has been hospitalised after she was attacked by a swarm of killer bees. She was stung all over her body and was only saved when firemen poured water over the woman and her attackers.

The bees were killer bees created by scientists in South America who were trying to breed American honey bees with stronger African bees. The insects escaped from their laboratory in 1957 and migrated north into the USA. So far an estimated 1,000 people have been killed after attacks by the swarms. Typically bees attack when there is a threat to their hives and will follow enemies for over a kilometre.

C Crocodiles, Australia

Diver Jeff Tanswell thought his life was over when he was seized by a huge saltwater crocodile while snorkelling over a reef in Queensland, Australia. The animal grabbed him and dragged him down into the deep water. This is normally the prelude to a 'death roll' where crocodiles dive to the depths and spin their prey round until they drown. But Jeff survived.

One explanation for the attack was that it may have been a female trying to protect a nest nearby from a potential danger. However, although Jeff had been unable to put up much resistance, the crocodile gave up the attack and just let him go. Wildlife experts suspect that the fight was over because the crocodile was just interested in what Jeff was. Because crocodiles lack fingers they have to inspect new things with their mouths, which is why it may have bitten the diver in the first place.

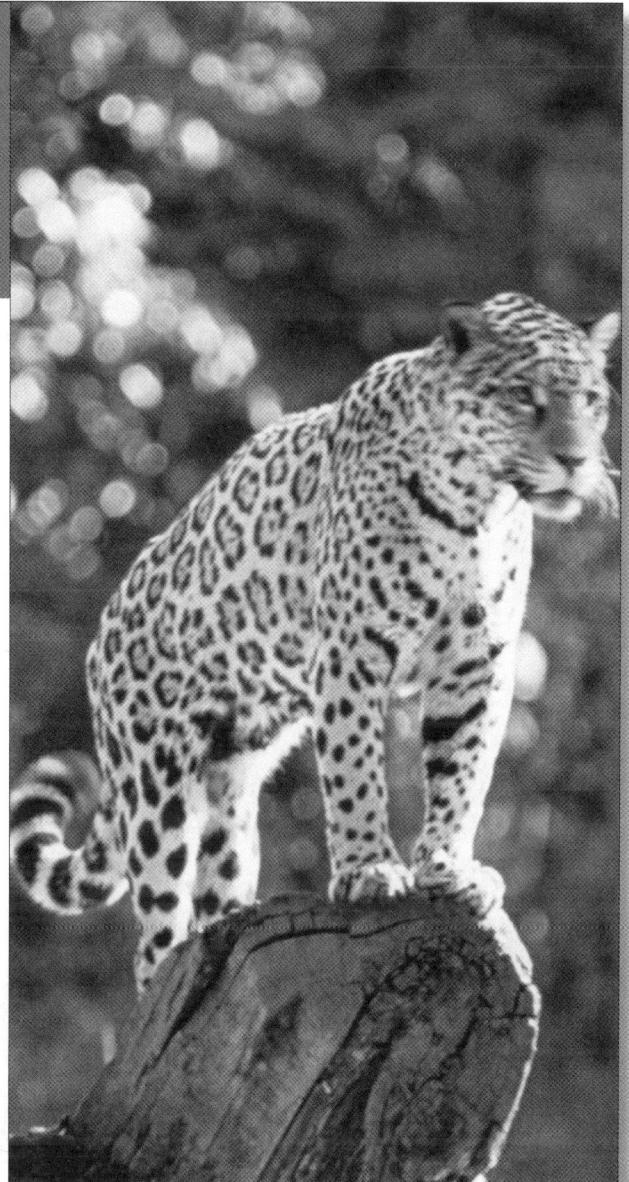

D Great white sharks, Australia

Another man lucky to escape a close encounter with a wild animal was Eric Nerhus. While diving for shellfish off Cape Howe, he found himself in sudden jeopardy. A 3.5 m great white shark shot towards him through the dark water. It grabbed his head, body and arms in its jaws. Although Eric said it felt like being trapped in a dark cave, miraculously his body was protected by a lead-weight vest. The shark started to shake him, whereupon the diver used his free hand to locate its eye which he stabbed with his diving chisel. As Eric escaped to the surface, the shark circled him until his son was able to drag him back into their boat.

Experts on marine behaviour theorise that in this case Eric was attacked because the shark had mistaken him for a seal and so it released him as soon as he started to put up a fight.

Vocabulary

NATURE AND ANIMALS

1 Complete the words. Write one letter in each space.

1 If you go on safari, you can see w _ l _ animals such as giraffes, lions and antelope.

2 In India and Thailand they use t _ _ e elephants to help lift heavy objects.

3 You see very few young pandas in zoos because the animals don't usually b _ _ _ d in captivity.

4 Animals behave on i _ s _ _ _ c _ .

5 Many animal species are now e _ d _ _ _ _ _ _ d: they could die out in the next 50 years.

6 Our family has a p _ _ cat called Tiger.

7 Sharks hunt seals as p _ _ y .

8 You can t _ _ _ n dogs to help blind people.

9 The natural h _ _ _ t _ t of the tiger is the jungles of Asia.

10 We have to do everything possible to save animal species from e _ t _ _ c _ _ _ _ so that they don't become like the dodo or the dinosaurs.

ADJECTIVES AND PREPOSITIONS

2 Underline the correct preposition.

1 We are leaving at two o'clock, so we need to be aware *for / of* the time.

2 I love cats, but I am allergic *with / to* them.

3 The kids want a dog, but I'm not keen *on / for* the idea.

4 I'm fed up *about / with* the cat: she keeps killing birds and mice.

5 I'm interested *in / for* doing something to help wild animals.

6 Jane Goodall is famous *from / for* her work with chimpanzees.

Spelling

Words with double letters
One of the biggest problems with spelling in English is that many words have double letters. As the pronunciation of the word does not tell you if the word is spelt with one letter or two, you often need to learn the spelling of each word individually.

1 Look at the words below which are commonly spelt wrongly. Circle the correct spelling.

1 a necessary
  b neccessary
  c neccesary

2 a acommodation
  b accomodation
  c accommodation

3 a misspel
  b misspell
  c mispell

4 a occasion
  b ocassion
  c occassion

5 a tommorow
  b tomorrow
  c tommorrow

6 a commision
  b comission
  c commission

7 a assistant
  b asisstant
  c assisttant

8 a milionnaire
  b millionaire
  c millionnaire

9 a possessions
  b posessions
  c possesions

10 a inacessible
   b innacesible
   c inaccessible

11 a oportunity
   b opportunity
   c opporttunity

12 a reccomendation
   b reccommendation
   c recommendation

Grammar

PHRASAL VERBS

1 Look at the sentences below. Six of them contain a mistake. Find and correct the mistakes.

1 Mark and Steve get on them well together. They are great friends.

2 I was so poor that I lived rice off. It was all I ate.

3 Some journalists have revealed that big business is destroying wild animal habitats in Africa. I wonder how they found out it.

4 It is an absolute tragedy that so many wonderful species are just dying out.

5 I have some complicated instructions that I want you to carry them out.

6 You shouldn't look down to environmental activists. They are trying to help all of us.

7 I didn't know they were criminals and they stole a lot of money from me. I was completely taken in.

8 One of the most exciting things about Indonesia is that explorers are coming new species across all the time.

2 Match the two halves of the sentences.

1 The world's oldest man passed

2 The neighbours look down

3 We couldn't find any ginger kittens, so we ended

4 My grandmother was in hospital for weeks with pneumonia. I don't know how she got

5 The kids are looking forward

6 We didn't know what to do tomorrow until my cousin came

a through it.

b on us because we aren't interested in opera and art and things like that.

c to doing a camel ride on holiday.

d away yesterday at the age of 116.

e up with a great idea.

f up getting a black one.

Reading and Use of English

MULTIPLE-CHOICE CLOZE: PAPER 1, PART 1

1 Read the text below and decide which answer (A, B, C or D) best fits each gap. There is an example at the beginning (0).

Michelle Whiteman has **(0)** .... *D* .... her life to protecting the orang-utan. For ten months of the year she works in the jungles of Borneo, watching and studying the great apes in their natural **(1)** ....
The rest of the time she spends in the UK raising **(2)** .... of the need for help. Like many of the animals in the islands of Indonesia, the orang-utan is in grave danger.

The destruction of the jungles is so severe that **(3)** .... to some experts the species may be extinct within ten years. In addition to the destruction of their jungle homes, the animals are also at **(4)** .... due to hunting and the capture of wild animals for the pet trade. Furthermore, their population does not increase rapidly: a female orang-utan has a single baby only once every eight years.

Orang-utans are solitary animals which spend almost all of their time in the trees, **(5)** .... for food or sleeping. They can weigh up to 77 kilos, which means they are also the largest tree-living animals in the world.

Michelle learnt about the orang-utans while studying zoology at Bristol University. 'When I read about the terrible situation in Indonesia, I could **(6)** .... believe it. There are a great number of new animal species there that could become extinct before we have had a chance to discover them! I knew I **(7)** .... do something, so I came out here. If we don't find a **(8)** .... soon to stop the destruction of their habitat, the orang-utan will simply disappear.'

0 A chosen	B selected	C decided	D dedicated
1 A places	B locations	C habitats	D sites
2 A knowledge	B appreciation	C awareness	D realisation
3 A relating	B furthermore	C further	D according
4 A risk	B trouble	C hazard	D threat
5 A finding	B locating	C seeking	D searching
6 A hardly	B almost	C just	D absolutely
7 A must	B had to	C can	D ought
8 A route	B path	C direction	D way

Writing: an essay

COMPULSORY TASK: PAPER 2 PART 1

1 In Part 1 of the Writing test, you will be asked to write an essay. Read the exam question below. Then put the paragraphs (A–E) in the correct order (1–5) to complete the student's answer.

1 _____   2 _____   3 _____   4 _____   5 _____

In your English class, you have been talking about endangered species. Now your English teacher has asked you to write an essay.

Write an essay using all the notes and give reasons for your point of view.

Write 140–190 words.

There are many animals around the world in danger of extinction.

Do you think this problem can be solved?

Write about:

1. animal habitats

2. hunting

3. .... (your own idea)

A
To begin with, many of their habitats are in danger. People are cutting down rainforests to make wood. This means there is nowhere for wild animals to live. If we cannot protect the jungle, we cannot protect the animals that live there.

B
So animals in the wild are in danger of extinction. However, there are some endangered species in captivity. Unfortunately, there is usually only a small number of these animals. What's more, many animals do not breed in these situations, so this is not a real solution to the problem.

C
Many animals like tigers and elephants are disappearing. The future looks very bad. It may be impossible to solve this problem.

D
In conclusion, animals around the world are in danger of extinction. It is possible that we cannot save them because there are too many problems to solve.

E
In addition, hunters are killing many endangered species. They kill tigers because people want to use their body parts in medicine. People in poor countries can get a lot of money for these body parts. However, this medicine does not work. Perhaps there is a solution here. We can educate people and tell them not to buy these body parts.

2 Look again at the student's answer. Tick (✔) the things (a–h) that he mentioned.

a charity work to help animals ☐

b government action to protect animals ☐

c fishing and animals in the sea ☐

d unnecessary killing of animals ☐

e pollution ☐

f tourism to see wild animals ☐

g selling wild animals as pets ☐

h endangered species in zoos ☐

SPOTLIGHT ON STUDY TECHNIQUES

When you see the compulsory Writing question, don't worry if you don't know all the key vocabulary that you need to discuss the topic. Use the words you know and don't try to guess or invent new words. The most important thing is to explain your ideas clearly.

3 Now write your own answer to the exam question in exercise 1. Use the points in exercise 2 to help you with your own ideas.

....

....

....

....

....

....

....

....

....

....

....

....

....

....

....

....

....

....

Listening: special animals

MULTIPLE MATCHING: PAPER 3, PART 3

1 🎧 4.1 **You will hear five different people talking about animals that have been important in their lives. For Speakers 1–5, choose from the list (A–H) the animal that each person is talking about. There are three extra letters which you do not need to use.**

Which animal

A was scared of people?

B was in the zoo?   Speaker 1 ____

C was in a circus?
                                     Speaker 2 ____
D had been trained to do a job?

E had to be given away?   Speaker 3 ____

F attacked someone?   Speaker 4 ____

G saved someone's life?   Speaker 5 ____

H was very rare?

Pronunciation

1 🎧 4.2 **Listen again to these two sentences from the Listening. Can you hear an extra sound which connects (links) the letters underlined?**

1 As it gre<u>w u</u>p, it became large<u>r a</u>nd larger.

2 You don't often se<u>e a</u> kingfisher in the wild.

SPOTLIGHT ON PRONUNCIATION

Linking sounds
Listening to native speakers can be difficult because they do not always say words separately. Instead, when they speak quickly, they use linking sounds to join words together. To become an effective listener, you need to expect to hear these linking sounds.

In the words gre<u>w up</u>, the linking sound /w/ comes from the final letter of the word grew. In the same way, in large<u>r and</u> the linking sound /r/ comes from the final letter of the word larger.

However, notice that in the words se<u>e a</u> there is a linking sound /j/, but there is no letter representing this sound in the spelling of the words: there is no y or j.

---

2 🎧 4.3 **Look at the sentences below and decide which sound is linking the words underlined: /j/, /r/ or /w/? Then listen to check your answers.**

1 My teache<u>r a</u>nd I were interviewed on TV.

2 Let's g<u>o a</u>nd see the parrots in the park.

3 Andre<u>w a</u>sked me if we could have a pet rabbit.

4 We want to se<u>e a</u>ll the animals while we're here.

5 The police sa<u>y a</u> wild puma has been seen.

6 We sa<u>w a</u> giraffe and some lions on safari.

3 Look again at the sentences (1–6) in exercise 2. Which sentences make the linking sound from a letter which is already in one of the words? Which sentences add a linking sound?

4 🎧 4.4 **Find the linking sounds in each sentence below. Then listen to check your answers.**

1 Grandad's too old to go for a two-hour walk.

2 Is there another way of working?

3 Here's the tea and coffee for Tina and Sarah.

5 **If you are working with a partner, practise together reading the sentences in exercise 4.**

Reading and Use of English

WORD FORMATION: PAPER 1, PART 3

1 Read the text below. Use the words given in capitals at the end of some of the lines to form a word that fits in the gap in the same line. There is an example at the beginning (0).

After the strange death last week of three sheep on a farm in Somerset, England, the police have begun an (0) .....*investigation*..... into reports	**INVESTIGATE**
of a big cat in the area. It is not the first time this has happened. Farmer Thomas Sudbury was walking home late last year when he had a (1)	**TERRIFY**
experience. 'I heard a noise behind me and when I turned around, I saw a big black cat, as big as a puma,' he said. 'I was so scared I could hardly (2) ....' Although	**BREATH**
critics say that the story is just a product of Mr Sudbury's (3) .... , the farmer	**IMAGINE**
defends his story. 'That was no (4) .... pet cat: it looked dangerous!'	**HARM**
While a few people have been (5) .... in getting	**SUCCESS**
a photograph of the beast on film, so far nobody has taken a clear picture of the (6) .... animal.	**MYSTERY**
In the majority of the photos, the shape and size of the animal are extremely vague. However, although no one can say for certain if a big cat is loose in Somerset, local people are (7) .... 'I don't	**NERVE**
know what killed my sheep,' says farmer Martin Hoggard, 'but I know this: the (8) .... was big, much	**ATTACK**
bigger than a fox. And it's out there now, roaming the countryside.'	

Speaking

INDIVIDUAL 'LONG TURN': PAPER 4, PART 2

1 🎧 4.5 Look at the study techniques box above. Julieta is practising before the speaking exam and she has prepared a list of useful phrases. Listen to her describing the pictures on page 37. Which of the phrases in the list does she use?

a *Well, let me see.* ☐

b *Both photos show ...* ☐

c *In the first photo there's a ...* ☐

d *The second photo shows ...* ☐

e *Perhaps ...* ☐

f *Maybe ...* ☐

g *In the first one, there's a ... whereas in the second photo, the bottom one, there are ...* ☐

h *In the first one, there's a ... while in the other one I can see a ...* ☐

i *Returning to the first picture ...* ☐

j *Anyway, going back to the first picture ...* ☐

2 If you are working with a partner, ask and answer the question below for the photographs.

> Compare the two photographs on page 37 and say which experience is more memorable.

Pronunciation

/r/ and /w/
Many people have problems pronouncing /r/ and /w/.
The difference between these sounds is that when you
say /w/, your lips start closed and then open.

1 🎧 4.6 **Listen and write the word you hear.**

1 _____

2 _____

3 _____

4 _____

5 _____

6 _____

/r/ and /l/
The pronunciation of /r/ and /l/ can also be difficult.
The difference between /r/ and /l/ is that when you say
/l/, your tongue should touch the top of your mouth.

2 🎧 4.7 **Listen and circle the words you hear.**

1 a light
  b right

2 a led
  b red

3 a lock
  b rock

4 a load
  b road

3 🎧 4.8 **Now listen and repeat the words.**

1 light   right   white

2 late   rate   wait

3 lock   rock   wok

4 led   red   wed

5 lay   ray   way

6 law   raw   war

4 **If you are working with a partner, take turns to say one
word from exercise 3. Your partner must point to the
word that you say.**

LANGUAGE CHECKLIST

☐ I know words to describe books and films, page 40.

☐ I know some gradable and non-gradable adjectives, page 40.

☐ I know some verbs of manner, page 41.

☐ I know how to use narrative tenses, page 41.

☐ I know how to place stress in long words, page 42.

EXAM CHECKLIST

☐ I have practised the multiple choice question from the Reading and Use of English paper, page 38.

☐ I have practised the Part 4 dialogue + multiple choice question from the Listening paper, page 42.

☐ I have practised the open cloze question from the Reading and Use of English paper, page 43.

☐ I have practised the multiple-choice cloze question from the Reading and Use of English paper, page 43.

☐ I have practised writing a short story from the Writing paper, page 44.

☐ I have practised the collaborative task from the Speaking paper, page 45.

Reading and Use of English

MULTIPLE CHOICE: PAPER 1, PART 5

1 **You are going to read an article about words that came from fictional characters. For questions 1–6, choose the answer (A, B, C or D) which you think fits best according to the text.**

1 The word 'quixotic'

   A is a compliment.

   B is a criticism.

   C can mean one of two things.

   D is very old-fashioned.

2 What was Ebenezer Scrooge?

   A a criminal

   B a very poor man

   C a hero

   D a businessman

3 What kind of people use the word 'Fagin'?

   A children

   B criminals

   C politicians

   D journalists

4 What does the writer mean by 'Stevenson also brought two of his characters into everyday speech'?

   A The names of the characters are used by people as part of a common expression.

   B The characters spoke very naturally.

   C The characters were named after words people used in their daily lives.

   D The author changed the characters' names to make them more popular.

5 How does the writer feel about genetically modified foods?

   A He is undecided.

   B He opposes them.

   C He thinks they taste horrible.

   D He thinks they are an amazing scientific achievement.

6 What is the effect of the posters of Big Brother?

   A They give people orders.

   B They are used in election campaigns.

   C They make people feel nervous.

   D They advertise a television programme.

Real-life Romeos

When we use the word *Romeo* for a romantic young man, we hardly think of the character from William Shakespeare's play *Romeo and Juliet*. But a sure sign of an author having created a successful character is that
5 the character's name enters the language and becomes a word. Despite only writing in Spanish, Shakespeare's contemporary Cervantes achieved the feat of creating a new word in a different language – English, the adjective *quixotic*. This word comes from the title
10 character of Cervantes' *Don Quixote*. It describes a person who has great imagination and makes incredible plans, but whose plans are unfortunately impossible to achieve.

One author who was particularly successful in
15 seeing his characters enter the language was the novelist Charles Dickens. In modern English a *scrooge* is used to describe someone who is mean and tries to avoid spending money at all. The word comes from the protagonist of Dickens's novella *A Christmas
20 Carol*, Ebenezer Scrooge, who treats the employees who work in his office poorly and makes them work in terrible conditions. As well as Scrooge, Dickens also had success with Fagin, the villain of *Oliver Twist*. In the novel Fagin controlled a group of child criminals.
25 His name is often used in the press to describe real-life adult leaders of youthful gangs.

The Victorian era (1837–1901) in which Dickens wrote was a major period for the English novel. At the end of the nineteenth century, the Scottish
30 author Robert Louis Stevenson achieved enormous success with his masterpiece *Treasure Island*. Stevenson also brought two of his characters into everyday speech. A *Jekyll and Hyde* character is a person whose personality can quickly change from
35 being kind to being angry, impolite or aggressive. The name comes from the scientist protagonist of *Dr Jekyll and Mr Hyde* whose strange experiments turn him from man to murderous monster, and back again. Stevenson was not alone in seeing success
40 from the field of Gothic Horror. At the age of twenty-one Mary Shelley wrote *Frankenstein*, and the name of her mad scientist is now used as an adjective to describe any kind of science that seems to be out of control. *Frankenstein foods*, for example, is a term that people can understand to describe genetically 45 modified ingredients.

It does seem strange that villains enter the language more often than heroes. Sometimes in fact these characters need hardly appear in the original work at all. The television series *Big Brother* is named after the 50 all-powerful dictator who rules the London of the future in George Orwell's novel *Nineteen Eighty-Four*. Big Brother himself is never encountered during the story: we only ever see his face on posters along with the ominous message 'Big Brother is Watching You'. This is 55 why the presence of more and more cameras watching the streets, and greater government controls over the everyday lives of people, has led to the suggestion that we live in a 'Big Brother society'.

Interestingly, Orwell achieved the double feat of 60 creating a character that has entered the language as well as entering the language himself. The word *Orwellian* is used to describe a society which tries to control every aspect of people's lives, as happened in the pages of *Nineteen Eighty-Four*. Like the novel, it's a word that seems 65 to be getting more and more popular all the time.

"ARE YOU COME FROM DR. JEKYLL?" I ASKED

Vocabulary

BOOKS AND FILMS

1 **Complete the puzzle. What is the word in grey?**

1 A very famous book or film which is accepted as being a very important work.

2 One part of a book.

3 The most important bad person in a film or book.

4 The most important female in a film or book.

5 The person who tells the story.

6 A book or film that was invented by a writer, not history or biography, for example.

7 The story of a book or film, what happens.

8 A long-running television programme.

9 The landscape that you see on stage in the theatre or in the background of a film.

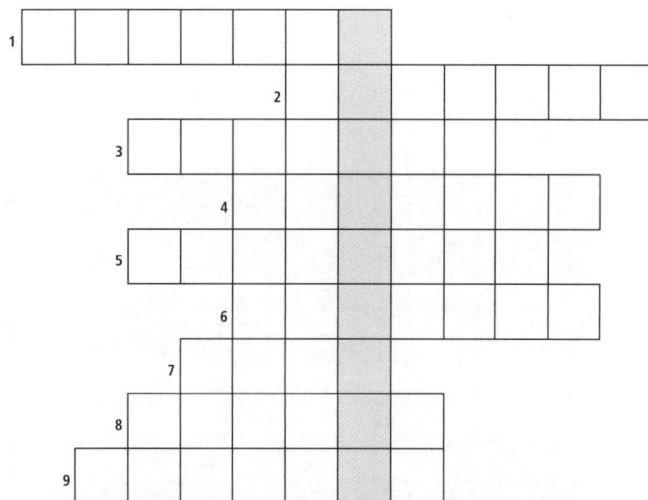

2 **Complete the blog text about *The Invisible Man* with the words from the box.**

| episodes | location | mythology | playwright | novel |
| novelists | scene | serial | set | |

The Invisible Man

Does anyone remember an old TV ¹_____ of *The Invisible Man*? It was adapted from the classic ²_____. I remember that it was split into six ³_____ and I watched them every Sunday with my family. I was only eight at the time and for me, one two-minute ⁴_____ was absolutely terrifying. The story is ⁵_____ in a typical nineteenth-century English village. The Invisible Man arrives and goes to a hotel room. Inside, he takes some bandages off his face – and underneath, you cannot see anything! It still makes me shiver today. Maybe it was because it was filmed on ⁶_____ in a village near my home, so everything looked very familiar to me.

Anyway, it's a great story by H.G. Wells, who was one of Britain's greatest ⁷_____. He also wrote *The War of the Worlds* and *The Time Machine*. His stories inspired me to become a writer and now I am a ⁸_____. In fact, my next work for the theatre is also about monsters and the unknown. It's based on a story from ancient Greek ⁹_____: Theseus and the Minotaur. I hope I can scare some kids in the audience in revenge for my childhood scare in front of the TV at home.

GRADABLE AND NON-GRADABLE ADJECTIVES

3 **Replace the words in bold with one word. Use a suitable non-gradable adjective so that the meaning of the sentence does not change.**

1 I presented an award and I read out the wrong person's name. I was **so embarrassed**.

_____

2 The film was **completely stupid**. We couldn't take it seriously. _____

3 The kids saw a film about ghosts and they were **very frightened**. _____

4 Frances bought seven DVDs and none of them worked. She was **very angry**! _____

5 Carlos got a big role in a movie, but the movie studio's money ran out and they couldn't make the film. He was **so disappointed**. _____

6 They were filming all night and that's why the actors are **really tired**. _____

7 Olivia has won a local poetry competition. Her parents are **really happy** for her. _____

VERBS OF MANNER

4 Complete the words. Write one letter in each space.

1 Can you drink more quietly? I hate it when you s _ u _ _ your coffee!

2 He is l _ _ p _ _ g because he hurt his leg playing football.

3 When I broke his glasses, he didn't say anything. He just g _ _ r _ _ at me angrily.

4 He told the girls to stop laughing at him, but they didn't listen and carried on g _ _ g _ _ _ g.

5 Everyone was g _ s _ _ _ g for breath because there was so much smoke in the room.

6 The tea was hot, so I s _ p _ _ d it slowly.

7 We s _ _ _ l _ _ d through the woods all afternoon. It was a lovely walk.

8 She's in love with a famous actor. She s _ g _ s every time she sees him on TV!

9 When I went to Russia, everyone s _ _ r _ _ at me because apparently, I look like a local celebrity.

10 My little brother is really annoying. If I say anything, he just s _ _ g _ _ _ s. I hate that laugh!

11 The movie was great. It begins when a mysterious man s _ _ g _ _ _ s into town. He can't walk because he has been in the desert for three days.

Grammar

NARRATIVE TENSES

1 Read the sentence beginnings (1–6). Match the endings (a–f) to the beginnings to make complete sentences.

1 I told him not to lend me the book because ___

2 That book is really boring. I fell asleep while ___

3 It was a great day for skiing. The sky was clear and ___

4 We decided to wait indoors while ___

5 The doctor didn't recognise the disease because ___

6 It wasn't possible to get an appointment with the doctor because ___

a I was reading it.

b he had never seen the symptoms before.

c it was snowing.

d he was seeing patients all afternoon.

e it had snowed the night before.

f I had read it before.

2 Look at the pictures below. They show past events. Complete the sentences using the words in brackets and the past perfect simple, past perfect continuous and past continuous.

1 When I got back to my car, I discovered
_____ (it / disappear).

2 He couldn't leave the stage because
_____ (audience / clap / ten minutes).

3 Gary was really tired in the morning because he
_____ (write / all night).

4 When I heard the bang, _____
(I / work / garden).

5 I missed my stop because _____
(I / read / novel).

6 The picture wasn't there – _____
(it / stole).

Listening: a ghostwriter

DIALOGUE + MULTIPLE CHOICE: PAPER 3, PART 4

1 🎧 5.1 **You will hear an interview with a ghostwriter, George Moore. For questions 1–7, choose the best answer (A, B or C).**

1 Why does George say that ghostwriters write the autobiographies of celebrities?

 A Celebrities are too lazy to write the book.

 B They are fans of the celebrities.

 C Celebrities do not have the time or skill to write the book.

2 What does George say about theatre actors?

 A They don't need a lot of help with the book.

 B They only write about half the book.

 C The ghostwriter writes all of the book for them.

3 Where does George get information about a teenage rock star's early career?

 A from the star's family

 B from national newspapers

 C from local libraries

4 How did George feel about writing the history of music festivals in the 1960s?

 A He preferred it to writing about teenage rock stars.

 B He thought it was boring.

 C He thought it was difficult.

5 How does George get paid?

 A The star gives him a percentage of his/her earnings from the book.

 B He receives a single payment for his work.

 C He gets royalties.

6 How did George start working as a ghostwriter?

 A His ex-boss gave up a job and George replaced him.

 B A star asked him to help write a book.

 C Through his business contacts.

7 Why does George not worry because his name is not on the cover of the book?

 A because he is embarrassed to be writing about pop music

 B because he gets a lot of money for his work

 C because his books are not as important as encyclopedias and other reference books

Pronunciation

Stress in long words
Placing the stress in new words can be very difficult. There is one guideline that can help you. When a word has more than three syllables, the stress is often on the third syllable from the end of the word.

1 🎧 5.2 **Look at the examples from the interview with George Moore. Listen to the pronunciation.**

autobiography

encyclopedia

negotiate

2 🎧 5.3 **Which words below have the stress on the second syllable from the end? Which words are exceptions? Listen to check your answers.**

appearances	experienced
appropriate	mysterious
centimetre	necessarily
characteristic	personality
disappearance	professional
disappointment	realistic
embarrassment	retirement
enthusiasm	sympathetic

3 🎧 5.3 **Listen again. Where is the stress in the adjectives that end -ic?**

4 🎧 5.4 **Now listen to these words of three or more syllables and complete the rule.**

When a word ends in -ion, the stress is on the

_____ syllable from the end.

association	restriction
definition	recognition
communication	suggestion
negotiation	

Reading and Use of English

OPEN CLOZE: PAPER 1, PART 2

1 Read the text below and think of the word which best fits each gap. Use only one word in each gap. There is an example at the beginning (0).

Heart of Darkness is **(0)** ....*a*.............. dark tale of colonial exploitation set **(1)** .... Africa during the nineteenth century. It was written **(2)** .... Joseph Conrad and published in English in 1902, despite the **(3)** .... that Conrad was born in modern Ukraine, and was of Polish nationality.

The narrator of the story is a sailor called Marlow **(4)** .... tells the tale while on a boat moored in the Thames. He recounts the story of how he travelled to Africa, excited by maps with empty spaces showing places that Europeans **(5)** .... not yet explored. Marlow takes a job on a boat travelling downriver into the African continent where he encounters an ivory trader, Mr Kurtz, who has become a kind of ruler over the local people.

The events of the novel are based on Conrad's own experience as the captain of a steamboat working in the Congo during the late nineteenth century. Although the African country in the book is **(6)** .... named in the novel, many readers assume that it is the Congo.

Conrad was a major novelist **(7)** .... novels have become even more popular since his death. The book has continued to influence later writers **(8)** .... well as Hollywood films such as *Apocalypse Now*.

Penguin Modern Classics

Joseph Conrad
Heart of Darkness

MULTIPLE-CHOICE CLOZE: PAPER 1, PART 1

2 Read the text below and decide which answer (A, B, C or D) best fits each gap. There is an example at the beginning (0).

If you want a different perspective on your friends' reading **(0)** ....*A*........... , why not ask them what was the worst book they ever read? Or what was the last book that they **(1)** .... to finish reading? When I asked a number of my friends this question, I got some surprising results.

The first surprise was one of my friends said that they had **(2)** .... on J.R.R. Tolkien's *The Lord of the Rings* after only ten pages! I was very disappointed because that is one of my all-time favourite reads. The same friend said that he had tried to read *Robinson Crusoe* by Daniel Defoe on several **(3)** .... , but had never finished it.

One of my friends said she had always **(4)** .... the modernist novelist Virginia Woolf, but that she had had problems reading her classic fantasy tale *Orlando*. The problem was that the book was difficult to read because of all its descriptions and adjectives. I have to admit that I felt the same: I finished the book, but it was **(5)** .... work.

Another interesting response was how many people said that they liked one kind of book when they were younger, but that their taste **(6)** .... as they got older. I remember my brother complaining at school when his teacher **(7)** .... him read *Great Expectations* by Charles Dickens. But when we were having dinner recently, he mentioned to me that now it is **(8)** .... of the books that he likes the most!

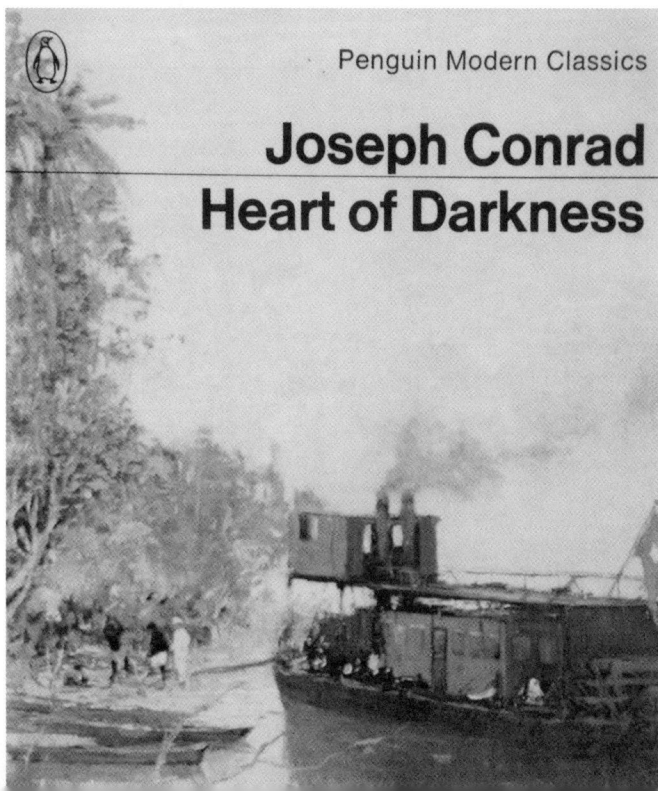

0	A habits	B hobbies	C activities	D pastimes
1	A objected	B passed	C failed	D lost
2	A gone away	B put down	C given up	D put away
3	A occasions	B events	C times	D dates
4	A admired	B delighted	C pleased	D preferred
5	A much	B hard	C heavy	D large
6	A grew	B changed	C distinguished	D turned
7	A said	B told	C let	D made
8	A one	B best	C included	D last

Writing: a short story

1   If you take the Cambridge English: First (FCE) for Schools exam, you may be asked to write a short story. Look at the exam question below and the student's answer, and answer the questions (1–5).

1   Does the story have a clear beginning and ending?

2   Does the story use paragraphs?

3   Does the story include the given sentence?

4   Is the story readable?

5   Is the story between 120 and 180 words?

> Your teacher has asked you to write a story for the school magazine. The story must include the sentence 'Suddenly we realised that we were lost.' Write your story in 120–180 words.

I was with my freind Martin and we were staying in a vilage in the mountains. We had decided to go walking because it was a sunny day. Unfortunately, the wether had changed in the afternoon and it had started to snow. Suddenly, everything was white. We were worried because we only had some sandwichs and a bottle of water. We didn't have a map so we didn't know wich way to go home. We wanted to phone our youth hostel to ask for help, but we had forgoten their phone number. It was a disaster! We were very frightend and we didn't know what to do. Luckily, after ten minutes, we saw a building on the road. There was a farmer outside and he was very surprised to see us. We explained what had happend and he agreed to help us. He was so nice because he gave us some food and then he drove us back to the youth hostel. We were lucky because it was a very dangerous situation.

(171 words)

2   Look again at the short story. Find and correct eight spelling mistakes. Then break the text into four paragraphs.

SPOTLIGHT ON STUDY TECHNIQUES

Make a note of your own common spelling errors while you are studying for the examination and learn the correct way to spell the words. When you check your written work, look for your common errors. If you cannot remember the correct spelling when doing the exam, cross out the word and replace it with another word that is easier to spell.

3   Write your own answer to the exam question in exercise 1. Remember to include the given sentence.

....

....

....

....

....

....

....

....

....

....

....

....

....

Speaking

COLLABORATIVE TASK: PAPER 4, PART 3

1 🎧 5.5 **In Part 3 of the Speaking test, you have to discuss something with your partner. Listen to two students discussing the question below and tick (✔) the options they choose.**

> You need to think of ways of encouraging schoolchildren in your country to read more. Discuss the list of possibilities below and choose the best two ideas.

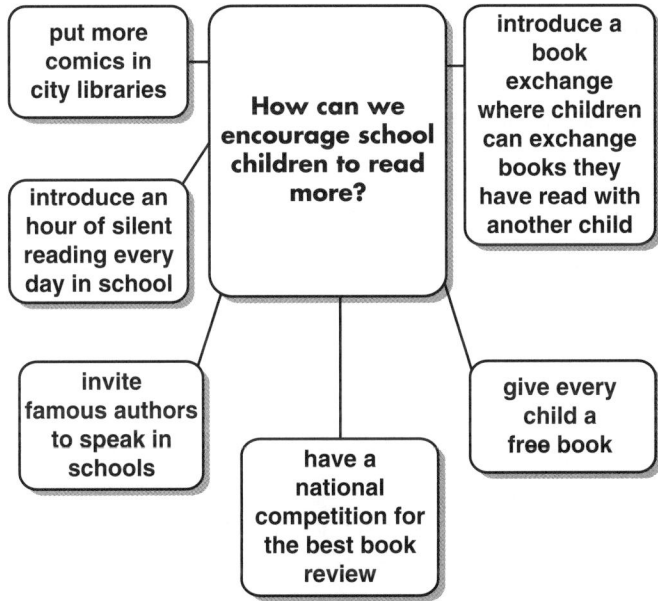

- put more comics in city libraries
- introduce an hour of silent reading every day in school
- invite famous authors to speak in schools
- **How can we encourage school children to read more?**
- have a national competition for the best book review
- introduce a book exchange where children can exchange books they have read with another child
- give every child a free book

2 🎧 5.5 **Correct the sentences (1–6) below. Then listen to the recording again to check your answers.**

1 There are options which appeal with different people.

2 I don't stand reading in the classroom.

3 It's not obvious choice, is it?

4 Anything that would appeal to me is to invite famous authors to schools.

5 Personal, I think this is difficult because it is expensive for the government.

6 Yes, I'm quite agree.

3 There are a number of phrasal verbs that you can use when you are discussing options in the collaborative task in the Speaking test. Look at the phrasal verbs in bold in the sentences (1–5) below. Match the definitions (a–e) to the phrasal verbs.

1 Let's **go through** the options one by one. ___

2 Let's **move on** to the second suggestion. ___

3 I think this is a good idea. I think we should **go for** it. ___

4 So to **sum up**, we have chosen the national competition. ___

5 I'm **weighing up** two possibilities: the famous authors and the book exchange. ___

a consider the benefits of

b progress

c discuss, examine

d conclude, end

e choose, select

4 🎧 5.5 **Listen to the discussion again. Try to hear the students using all of the phrasal verbs in exercise 3.**

5 If you are working with a partner, do the exam task in exercise 1 together.

Transport and travel

LANGUAGE CHECKLIST

☐ I know words to describe travel, page 48.

☐ I know some travel phrasal verbs, page 48.

☐ I know how to use ways of expressing the future, page 49.

☐ I know the spelling of some words in British and American English, page 49.

☐ I know how to pronounce /dʒ/, /tʃ/ and /j/, page 50.

EXAM CHECKLIST

☐ I have practised the multiple matching question from the Reading and Use of English paper, page 46.

☐ I have practised the Part 1 extracts + multiple choice question from the Listening paper, page 50.

☐ I have practised the open cloze question from the Reading and Use of English paper, page 51.

☐ I have practised the key word transformation question from the Reading and Use of English paper, page 51.

☐ I have practised writing a report from the Writing paper, page 52.

☐ I have practised the collaborative task from the Speaking paper, page 53.

Reading and Use of English

MULTIPLE MATCHING: PAPER 1, PART 7

1 You are going to read an article about four ancient sites. For questions 1–10, choose from the sites (A–D). The sites may be chosen more than once.

Which site

1 used to be a very important urban area? ____

2 was damaged by a natural disaster? ____

3 is used as a symbol of its country? ____

4 is less famous than another site in the same country? ____

5 has very many visitors? ____

6 has buildings which were used by more than one religion? ____

7 can be reached by public transport? ____

8 was used by people to build their homes? ____

9 was restored by a businessman? ____

10 is it best to visit early in the morning? ____

2 Now match the phrases in bold in the text to the definitions (1–10) below.

1 some _____

2 without having to share it with other people, alone _____

3 the best thing _____

4 something very special _____

5 in the end / after some time _____

6 despite this _____

7 similar to a thing that comes from _____

8 not less than _____

9 nothing is a better example of this _____

10 which is surprising because it is part of something very special

_____

LOOKING FOR THE ANCIENT WORLD

A Avebury, England

Stonehenge is one of the first things people want to see when they arrive in the UK. But there is one disadvantage to Stonehenge, which is that you are not allowed to touch the stones. And yet just a short distance away, there is another stone circle, not as well known, where you can walk and touch and explore the real stones: the Avebury stone circle.

Unlike Stonehenge, the Avebury stones are just large rocks which stand upright on the ground. The survival of the ring is **nothing short of** miraculous. The stones were once broken and buried by people who tried to eradicate evidence of the old religions. Later the stones were broken and used as building materials for local residences, as the stone circle surrounds the village of Avebury. **Eventually** the site was rescued by Alexander Keiller, a marmalade manufacturer, who paid for the buried stones to be raised up and for the circle to be restored. And now it can be visited again.

B Tarragona, Spain

The city of Tarragona in Catalonia was once the capital city of Roman Spain, when it was known as Tarraco. Today it is a very beautiful city with **a number of** excellent Roman sites. Very near the modern railway station, it is possible to visit the Roman amphitheatre, the city forum (the old marketplace), and a Roman tower, although Tarragona's best ancient site is outside the city walls.

A short bus ride from the city centre will take you to a desolate spot by the roadside. The bus driver will point at you to get off and you will find yourself wandering through hills and trees with no tourist centre, no cafés and bars, and hardly any tourists. And why? To see the ruins of a Roman aqueduct which used to bring water to the city. These ruins are **like something out of** another world. They are covered in weeds and the site is silent. You can walk along the top of the aqueduct marvelling at the view of the valley below. It's a rare treat nowadays: to find an ancient site and to have it **all to yourself**.

C Agrigento, Italy

In ancient times, the island of Sicily was an important part of the Greek world. Cities such as Siracuse were able to win famous battles over Athens and other Greek states. All of this colourful history means that Sicily is **a treat** for history buffs: and **nowhere more so** than Agrigento, the Valley of the Temples.

The sites themselves are scattered over a large area. **The highlight** of the trip is the Tempio della Concordia, a beautiful yellow temple saved from destruction because it was later converted into a Christian church. Other temples were not so lucky. All that remains of the Temple of Jupiter is the base of its columns and rubble after it was destroyed by an earthquake.

One further piece of advice is to drop into the museum on the site, which contains a number of important sculptures, mosaics and artwork.

D Nemrut Daği, Turkey

Turkey is rich with ancient sites, but the mountain of Nemrut Daği is special **even by its standards**. It is home to the massive stone heads which have become one of the iconic images of the country. Nemrut Daği lies in the far south-eastern corner of Turkey, but **even so** the fame of this remote site has meant that today the road to the sculptures is full of tourists.

However, there are still a few moments when you can enjoy the magic of the site with its giant stone heads of ancient gods, eagles and lions. If you arrive at dawn, you can watch the sun rise over the mountain illuminating the monuments.

Vocabulary

TRAVEL

1 Complete the words. Write one letter in each space.

In the Aegean Sea

I was once on a ¹ p _ _ k _ _ _ holiday in the Greek islands. I was staying with my boyfriend in a typical holiday ² r _ _ _ _ t and we were getting bored. There was nowhere to go ³ s _ g _ _ s _ _ _ _ g: no ruins or temples or anything like that. So we looked in our ⁴ g _ _ d _ b _ _ k. It recommended a boat ⁵ t _ _ p to a nearby island. It sounded great, so we went to the ⁶ t _ _ r _ _ _ information office to find out how to get there. However, when we asked for a ⁷ t _ _ _ t _ b _ _ to know when the boats left, the lady said 'there isn't one'. We were surprised and she explained that there was just one man and his boat. He didn't have any fixed schedules or ⁸ i _ _ n _ _ ar _ . He just left when he had enough tourists to go there.

So we went to the harbour, which was full of shops selling ⁹ s _ _ v _ _ ir _ . We were lucky to find the boat because there was no notice or advert for the tours. The boat was run by a man who had no watch and a T-shirt saying 'No problem'. He told us his name was Panos and he agreed to take us on an ¹⁰ e _ c _ r _ _ _ n to this little island.

It was one of the best days of my life. Panos stopped the boat so we could swim in the sea and he cooked fresh fish for us for lunch. He then joined us for a walk around the island and told us all about the local Greek history. He was very proud of his country's ¹¹ h _ r _ _ _ g _ and had loads of interesting things to tell us.

We came back at sunset and I wanted the day to go on forever. It just showed me that there is a different way to live life. I'm now back in London and I go to work every day with all the other ¹² c _ m _ _ t _ _ s, but in my heart, I'm still on Panos's boat, sailing on the timeless Mediterranean.

TRAVEL PHRASAL VERBS

2 Look at the sentences below. Six of them contain a mistake. Find and correct the mistakes.

1 Don't stay in a hotel. We can put you up while you're in London.

2 What time are you checking in your hotel?

3 We'll show around you the old town this afternoon.

4 When we get to Vilnius, we're meeting up from some friends.

5 Call me when you arrive and I'll pick you up from the airport.

6 We're setting to at 5 p.m. That's when we're leaving.

7 We were waiting for Rachel and Robert all afternoon, but they never turned them up.

8 The match is kicking out in five minutes!

3 Complete the phrasal verbs. Try to predict whether the phrasal verb will be made with *off*, *up* or *back*.

1 The explorers have started _____ on their journey to the North Pole.

2 If you want to take an English course next year, you can sign _____ here.

3 Some teenagers were writing graffiti on the walls. But when they saw the police, they ran _____.

4 Yvette sent me an email yesterday and I'm writing _____ to her this afternoon.

5 After he left school, Dan joined _____. He went into the army for seven years.

6 The glasses I had bought were broken, so I took them _____ to the shop.

4 Complete the sentences with the correct form of the phrasal verbs in the box.

drop off   phone back   take off   take out   travel around

1 The hotel you called this morning has _____ us _____ to find out what time we're arriving.

2 I'll be driving past the bus station on my way to work, so I can _____ you _____ there in time.

3 We're going to _____ _____ France in our motor home.

4 My wife is _____ me _____ for dinner this evening, but I don't know where we're going.

5 There was heavy snow at the airport, so our plane _____ _____ four hours late.

Grammar

EXPRESSING THE FUTURE

1 Read the sentences (1–6) below. Match the pictures (a–f) to the sentences.

1 We've just missed it, but don't worry, **I'll get** a taxi. ___

2 **We're going to go** to the beach this afternoon. ___

3 **There's bound to be** a tourist information office when we get there. ___

4 What time **does the first train leave tomorrow**? ___

5 We're just getting ready. We**'re leaving** in ten minutes, OK? ___

6 I've made some sandwiches because **she's likely to be** hungry after her long journey. ___

2 <u>Underline</u> the correct option.

1 According to the agenda, the meeting is *due / bound* to start now.

2 We're likely to *receive / receiving* an answer tomorrow.

3 Sorry, my mobile's ringing. *I'm just answering / I'll just answer* it.

4 Bill's carrying a lot of bags. *Will / Shall* I help him?

5 By the time Marie arrives tomorrow, Urs *will have gone / will be going* home.

6 Dad has to have an early night because he *is driving / will drive* to Manchester tomorrow.

7 Will you *have flown / be flying* to Spain or will you *have gone / be going* there by ferry?

8 Let's look for Nick in the café. He's *bound / due* to be waiting there.

Spelling

British and American English
In the Cambridge English: First (FCE) exam candidates are permitted to use British English, American English or other varieties of native speaker English. However, you should try to be consistent in your use of spelling as much as possible. There are a number of spelling differences between British and American English.

1 Look at the spelling table. Then look at the words below. Decide if the word is American or British English, as in the example.

British English	American English
-our, e.g. *rumour*	*-or*, e.g. *rumor*
-ise, e.g. *realise*	*-ize*, e.g. *realize*
-re, e.g. *centre*	*-er*, e.g. *center*
-ogue, e.g. *catalogue*	*-og*, e.g. *catalog*

1 odor *American English*

2 metre _____

3 dialog _____

4 organize _____

5 labour _____

6 specialisation _____

7 theater _____

8 litre _____

9 honor _____

10 colour _____

11 analogue _____

12 memorize _____

Listening: travel and visits

EXTRACTS + MULTIPLE CHOICE: PAPER 3, PART 1

1 🎧 6.1 **You will hear eight people talking about travel and visits. For questions 1–8, choose the best answer (A, B or C).**

1 You hear a man and woman speaking. What does the woman agree to do?

   A Drive the man in her car.

   B Let the man stay in her house.

   C Go with the man on his journey.

2 You hear a woman talking about her holiday. Why does she complain?

   A She received incorrect information about her hotel.

   B She did not like her hotel.

   C She did not like the beach.

3 You hear a boy talking about his holidays. What was the problem on the train?

   A It was too early.

   B It cost too much.

   C It was full of people.

4 You hear a man talking about his holiday. What did he buy?

   A A guidebook.

   B A souvenir.

   C A photograph.

5 You hear a man and a woman talking. Where are they?

   A A car park.

   B An airport.

   C A train station.

6 You hear a man and woman talking. What does the woman want to do?

   A She wants to go sightseeing every day.

   B She wants to save as much money as possible.

   C She wants to arrange the trip herself.

7 You hear a man talking about an excursion. Why was he unable to go?

   A He had a medical problem.

   B The weather was horrible.

   C He was not able to pay for it.

8 You hear a woman talking. What is she describing?

   A Being a tourist.

   B Being a taxi driver.

   C Being a tour guide.

Pronunciation

/dʒ/, /tʃ/ **and** /j/

The phonetic symbols /dʒ/, /tʃ/ and /j/ explain how to make the sounds.

/dʒ/ is d + z as in *John*.

/tʃ/ is t + sh as in *Czech*.

/j/ is pronounced *y* as in *yes*.

1 **Look at the sentences below. Which phonetic sound is used for the letters in bold?**

1 **J**im is a **j**azz **g**enius. ____

2 **Ch**eryl plays **ch**ess. ____

3 **Y**our **y**ogurt's **y**ellow. ____

4 **J**ane's **j**ust made some **j**ars of **j**am. ____

5 **Ch**arles's **ch**airs are **Ch**inese. ____

6 Mr **Y**oung works at **y**our **u**niversity. ____

2 🎧 6.2 **Listen and check your answers. Then listen and repeat.**

3 🎧 6.3 **Listen and circle the words you hear.**

> **chews** use **juice** cheese **jewel** **you'll**
> your *giraffe* **general** church *yeah*
> jaw *chair* yet *chin* judge jet *gin*

4 **If you are working with a partner, practise together reading all the words in exercise 3.**

Reading and Use of English

OPEN CLOZE: PAPER 1, PART 2

1 Read the text below and think of the word which best fits each gap. Use only one word in each gap. There is an example at the beginning (0).

For travellers on long-haul flights (flights of five hours or more), **(0)** ...._there_.......... are two main health problems: jet lag and the risk of DVT (deep vein thrombosis). Jet lag is **(1)** .... happens when you travel across time zones. Having jet lag means that your body's biological clock is running at a different time from the time in your destination country. Travellers suffering **(2)** .... jet lag feel tired and have problems sleeping. DVT is a serious medical condition that can be caused **(3)** .... sitting in the same position for a long period of time.

There are a number of things that can **(4)** .... done to prevent jet lag. First, it is better to take a night flight than a daytime flight so that you feel rested when you arrive. Secondly, you should try to drink a lot of water before you fly as well as during your flight. Medical evidence suggests that jet lag is caused by dehydration, so you should also avoid consumption of alcohol. In **(5)** .... to this, also avoid sleeping pills.

A number of health recommendations **(6)** .... been released that show you how to protect yourself against DVT. On long-haul flights, take the opportunity to walk up and down the aisle. There are a number of exercises that can be done without leaving your seat. **(7)** .... your flight includes a stopover in a foreign city, go for a short walk off the plane.

To help relax, wear sensible clothing and comfortable shoes. **(8)** .... your shoes off during the flight. To help you sleep, you should also wear dark glasses or bring your own eyeshades on board.

KEY WORD TRANSFORMATIONS: PAPER 1, PART 4

2 Complete the second sentence so that it has a similar meaning to the first sentence, using the word given. Do not change the word given. You must use between two and five words, including the word given. There is an example at the beginning (0).

0 She is the only one who doesn't want to fly to Morocco.

APART

Everyone wants to fly to Morocco ....*apart from her*........... .

1 We prefer to go to Switzerland.

RATHER

We .... to Switzerland.

2 I think that we should buy the flight tickets now.

TIME

It's .... the flight tickets.

3 I advise you to book a hotel before you leave.

HAD

You .... a hotel before you leave.

4 One possibility is to go on a walking holiday.

ALWAYS

We .... on a walking holiday.

5 I've never been on a plane before.

FIRST

This is .... I've been on a plane.

6 I'll call you the minute I get to Munich.

AS

I'll call you .... to Munich.

7 How long is the flight from London to Madrid?

TAKE

How long .... from London to Madrid?

8 I'd prefer us not to eat dinner at the hotel.

IF

I'd prefer it .... dinner at the hotel.

Writing: a report

OPTIONAL TASK: PAPER 2, PART 2

1 In Part 2 of the Writing test, you may be asked to write a report. Look at the exam question below and answer the questions.

1 What is the situation?

2 What is the purpose of the report?

3 Who is the target reader?

A travel website is preparing a short online guide to cities. They want a report on every city in the world for budget travellers.

Each report should explain:

- free or cheap places to visit
- ways to save money on transport
- cheap places to eat out.

The website has invited you to write a report for the guide about a city you know well. Write 140–190 words.

---

2 Look at a student's answer to the exam question in exercise 1. Complete the text with the words from the box.

all however including instead instance lastly
necessarily secondly

3 Now write your own answer to the exam question in exercise 1. Use as many phrases from exercise 2 as you can.

....
....
....
....
....
....
....
....
....
....
....
....
....
....
....
....
....

<u>London ... on a budget</u>

London is one of the most expensive cities in the world. ¹_____, it is possible to see the city without spending a lot of money.

First of ²_____, transport is expensive, especially the London Underground. A better way to see the city is to walk. Many underground stations are all in one street. For ³_____, Marble Arch, Bond Street and Tottenham Court Road Stations are all on Oxford Street so it is easy to explore the city on foot.

⁴_____, London restaurants are not cheap. ⁵_____ of eating a big lunch, buy sandwiches. Everyone eats them in the city parks, which are all free to enter. When it rains, go to Borough Market near London Bridge. There are lots of stalls there where you can buy food from all around the world at a very good price.

⁶_____, to save money and enjoy some culture, go to one of the city's museums. All the major galleries and museums are free, ⁷_____ the National Gallery and the British Museum.

In conclusion, London is not ⁸_____ a very expensive city. There are lots of affordable things to do if you plan your trip carefully.

Speaking

COLLABORATIVE TASK: PAPER 4, PART 3

SPOTLIGHT ON STUDY TECHNIQUES

In Part 3 of the speaking exam, the examiner ('the interlocutor') will ask you to discuss a question together. You will be shown a booklet with a diagram on it. This diagram will include a series of options. You will have two minutes to answer a general question about the options.

Then the examiner will ask you another question. In this question, the examiner will usually ask you to choose one or two of the options, and ask you to give a reason for your decision.

Listen carefully to the examiner's question and do exactly what they ask.

1 **Complete the sentences spoken by a Cambridge English: First (FCE) exam interlocutor. The interlocutor is showing the students the diagram below. Write one word in each gap.**

1 Now I'd like you to talk about something _____ for about two minutes.

2 I'd like you to _____ that you are in charge of organising a one-day school trip for teenagers aged 14 to 15.

3 Here are some of the places that you _____ go.

4 Talk to _____ other about what the students could learn by visiting these different places.

5 You now have some time to look at the _____.

6 All _____ ? Could you start now please?

7 Thank you. Now you have a _____ to decide which two places would be most interesting for the students to visit.

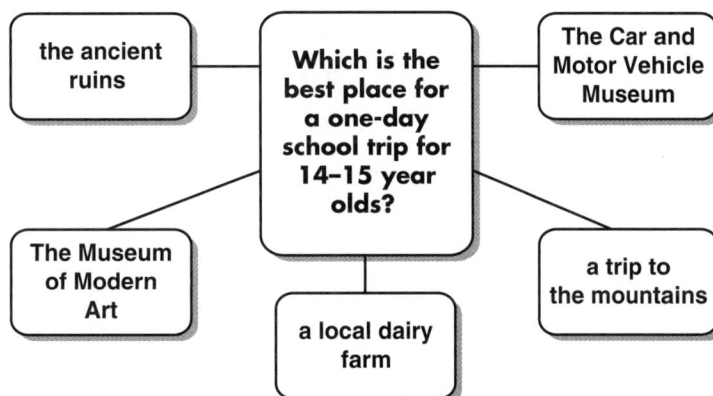

2 🎧 6.4 **Listen to the interlocutor in Part 3 of the Speaking test. Check your answers to exercise 1.**

3 🎧 6.5 **Listen to Bastien and Victoria doing Part 3 of the Speaking test. Number the trips (1–5) in the order they are mentioned.**

___ The ancient ruins

___ The Car and Motor Vehicle Museum

___ A trip to the mountains

___ A local dairy farm

___ The Museum of Modern Art

4 🎧 6.5 **Correct the mistakes in the sentences below. Then listen again to check your answers.**

1 It depends of the ruins. Sometimes there is not a lot to see.

2 Yes, that's true, Bastien. I think it's the good option. It's a better one than the Museum of Modern Art.

3 I think teenagers wouldn't learn nothing in the Museum of Modern Art.

4 It would be educational but personally, I'm not really interested of cars.

5 I mean, walking in the mountains is a good idea, don't it?

6 I no see why the trip to the mountains is a good option.

5 🎧 6.6 **Now listen to the interlocutor's next question. Answer these questions.**

1 Which two places do Bastien and Victoria choose?

....

2 What does the interlocutor ask for at the end?

....

6 **If you are working with a partner, ask and answer the exam questions in exercise 1.**

```
the ancient ruins — Which is the best place for a one-day school trip for 14–15 year olds? — The Car and Motor Vehicle Museum
The Museum of Modern Art — a local dairy farm — a trip to the mountains
```

LANGUAGE CHECKLIST

- [ ] I know words to describe inventors and inventing, page 56.
- [ ] I know some verbs which are followed by the gerund or the infinitive, page 57.
- [ ] I know how to spell nouns ending *-ment*, page 58.
- [ ] I know how to pronounce /ɪ/ and /iː/, page 59.

EXAM CHECKLIST

- [ ] I have practised the gapped text question from the Reading and Use of English paper, page 54.
- [ ] I have practised the sentence completion question from the Listening paper, page 58.
- [ ] I have practised the word formation question from the Reading and Use of English paper, page 59.
- [ ] I have practised writing a review from the Writing paper, page 60.
- [ ] I have practised the key word transformation question from the Reading and Use of English paper, page 61.
- [ ] I have practised the collaborative task from the Speaking paper, page 61.

Reading and Use of English

GAPPED TEXT: PAPER 1, PART 6

1 **You are going to read an article about professional computer games players. Six sentences have been removed from the article. Choose from the sentences (A–G) the one which fits each gap (1–6). There is one extra sentence which you do not need to use.**

A Row upon row of fans seated in the giant arena cheered, clapped and stamped their feet as the action unfolded on giant screens above the players.

B He used to play badminton at county level but began gaming after being injured at 15.

C Most gamers only play one game which they practise for up to twelve hours a day.

D By day, Anja Møller studies Nordic languages, but by night she is captain of the Aurora-Gaming Danish Women's Counter-Strike team.

E While he cannot match the top gamers in South Korea, the best of whom earn up to £500,000 per year, Liquid is still doing well.

F While gaming has not reached this level of excitement in Europe, it is heading in that direction.

G In front of him, the five members of the UK Four Kings Counter-Strike team shouted warnings and commands to each other.

2 **Now read the text again and find words that mean the following:**

1 only just (paragraph 1) _____

2 people who fight in a war (paragraph 1) _____

3 walked with big steps (paragraph 3) _____

4 to compete at the same standard (paragraph 3) _____

5 recruited (paragraph 5) _____

6 only just (paragraph 7) _____

7 a place where there is nothing (paragraph 7) _____

8 becoming smaller (paragraph 9) _____

£60,000 A YEAR, AND ALL YOU'VE GOT TO DO IS ZAP THE BAD GUYS

❶ **They look as if they are barely out of school, but when their zapping finger hits form, these computer game warriors can earn nearly £60,000 a year. Long gone are the days when playing video games was simply for teenage boys who spent too long in their bedrooms. Today's leading players are professional 'gamers' earning a good living from a basic salary, prize money and sponsorship.**

❷ In some parts of the world the elite players date models and need bodyguards to protect them from over-eager fans. **(1)** _____ Britain has 13 professional players, some of whom were at the Electronic Sports World Cup in Paris, which finished last night.

❸ In the heat of the competition, coach Ed Harborne paced up and down shouting instructions between the computer screens in front of his young stars. **(2)** _____ They were attempting to hold their own against strong Chinese opponents.

❹ 'C'est bien, allez, continuez,' called the female coach of the nearby French girls team. **(3)** _____ Approximately 25,000 supporters ignored the sunshine to watch the games.

❺ The 750 players from 53 nations were fighting to win a total of £216,000. It's a small amount in an industry worth £20 billion a year worldwide but a sign of things to come. Marc Mangiacapra, also known as Liquid, put his computer engineering degree on hold when he was signed by the Four Kings team two years ago.

❻ So far this year he has won £10,000 in prize money and spent one month each playing in Finland, China and Denmark. On Wednesday he will fly to Dallas for the World Series of Video Games. **(4)** _____ On top of his £19,000 salary from the team's Intel sponsorship deal, he expects to make around £20,000 in prize money this year, and in his most successful year earned close to £60,000. Last year he won £11,000 in one game. Earlier this year in China, he was chased down the street by autograph hunters and his team was treated to a limousine.

❼ 'All my friends think I'm the luckiest person ever, earning much more than them for flying around the world playing games and having fun.' James Harding, 23, from Glastonbury, Somerset, is known as 2GD to other gamers. **(5)** _____ In Paris yesterday he narrowly lost to the eventual winner in the quarter finals, earning himself £1,080. He said: 'I loved the competitive element of playing badminton and gaming has filled the void my injury left.'

❽ 'It should be classed as a sport. It requires just as much hand-eye co-ordination as tennis, and you need the same level of strategic and tactical ability as in chess.'

❾ Gaming is still a male-dominated activity, but the girls are catching up. **(6)** _____ She said: 'Girl gaming is getting much more competitive these days. We are not at the level of the guys yet, but the skill level gap is narrowing every day.'

Vocabulary

INVENTORS AND INVENTING

1 Complete the words. Write one letter in each space.

1 Dr Christiaan Barnard was a p _ _ n _ _ r of heart surgery. He performed the first successful heart transplant.

2 We don't know what caused the pollution in the river, but government scientists are running ex _ _ _ _ m _ _ _ s on the water to find out what is wrong.

3 The Wright brothers performed the first flight in an aeroplane, but it wasn't easy. They had many s _ _ b _ c _ s that stopped their work before they were finally successful.

4 Archimedes had the most famous b _ _ _ nw _ _ _ in history when he solved the problem of measuring volume in his bath.

5 When it first appeared, the Apple iPad was an amazing i _ n _ v _ _ _ _ n. No one had seen anything like it before.

6 Our holiday started really badly. A lorry had a b _ _ _ kd _ _ n on the motorway and we had to wait hours on the road before they moved it.

7 Thomas Edison's most famous i _ v _ _ t _ _ n is the lightbulb, but one of his other ideas was the first movie camera.

8 We couldn't find any explanation for the disease until the doctor finally made a b _ _ _ kt _ _ _ _ g _ when she was looking at a blood test.

2 Underline the correct part of the phrasal verb.

1 He hacked *into / over* the bank's computer system.

2 Click *at / on* the icon at the top of the page.

3 We've set *off / up* a new website.

4 I can't log *across / into* the system because I've forgotten my password.

5 The printer isn't working – it isn't plugged *in / on*.

6 I'll back the work *down / up* on another computer.

3 Complete the news article with the words from the box.

| brainchild | drawback | imagination |
| obsession | prototype | tests |

As easy as boiling an egg

I have an ¹_____ with the perfect boiled egg. I have one every morning and it has to be cooked for exactly three minutes, thirty seconds. So I was fascinated to read about the 'hot' new invention from Russia. The 'Gogol Mogol' is a special cardboard box with an egg inside. To make it work, you pull a tab to release chemicals inside the box. These then 'cook' the egg in two minutes, with no water required. It's the ²_____ of a team of scientists called KIAN. They have performed a series of ³_____ on the Gogol Mogol and they are confident it will work.

Unfortunately, there is just one big ⁴_____. The Gogol Mogol is not yet available in the shops: the scientists only have a ⁵_____ in their laboratory. All they need is a big food company with enough ⁶_____ to make the Gogol Mogol work and then my breakfast time will never be the same again. It will be one minute, thirty seconds shorter, to be precise.

TECHNOLOGY

4 Complete the puzzle with words for technology. What is the word in grey?

1 This is a document or a file that you add to an email message.

2 This is where new emails arrive for you.

3 You move this object with your hand to use the computer.

4 You use this device to make videocalls etc. online, e.g. by Skype.

5 Programs like Google and Bing are examples of _____ engines.

6 You put these in a page on the Internet to connect to other pages. You click on them and then you go to a new page.

7 This part of an email tells you what the message is about.

8 You use this to type information into your computer. It contains lots of letters and numbers.

9 You save and organise files in one of these on your computer.

10 Another name for the Internet.

11 When you are on the Internet, you are _____.

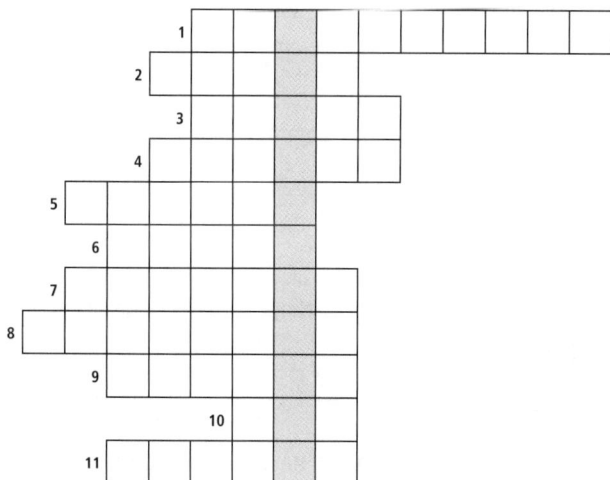

Grammar

VERBS FOLLOWED BY THE GERUND OR THE INFINITIVE

1 Look at the sentences below. Six of them contain a mistake. Find and correct the mistakes.

1 Oh no! I've forgotten telling Mika about the party!

2 I would like see what the world is like in 100 years' time.

3 Would you prefer to communicate by phone or email?

4 Do you remember to visit the Kremlin when we were in Russia?

5 He started as an assistant engineer and went on to be the chief designer.

6 Sorry, I didn't mean stopping you while you were working.

7 This equipment is out of date. It needs replace.

8 I told them to do some work, but they went on read the newspaper.

2 Underline the correct form of the verb.

1 In the future they will succeed *to develop / in developing* a robot that can think.

2 These robots could be designed to *look after / looking after* patients in hospitals.

3 I expect *to see / seeing* these robots in hospitals in my lifetime.

4 But can we risk *to have / having* robots to do a nurse's job?

5 The government would need *to think / thinking* carefully before it uses machines in a medical environment.

6 When I told this theory to my friends, they just laughed at me. I regret *to tell / telling* them now.

Spelling

Nouns with *-ment*

Many nouns in English end with the letters *-ment*. Usually these words are spelt by adding *-ment* to a verb, and the spelling of the verb does not change.

Example: manage ➡ management

1 Find ten nouns ending *-ment* in the wordsearch. Words can be found vertically, horizontally and diagonally.

e	s	p	j	u	d	g	e	m	e	n	t	a
n	a	a	f	g	o	l	z	o	i	b	v	i
c	c	r	y	e	b	q	a	v	u	k	u	z
o	h	j	r	v	n	t	y	e	e	l	l	y
u	i	e	f	a	r	g	u	m	e	n	t	a
r	e	s	u	l	n	k	q	e	t	o	d	d
a	v	q	p	e	e	g	u	n	c	n	f	v
g	e	r	o	n	p	k	e	t	s	s	e	e
e	m	g	o	v	e	r	n	m	e	n	t	r
m	e	b	d	i	b	v	v	o	e	k	e	t
e	n	a	e	r	c	o	d	g	x	n	v	i
n	t	x	d	o	e	n	t	f	p	g	t	s
t	a	w	z	n	p	w	j	w	i	y	o	e
y	f	l	k	m	b	l	e	j	b	e	i	m
p	l	a	c	e	m	e	n	t	s	n	k	e
i	v	o	d	n	y	a	n	g	y	t	c	n
g	l	i	x	t	z	d	w	t	e	x	s	t

2 Look again at your answers to exercise 1 and answer the questions.

1 Which word does not come from a verb?

2 Which word loses one letter when it changes from a verb to a noun?

Remember that in the Listening test, you will always hear the recording twice. As you work through the listening practice in this book, listen twice before checking your answers. The first time you listen, try to note down as many of the answers as you can without being distracted by the parts you do not understand. You will only find some of the answers when you listen the second time: do not panic the first time around!

Listening: Yume

SENTENCE COMPLETION: PAPER 3, PART 2

1 🎧 7.1 **You will hear a news report by Oliver Feldmann, a technology journalist, about the robots Yume and Geminoid. For questions 1–10, complete the sentences. You will need to write a word or a short phrase in each gap.**

People now use robots to

(1) ....

The robot Yume's name means

(2) .... in Japanese.

To develop Yume, researchers have already spent over

(3) ....

Yume cannot always recognise

(4) ....

The robot Yume cannot close her

(5) ....

People are friendlier to Yume if the robot tells

them that it (6) .... from time to time.

Yume's inventor Hiroshi Ishiguro has invented another robot called Geminoid, which looks like his

(7) ....

Hiroshi wants to put Geminoid in

(8) ....

The scientists want robots to look after

(9) ....

The ethical problem is that robots may be used as

(10) ....

2 🎧 7.1 **Now listen to the news report again and check your answers.**

Pronunciation

/ɪ/ and /iː/
To make an /iː/ sound, open your mouth wider so that you are grinning.

1 🎧 7.2 **Listen and number the pictures 1–6.**

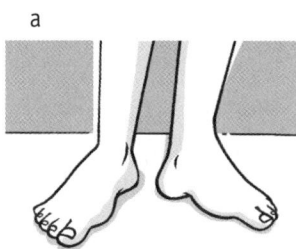

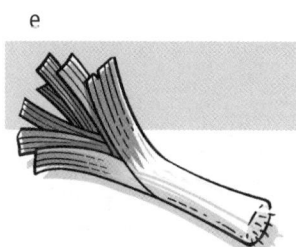

a

b

c

d

e

f

2 **Work with a partner. Say the words in exercise 1 to each other.**

3 🎧 7.3 **Now listen and repeat.**

	/ɪ/	/iː/			/ɪ/	/iː/
1	grin	green	5	rid	read
2	pick	peek	6	this	these
3	bit	beat	7	it	eat
4	sit	seat	8	chip	cheap

4 **If you are working with a partner, take turns to say one word from exercise 3. Your partner must point to the word that you say.**

Reading and Use of English

WORD FORMATION: PAPER 1, PART 3

1 **Read the text below. Use the words given in capitals at the end of some of the lines to form a word that fits in the gap in the same line. Use the endings in the box. There is an example at the beginning (0).**

ing	-er	~~-ment~~	-ical	-ant
-ity	-al	-ism	-ment	

When I first bought a computer fifteen years ago, I thought turning the machine on was an
(0) ......*achievement*...... . As far as I   **ACHIEVE**
was concerned, it was just a glorified typewriter. I had no internet connection, no printer, nothing. But after the
(1) .... revolution of   **TECHNOLOGY**
the last few years, I can't believe how my computer has changed my life.

When I first bought my computer, the main problem I had was my children having an (2) ....   **ARGUE**
over who could play a game on it. Now my main concern is
(3) .... Nevertheless,   **SECURE**
I do use the Internet for shopping and I get all my groceries online. I know there has been (4) .... of   **CRITICISE**
the effect online shopping is having on high street shops, but the Internet offers a (5) ....   **WIDE**
choice of books, DVDs and music than I can find in my local stores.

But perhaps the biggest change has been in my working life. My husband is an artist and he now does a lot of
(6) .... using the   **DRAW**
computer. And as for me, I work as a
(7) .... and I now   **CONSULT**
work from home. Fifteen years ago that would have been just a dream, but now it seems completely
(8) .... to work in my   **NATURE**
living room.

Writing: a review

1 Complete the student's answer to the exam question below with the phrases (a–g).

a The best moment

b it is worth

c All in all

d It is set

e My favourite film is

f The only downside of

g One thing I liked

Your school magazine has a section called *My favourite film*. Write a **review** of your favourite film, explaining why you like it. Write your answer in 140–190 words.

---

2 Now write your own answer to the exam question in exercise 1.

....
....
....
....
....
....
....
....
....
....
....
....
....
....
....
....
....
....

The Silver Linings Playbook

1_____ `The Silver Linings Playbook', a romantic comedy which was directed by David O. Russell. 2_____ in Pennsylvania, USA and it's about two people whose relationships have recently ended. Pat (Bradley Cooper) and Tiffany (Jennifer Lawrence) meet when they are jogging. They become friends and then they start to practise together for a dance competition. Slowly, they fall in love.

3_____ about the film was the intelligent script, which had lots of interesting ideas about modern life. It also has a surprise in the final scene, which is different from the normal Hollywood ending.

The cast is excellent, especially Jennifer Lawrence. There is also a great performance by Chris Tucker, who plays Pat's friend. 4_____ in the film is when he shows Pat how to dance with more emotion. The music is great too and 5_____ watching the film just for the soundtrack. 6_____ the film is that it deals with very serious issues, so it is not really appropriate to watch with children.

7_____, `The Silver Linings Playbook' is a great movie and you really feel good after watching it. Personally, I loved it.

Love hurts.

BRADLEY COOPER   JENNIFER LAWRENCE   ROBERT DE NIRO   JACKI WEAVER   CHRIS TUCKER

SILVER LININGS PLAYBOOK

Reading and Use of English

KEY WORD TRANSFORMATIONS: PAPER 1, PART 4

1 Complete the second sentence so that it has a similar meaning to the first sentence, using the word given. Do not change the word given. You must use between two and five words, including the word given. There is an example at the beginning (0).

0 Your computer might crash, so save all your work.
CASE
Save all your work *...in case your computer crashes...* .

1 We forgot to buy a mouse for the new computer.
REMEMBER

We .... a mouse for the new computer.

2 They ignored me and continued playing their game.
WENT

They ignored me and .... their game.

3 I shouldn't have deleted those computer files.
REGRET

I .... those computer files.

4 We wanted to fix the printer, but we didn't succeed.
TRIED

We .... the printer, but we didn't succeed.

5 Jill hasn't used her phone since she got Skype.
STOPPED

Jill .... her phone when she got Skype.

6 Finally, we managed to solve the problem!
SUCCEEDED

Finally, we .... the problem.

7 I can't wait to go to the technology fair.
FORWARD

I'm really .... the technology fair.

8 Someone should check to see if the website is working.
NEEDS

The website .... to see if it is working.

Speaking

COLLABORATIVE TASK: PAPER 4, PART 3

1 🎧 7.4 You will hear some students doing the collaborative task in the Speaking test. They have to decide which of the six suggestions below would be most useful for a website that helps to teach people to speak English. Listen and decide which point they are discussing.

Pair 1 ____   Pair 3 ____   Pair 5 ____

Pair 2 ____   Pair 4 ____

> a video of people in real situations (in the bank, etc.)
> b online exercises with words to complete
> c an online translation device
> d written models of letters, essays, etc. to print off
> e lists of common errors that people make in English
> f games and songs
> g reading exercises with questions

2 🎧 7.4 Listen again and complete the sentences with the useful words for exchanging ideas, and expressing and justifying opinions.

1 I think this would be _____ for people learning English. (extract 1)

2 I know what _____, but I don't think you can have a list for every language. (extract 1)

3 I don't _____ this. I mean, if you use the Internet, it's easy to find an article in English. (extract 2)

4 _____ good idea. I never get the opportunity to see English as it's used in real life. (extract 3)

5 Yes, I think _____. (extract 3)

6 For me, _____ one. (extract 4)

7 And we _____ highlight useful words and phrases that students can learn. (extract 4)

8 I don't think this is a good idea _____. (extract 5)

9 This kind _____ never works. (extract 5)

10 Sure. I think it's _____ too. (extract 5)

3 If you are working with a partner, do the exam task in exercise 1 together. In the Speaking test, you will have about three minutes to do the collaborative task.

Reading and Use of English

MULTIPLE MATCHING: PAPER 1, PART 7

1 **You are going to read an article about four prisons. For questions 1–10, choose from the prisons (A–D). The prisons may be chosen more than once.**

In which prison

1 are there places where you can go shopping? ___

2 are prisoners allowed to get takeaway food? ___

3 were there restrictions on washing? ___

4 can you play racket sports? ___

5 are cells traded as property? ___

6 is excellent cuisine served? ___

7 can sports skills improve the lives of prisoners? ___

8 do some people meet a wife or husband? ___

9 is there nowhere to borrow books? ___

10 do people want to become prisoners at the jail? ___

2 **Now match the words in bold in the text to the definitions (1–8) below.**

1 many _____

2 a building and organisation like a school, a prison or a hospital

   _____

3 made to do something that you do not want to do _____

4 the government and the organisations that it controls, such as the police, the army, etc. _____

5 absolutely enormous _____

6 inside _____

7 in a very bad condition (especially for a building) _____

8 money you can pay so that you can wait for trial in your home and not in prison _____

Prison tales

This week we profile four rather unusual prisons and prison systems.

A Bolivia

On arriving at the San Pedro prison in La Paz, Bolivia, you could be forgiven for thinking you weren't in jail at all. The jail seems like a city **within** a city. The prisoners have a market and restaurants, and children are running around the streets. It seems almost surreal, but this is a jail: everything is surrounded by huge walls, and all the entrances and exits are guarded.

Uniquely at San Pedro, the world of commerce rules the prison world. Inmates have to pay for their cells, which means that they need to work to earn money. There's just one problem: they still have to spend their time in jail! There are even wealthy areas of the prison where cells can be traded for as much as £1,500. Not everyone lives in this luxury and other prisoners are **forced to** share small cells elsewhere in the prison complex.

You might wonder where people get the money to support this sort of lifestyle, but in fact, it is not that much different from life outside. For example, there is a football pitch in the prison and games are played by **numerous** teams. A top player can be signed up by a team with more money, which is a ticket to living in the nicer end of 'town'.

B India

Once the prison at Parappana Agrahara in Bangalore was **an institution** with serious problems. In a country with intense heat and high population, the prison suffered for many years from a serious water shortage. The prison needed almost 30,000 gallons every day, which was an unsustainable rate of consumption. It affected everyone at the prison, and forced the authorities to reduce the amount of water available for bathing.

That was some years ago and now the prison is enjoying a resurgence in popularity from its own inmates. The prison cooking has been taken over by the International Society of Krishna Consciousness and the prisoners are delighted with the delicious meals that are being served. Some prisoners are even neglecting to apply for **bail** and opting to remain locked up. 'When we are getting tasty, nutritious food three times a day, why should we go out and commit crimes?' one burglar inquired. There are even reports of criminals wanting to get in!

C Spain

Popular prisons are not the sole preserve of Asia, however. In his excellent book *Ghosts of Spain*, the author Giles Tremlett describes Spanish jails in a similarly positive way.

'Spanish jails are remarkably modern, well equipped and tolerant places,' he writes. 'Some boast glass-backed squash courts, swimming pools and theatres. Most of the British prisoners in them do not apply to serve their time back home in Britain's **run-down**, aggressive Victorian-built prisons.'

Most surprising of all is the fact that prisons are not separated into male and female prisons. Some prisoners even meet their future spouses while serving time for their crimes.

D Switzerland

The more comfortable prison is nothing new, however. In 1970 the writer Paul Erdman was arrested after the bank he was running went out of business with **colossal** debts. He was incarcerated in a three-hundred-year-old dungeon in the Swiss city of Basel, but was lucky to avoid the terrible conditions of eighteenth-century justice.

Instead he found himself living in near luxury. The dungeon was much improved. Prison life included room service which brought him his evening dinner. This service was not delivered by **the state** as Erdman had enough money in his own bank account to pay for this food to be delivered to him from local restaurants.

Untroubled by the usual conflicts and noise of prison life, Erdman passed the time writing his first novel, having brought along a typewriter to his cell. In many ways it was the deficiency of the jail that caused his career change. The prison lacked a library, preventing him from doing research. This meant Erdman decided to work on a novel instead of non-fiction and became a best-selling novelist once he was released.

Vocabulary

CRIME AND CRIMINALS

1 Complete the crimes in the police Twitter feed. Write one letter in each gap.

National Police @NationalPolice

↩ Reply ⇄ Retweet ★ Favorite ••• More

1 Watch out for fake banknotes in the city area. We have discovered a case of f _ _ _ _ r _ using notes of €50.

2 We advise all shopkeepers to install security cameras to prevent s _ _ p _ _ f _ _ _ _ . Help us prevent crime!

3 Today is the fifth anniversary of the k _ _ _ _ _ p _ _ g of the race horse Titan. His location is still unknown.

4 We now believe that the fire at the Football Club was a case of a _ _ o _ . We invite members of the public to contact us if they have any information.

5 News reports of the death of Mr F Welsh are inaccurate. We believe his death to be a tragic accident, not m _ _ _ _ r , as reported in some parts of the media.

6 After a violent m _ g _ _ _ g on an intercity train where a gang stole money from an elderly couple, security guards will now travel on board at all times.

7 Remember to change your passwords regularly to prevent people from h _ _ k _ _ g into your account.

8 Thanks to action from the local community, there is much less v _ _ d _ _ _ _ m of bus stops and vending machines in the area. Thanks to all our volunteers!

9 There were four cases of b _ _ g _ _ _ y in the harbour area last month, where homes were broken into and electrical goods taken.

10 Customs officers last night prevented a case of s _ _ g _ _ _ _ g rare birds into the country.

---

2 Find ten words for criminals in the wordsearch.

S	H	O	P	L	I	F	T	E	R
Z	X	S	V	A	N	D	A	L	A
Q	J	M	U	R	D	E	R	E	R
W	B	U	R	G	L	A	R	H	S
K	V	G	K	J	J	Y	Z	A	O
M	U	G	G	E	R	N	Q	C	N
W	P	L	Q	V	F	D	X	K	I
V	N	E	M	W	Z	Y	Y	E	S
F	O	R	G	E	R	G	Y	R	T
K	I	D	N	A	P	P	E	R	W

Grammar

RELATIVE CLAUSES

1 Combine the two sentences with a relative clause to make a single sentence, as in the example.

1 Sherlock Holmes was the detective. He solved the crime.

Sherlock Holmes was the detective who solved the crime.

2 This is the hotel. The murderer was caught here.

_____

3 The police want to speak to the man. His car was parked outside the bank during the robbery.

_____

4 Three people were working in the jewellery store on Wednesday. Several watches and pairs of sunglasses were stolen then.

_____

5 The police interviewed five people. They had reported the vandalism in the railway station.

_____

6 No one knew the reason. The crime had taken place.

_____

7 These are the keys. The keys were stolen last night at 11 p.m.

_____

2 **Non-defining relative clauses add extra information to a sentence. Unlike defining relative clauses, they are separated from the main sentence with commas. Add commas to the sentences, if necessary.**

1 Martina Kruger is the person that asked to speak to you.

2 The police released the man who then sold his story to the newspapers.

3 My father who you met last year is now writing a detective novel.

4 Our head office which is being decorated at the moment is on the top floor of this building.

5 The police have found the place where the murder happened.

6 Leonardo DiCaprio starred in *The Great Gatsby* which was directed by Baz Luhrmann.

3 **Look at the sentences below. Five of them contain a mistake. Find and correct the mistakes.**

1 This is the building where was built by Sir Norman Foster.

2 That is the man who dog is outside.

3 The reporters interviewed the man that was accused of murder.

4 This is the book which you gave me.

5 Denise is the woman what comes from France.

6 Do you know the name of the man whom is working here tomorrow?

7 I know the reason why you helped me.

8 I think 19th November is the day which we are having the party.

4 **Complete the sentences with a preposition to make more formal relative clauses.**

1 This is a list of the addresses of all the people _____ whom the invitations should be sent.

2 11 July is the date _____ which the trial will begin.

3 We have selected the building _____ which the ceremony will be held.

4 Do you know _____ which reason these documents are required?

Spelling

Negative adjectives
The negative of many adjectives is spelt with the prefix *un-*.
Example: comfortable ➜ uncomfortable

However, there are other adjectives which use a prefix starting with *in-*.
Example: effective ➜ ineffective

Some negative adjectives are made by adding *i-* and doubling the first consonant. These words may start with *l*, *m* or *r* and you need to learn them in each case.
Example: legal ➜ illegal

Many adjectives that begin with *p* use a prefix starting with *im-*.
Example: possible ➜ impossible

1 **Look at the adjectives below. Write the negative adjective.**

1 responsible _____

2 mature _____

3 accurate _____

4 logical _____

5 relevant _____

6 moral _____

7 regular _____

8 probable _____

9 appropriate _____

10 literate _____

11 precise _____

12 mortal _____

13 resistible _____

14 capable _____

15 polite _____

Listening: victims of crime

MULTIPLE MATCHING: PAPER 3, PART 3

1　When you do the multiple matching task, look at the options and identify the key words. Try to think of related words that you might hear in the recording. These related words might help you to match the options. You are going to listen to some extracts about victims of crime. Before you listen, try to match the key words in the box to the crimes (1–6) below. Write the words next to the crimes.

> a bag　a bank statement　to break　to break in
> to clone　a credit card　the fire brigade
> the front door　to hit　holiday　a knife　matches
> the number　to scratch　a shelf　a store　a till
> a wallet　a window

1　arson _____

2　shoplifting _____

3　vandalism _____

4　mugging _____

5　forgery _____

6　burglary _____

2　🎧 8.1 Now do the listening task. You will hear five people talking about being victims of crime. For Speakers 1–5, choose from the list (A–H) the crime that each person was a victim of. There are three extra letters which you do not need to use.

Which speaker

A　was a victim of a pickpocket?

B　was a victim of arson?　　　　　Speaker 1 ___

C　was a victim of shoplifting?　　Speaker 2 ___

D　was a victim of vandalism?

E　was a victim of online hacking?　Speaker 3 ___

F　was a victim of mugging?　　　Speaker 4 ___

G　was a victim of forgery?　　　Speaker 5 ___

H　was a victim of burglary?

Pronunciation

Nouns and verbs with changing pronunciation (1)
Some words are stressed differently, depending on whether the word is a noun or a verb. This only affects a small number of words, fortunately. Errors here rarely cause misunderstanding.

1　Look at the sentences below. What kind of word is the word in bold in each sentence?

1　a　I have bought Joe a **present** for his birthday. ___

　　b　Who is going to **present** the report? ___

2　a　The plates were cheap because they were **rejects** from the factory. ___

　　b　The problem with Dieter is that he **rejects** everyone else's suggestions. ___

3　a　I'm going to **conduct** the orchestra at a concert next week. ___

　　b　All members of the club have to obey our code of **conduct**. ___

4　a　I was shocked that the police had no **record** of the crime. ___

　　b　You can't use the video because I'm going to **record** something on TV. ___

5　a　We only stock fresh **produce** in the store. ___

　　b　If you accuse someone of a crime, you need to **produce** some evidence. ___

6　a　Here is all the equipment you need to **project** your presentation from your computer. ___

　　b　Karen is working on a very difficult **project** at the moment. ___

2　🎧 8.2 Now listen and underline the stress on the words in bold, as in the first sentence.

Reading and Use of English

OPEN CLOZE: PAPER 1, PART 2

1 Read the text below and think of the word which best fits each gap. Use only one word in each gap. There is an example at the beginning (0).

Middlesbrough **(0)** ......*has*...... become the first town in Britain **(1)** .... introduce talking CCTV cameras. Faced with problems like littering, drunkenness and antisocial behaviour, the city mayor started placing loudspeakers next **(2)** .... security cameras last year. Now, when people are breaking the law, they will hear a voice warning **(3)** .... that they are being watched. This affects all sorts of petty offences, including riding a bicycle through **(4)** .... pedestrianised zone.

If you are foolish enough to ignore the law inside the system's zone, you **(5)** .... be very quickly told to change your behaviour. For example, people who throw litter on the streets will hear themselves being described and an instruction to pick up their rubbish and throw it away **(6)** .... the correct place.

This system is the brainchild **(7)** .... the local mayor, Ray Mallon, an ex-policeman who **(8)** .... known as Robocop for his hard stance against law-breaking. Of course, as this is England, the voices are very polite. They use 'please' and 'thank you' while the women are addressed as 'madam' and the men as 'sir'.

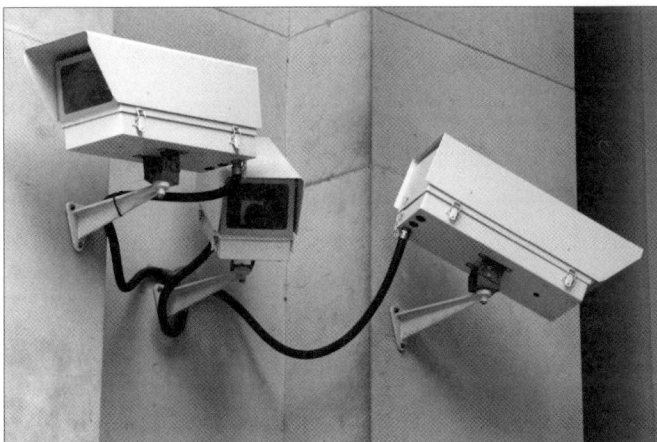

MULTIPLE-CHOICE CLOZE: PAPER 1, PART 1

2 Read the text below and decide which answer (A, B, C or D) best fits each gap. There is an example at the beginning (0).

The police have announced that **(0)** ....*D*.......... figures in the capital have increased yet again. A police spokesperson warned that small offences were increasing and warned the public to be on their guard against attacks in the streets, such as **(1)** ....

The police did report a crackdown on offenders after they made a number of **(2)** .... of gangs of thieves who work on the underground network. This attracted a great deal of **(3)** .... attention and the photographs of the suspects appeared in all major newspapers. The police have also encouraged local storekeepers to install security cameras to reduce the amount of **(4)** .... throughout the city.

Nevertheless, it is the organised gangs that remain public **(5)** .... number one. They have been responsible for graffiti, vandalism and violent attacks on the major housing estates north of the city. Many elderly people suffer from intimidation from the gangs and some are afraid even to leave their own homes. The police have **(6)** .... for witnesses who may be able to give evidence against these people. The police commissioner has stated that this situation cannot continue. 'We cannot **(7)** .... these hooligans ruin the lives of everyone else in the community,' she said yesterday. 'But whether we can catch the leaders of the gangs **(8)** .... on us getting information from the public.' She also emphasised the increased threat to the city's essential tourist industry if future conditions do not improve.

0	A illegal	B suspect	C police	D crime
1	A burglary	B mugging	C arson	D forgery
2	A arrests	B stops	C escapes	D catches
3	A journalist	B media	C presentation	D report
4	A blackmailing	B hacking	C shoplifting	D kidnapping
5	A opponent	B protestor	C enemy	D fear
6	A demanded	B complained	C applied	D appealed
7	A permit	B accept	C let	D allow
8	A requires	B needs	C follows	D depends

Writing: an article

OPTIONAL TASK: PAPER 2, PART 2

1 In Part 2 of the Writing test, you may be asked to write an article. Complete the student's answer to the exam question below with the phrases (a–i).

a So why not
b A second way
c In conclusion
d So it is clear to see
e Take, for example,
f There are three main things
g There is no doubt that
h Finally
i Firstly

> Read this advertisement from a website. Write an article for the website.
>
> We are looking for suggestions for three ways that local people can get involved to help improve our city and make it a nicer place to live in.
>
> Write your answer in 140–190 words.

<u>GET INVOLVED!</u>

1 _____ our city needs improvement. 2 _____ the litter and the graffiti which are everywhere. Many public places have also been damaged by vandalism. 3 _____ that we need to do something to encourage people to help improve our city.

4 _____ that we can do. 5 _____, it is difficult to stop people littering. 6 _____ start groups to pick up the litter? If we keep the streets clean, people will think carefully before dropping rubbish. 7 _____ is to ask people to plant more trees in the parks. People will want to get involved if they are helping the environment. If the city is a nice place to live, it will discourage vandalism. 8 _____, we need to set up special spaces for graffiti. Then graffiti artists can paint in these special places and not on public buildings.

9 _____, if we want to live in a nice city, we all have to do something to make our environment pleasant to live in.

2 Now write your own answer to the exam question in exercise 1. Use this plan:

Paragraph 1: introduction and explanation of the problem

Paragraph 2: three solutions and explanations of the solutions

Paragraph 3: conclusion

....
....
....
....
....
....
....
....
....
....
....
....
....
....
....
....
....
....

Speaking

COLLABORATIVE TASK: PAPER 4, PART 3

1 🎧 8.3 Sometimes in the Speaking test you might work in a group of three rather than two. It is even more important to use phrases to show that you are listening. Listen to five extracts of Bastien, Natalya and Victoria discussing the exam question below, and decide which method of crime prevention (a–e) they are talking about.

Extract 1 ___   Extract 4 ___

Extract 2 ___   Extract 5 ___

Extract 3 ___

a. car alarms	**Are these good ways of preventing crime and bad behaviour?**	**e. instant fines for dangerous driving**
b. asking for photo ID when paying by credit card	**c. security cameras in public places**	**d. put up warning posters about pickpockets**

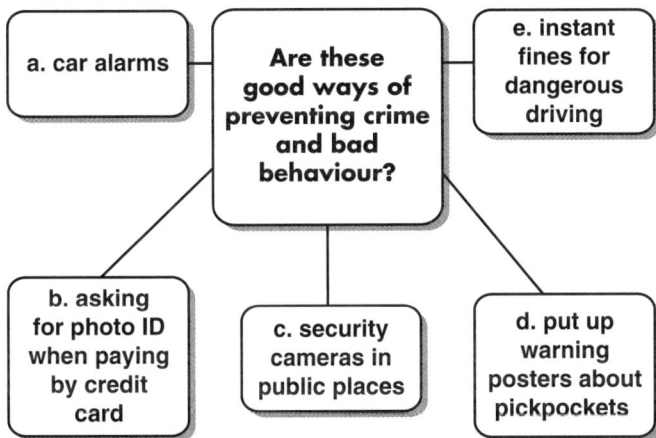

2 🎧 8.3 **Listen again and write the words that Natalya (N), Victoria (V), and Bastien (B) use to respond to suggestions, and to show that they are listening.**

1 **N** The problem is that you hear these alarms all the time.

  V _____.

2 **N** You think, 'Oh, there's another alarm. How noisy!'

  V I'm _____ on that.

3 **B** I think that drivers don't care if they drive very fast.

  N _____.

  B You know, the drivers, they don't really care, so you have to do something else. To …

  V _____. You have to force them to drive with more care.

  B Yes. _____. To force.

4 **V** In my country this is very common.

  N _____, Victoria?

  V _____ . Every time you buy with your credit card, they ask to see your identity card. It's normal.

  B _____.

5 **V** If you don't have an identity card, the police don't know who you are, who anyone is.

  N _____, but I don't think that they are very useful.

6 **N** This is a very quick way to tell people to look out.

  B _____ you mean, but I really don't agree. Posters won't stop pickpockets. It's just a waste of money.

  N _____, but it is important to say to people, 'Be careful'.

  V _____, so do we think this is a good idea or not?

7 **V** And also you can cover your face so nobody sees you.

  B _____. Anyway, the pictures you get from these cameras are often not very clear.

  N _____. But sometimes they are useful after a crime. The police have caught lots of criminals by using these cameras.

  V _____.

3 **If you are working with a partner, do the exam task in exercise 1 together. Try to use the words and phrases from exercise 2.**

Reading and Use of English

GAPPED TEXT: PAPER 1, PART 6

1 **You are going to read an article about the history of food. Six sentences have been removed from the article. Choose from the sentences (A–G) the one which fits each gap (1–6). There is one extra sentence which you do not need to use.**

A The avocado was known to the Maya, one of the ancient peoples of Mexico.

B Elsewhere, in Ecuador, there is evidence that chillis have been used in cooking for over 6,000 years.

C At first the local people were shocked and believed that the animal and its rider were the same creature.

D This impacted our diet and our languages.

E Instead they were grown for decoration.

F Supermarket shelves are full of every imaginable type of fruit and vegetable.

G It was known in ancient times: Alexander the Great had encountered the fruit while he was travelling in India.

2 **Now read the text again and find words or phrases that mean the following:**

1 come from (paragraph 2) _____

2 a large variety of (paragraph 3) _____

3 in the beginning (paragraph 4) _____

4 the parts of a plant that grow under the ground (paragraph 4)

   _____

5 is the largest participant in (paragraph 6) _____

6 to change an animal species from wild to tame (paragraph 7)

   _____

The first food revolution

❶ Can you imagine goulash, the national dish of Hungary, without its spicy paprika? Or Italian cooking without the tomato? These foods are a huge part of each country's national cuisine. So it comes as rather a shock to know that both countries have been using these ingredients for little more than 600 years. This is because both paprika and the tomato came to Europe from the New World, after the arrival of Columbus in the Americas in 1492.

❷ After the first encounter of Europeans and native Americans, there was an enormous movement of food from the Old World to the New World, and vice-versa. **(1)** _____ The words *tomato*, *avocado* and *chocolate* all originate from the civilisations of the New World, such as the Aztecs.

❸ Agriculture in the 'New' World was very old indeed. Peoples such as the Maya and Aztecs in modern Mexico had developed a wide range of interesting foodstuffs. For example, the Spanish conquistadors were astonished to see the Aztec ruler Montezuma drinking chocolate. They soon exported this drink to Europe. **(2)** _____ The spice would be mixed with corn, which was also grown on ancient farms.

❹ Like all new things, there was suspicion of the discoveries made by the European explorers. Originally, both the turkey and the tomato were not used as food in some parts of Europe. **(3)** _____ The turkey was kept for its beautiful feathers and the tomato as a plant for gardens. In the past, experts believed the tomato was a similar plant to *belladonna* and so many people believed that it was dangerous to eat. There is some truth in this, as the leaves and roots of the plant are actually poisonous.

❺ The huge movement of foods which took place after 1492 has become known as the Columbian Exchange. This is because the traffic was not all one-way. In addition to new crops moving to Europe and Asia, Old World crops were planted across North and South America.

❻ One example is the banana. **(4)** _____ Once it moved to the Caribbean islands, it soon became an enormously important crop throughout the area. In the same way, coffee was discovered in Africa and then transported to South America. We now have a situation where the world's largest producer of the drink is Brazil, which dominates world production.

❼ The arrival of the horse into the Americas also had dramatic effects. **(5)** _____ Quickly, they learnt how to domesticate and use the animals themselves. In North America, the horse revolutionised the native American's way of life. On horseback, the local tribes were able to hunt the wild buffalo, which were then common across the continent.

❽ From the Columbian Exchange we can see that globalisation is not a new process, but rather the result of centuries of cultural exchange. In our modern world we are now able to buy and grow all of these food products with ease. **(6)** _____ This makes it difficult to imagine a world where a tomato was looked at with fear and a horse was something magical. This is one of the greatest losses of our era: that we are no longer excited by the extraordinary world around us.

Vocabulary

FOOD AND DRINK

1 Complete the sentences with the word pairs. Write one word in each gap.

> bitter / tasty   bland / salty   cold / mild
> cooked / raw   rare / well-done   sour / sweet
> sparkling / still   hot / spicy

1 Some people think that all curries are

_____ but actually many of them are

quite mild. They can still be _____
when they're mild, though, because they use lots of
exotic ingredients.

2 I found a recipe online for a _____
cauliflower salad. I wasn't sure about it because I

had only ever eaten _____ cauliflower
before, usually boiled, but it was actually very nice.

3 I prefer my steak _____. I don't want
any blood in it. My brother likes them

_____: they only cook it for a few
seconds on each side. Yuk!

4 At first the stew was a bit _____ and
tasteless but after we seasoned it, it was too

_____ and it was impossible to eat.

5 If I'm buying water, then I'd always

choose _____. If you want

_____, you may as well drink tap water.

6 I made a big mistake with my cake. Because the

lemons were quite _____, I added lots
of sugar. But in the end, it was too much and the cake

was too _____.

7 I've made you a summer soup with pea and mint. It's

very _____ – it doesn't have a very

strong taste. It's better eaten _____, so
we don't heat it.

8 Turkish coffee is very _____, so they
always serve it with water. But it goes very well with
their cakes, like baklava. They're really

_____, delicious!

2 Cross out the word that doesn't work in each sentence.

1 Get a knife and *chop / grate / slice* these onions for
me, please.

2 Let's *boil / fry / grill* these steaks.

3 You need to *grate / peel / sprinkle* some cheese on the
pasta.

4 Now we need to *mix / slice / stir* the cream and the
chocolate sauce together.

5 You need to *boil / peel / pour* those potatoes before
we eat them.

6 We'll *bake / fry / roast* this salmon in the oven for
about half an hour.

7 How's the lasagne doing? Could you *add / chop / stir*
the sauce?

8 I'll just *bake / stir / pour* the soup for you. OK. Is that
enough?

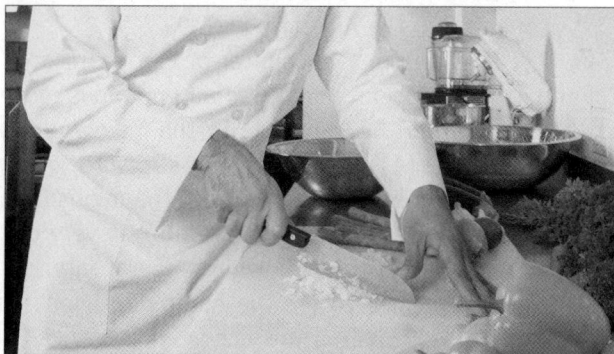

Pronunciation

Silent letters
English words frequently contain silent letters. Be
careful that you do not pronounce these letters when
you say the words.
Example: iron ➔ i~~r~~on /aɪən/

1 ♩ 9.1 **Cross out the silent letters in each word, as in
the example above. Then listen to check your answers.**

answer	island	sandwich
calm	knight	sword
castle	knitting	vegetable
chocolate	palm	Wednesday
cupboard	pneumonia	whole
guardian	psychiatrist	yacht
guess	salmon	

2 **If you are working with a partner, read the words
to each other. Remember not to pronounce the
silent letters.**

Grammar

USED TO AND WOULD

1 <u>Underline</u> the correct form of *used to*.

1 When I was a child, I *used to love / got used to loving* watching my mother making biscuits.

2 I've been living in this country for 20 years, but I still *can't be used to / can't get used to* the appalling weather!

3 They *used to / were used to* wrap fish and chips in newspaper, but they don't do that any more.

4 When we first moved to this country, we didn't like all the hot food. But we *are used to / get used to* it now.

5 Many foreigners don't like the idea of eating rice for breakfast. But, after living here in Korea for over ten years, I *have been used to / have got used to* it!

6 The kids have fallen asleep. They *used not to eat / aren't used to eating* this late.

2 In four of the sentences below, it is not possible to use *used to*. Decide which sentences are incorrect. Then rewrite the incorrect sentences, replacing *used to* with the past simple.

1 My father used to work for the post office for five years.

_____

2 My mother used to ride a motorbike.

_____

3 I used to study at Bristol University from 2005 to 2009.

_____

4 He used to be an English teacher.

_____

5 Bill Clinton used to be President of the USA for eight years.

_____

6 We used to travel across Asia from January to June 2013.

_____

3 Look at the sentences below. All the sentences are correct. However, if it is also possible to replace *used to* with *would*, rewrite the sentences.

1 Gabriele used to own a toy kitchen when she was a little girl.

2 My family always used to eat lunch together on Sundays.

3 We always used to go on holiday to the same seaside village.

4 I used to like sweets when I was younger, but I can't stand them now.

5 I used to know how to make a really nice fish pie, but I've forgotten the recipe now.

Spelling

Adjectives ending -y
Many English adjectives are made by adding *-y* to the end of a noun.
Example: salt ➔ salty
Spelling problems occur when the noun ends in -e. In this case the final -e is usually dropped and replaced by *-y*.
Example: grime ➔ grimy ~~grimey~~

1 Find ten adjectives ending *-y* in the wordsearch. Words can be found vertically, horizontally and diagonally.

p	m	y	n	o	i	s	y	i	c
g	s	t	o	n	y	u	y	t	o
k	g	a	r	l	i	c	k	y	l
w	a	s	h	a	b	c	b	d	k
e	p	t	p	a	s	m	o	k	y
j	i	y	g	i	f	q	n	p	o
z	u	g	h	x	c	k	y	i	r
a	t	i	u	r	r	y	a	i	p
g	t	i	c	y	b	o	j	o	q
o	v	m	s	y	d	n	o	s	y

2 Which adjective in the wordsearch comes from a noun that does not end *-e*? What extra letter is added to this adjective before the *-y* ending?

Writing: a review

1 **Look at the student's answers to the exam question below. Before the student started writing, she made a plan. Read the review and number the paragraphs in her plan in the correct order 1–5.**

___ an interesting fact from historical Italy

___ who would enjoy it

___ general description of the book

___ food in modern Italy

___ my favourite thing in the book

You see this announcement in your college English-language magazine.

> **Book reviews wanted**
>
> Have you read a great non-fiction book?
>
> Write us a review of the book, explaining what it is about. Also tell us who would enjoy reading the book. Include one interesting fact that you remember from the book.
>
> The best reviews will be published in the magazine.
>
> Write your **review**. Write your answer in 140–190 words.

---

2 **Complete the sentences below from another student's answer about the book *Cod* by Mark Kurlansky. Use the underlined phrases from the student's answer in exercise 1.**

1 _____, Kurlansky travels with local fisherman to see what life is like on board a traditional boat.

2 _____ people who are interested in boats and the sea.

3 _____ was the recipes at the end. I even tried some at home.

4 *Cod* by Mark Kurlansky _____ of the world's most popular fish.

5 _____, cod was cheap food, but today it is very expensive.

6 It _____ over-fishing destroyed the number of cod in the sea.

'Delizia!' by John Dickie

'Delizia!' is a fascinating history of Italian food. It talks about everyday life in Italy from the Middle Ages to today.

In one interesting chapter, *'Delizia!'* describes the history of spaghetti. In old Naples, people didn't eat spaghetti on plates with a knife and fork. They ate it in the street with their hands because it was a cheap dish for poor people.

'Delizia!' also explains how Italian food became popular all over the world. It describes how companies like Rana produce pasta that is very easy to make. In the past, people used to spend hours making ravioli, but with Rana's pasta, a family could prepare dinner in minutes. It changed people's lives.

What I liked best about the book were the photos and illustrations. They include images from old Italian films and adverts which are a lot of fun to see.

'Delizia!' is a well-written book which includes hundreds of interesting facts. It is the perfect book for anyone who is going on holiday to Italy because it describes life all over the country, from Sicily to Milan.

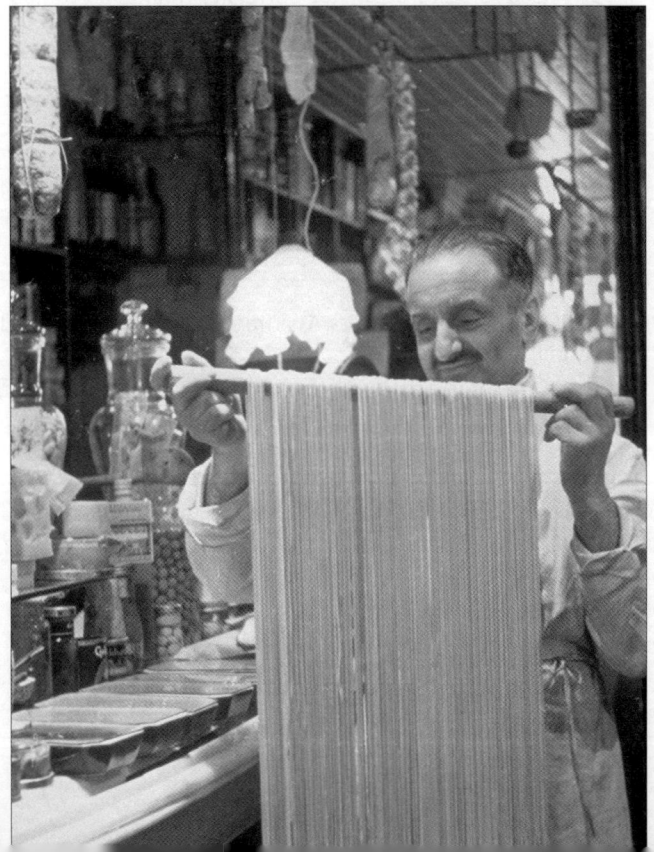

3 Now write your own answer to the exam question in exercise 1.

....

....

....

....

....

....

....

....

....

....

....

....

....

....

....

....

....

Listening: favourite dish

MULTIPLE MATCHING: PAPER 3, PART 3

1 🎧 9.2 **You will hear five different people talking about the dish they most enjoy cooking. For Speakers 1–5, choose from the list (A–H). Use the letters only once. There are three extra letters which you do not need to use.**

Which speaker

A does not eat any animal products?

B cooks fish?

C cooks something garlicky?

D thinks their country's cuisine is different in other countries?

E has to stir their recipe for a long time?

F uses ingredients that other people normally throw away?

G uses only raw vegetables?

H does not cook their dish at home?

Speaker 1 ___

Speaker 2 ___

Speaker 3 ___

Speaker 4 ___

Speaker 5 ___

Vocabulary

EXTENSION: PHRASAL VERBS WITH *UP*

1 *Up* has many different meanings in phrasal verbs. Look at the phrasal verbs in **bold** in the sentences (1–5) below. Match the definitions (a–e) to the phrasal verbs.

1 People don't eat lunch on Sundays together any more because the traditional family is **breaking up.** ___

2 You need to **chop** all the vegetables **up** and put them in a saucepan. ___

3 I always add extra chilli to **spice** it **up**. ___

4 People have been eating this for hundreds of years and I think it's important to **keep** the old traditions **up.** ___

5 Although the food tastes different, they always **eat** everything **up.** ___

a into little pieces

b going

c more

d all, completely

e into separate parts

2 Now complete the sentences with the correct form of the phrasal verbs in exercise 1.

1 You've been doing some really good work.

_____ it _____!

2 It tastes really bland. What can I add to

_____ it _____?

3 The team played together for years, but now it is

_____ because lots of players are leaving.

4 That piece of meat is too big for the cats to eat. You

need to _____ it _____.

5 I was worried that no one would like the dinner

I prepared, but they _____ everything

_____.

Reading and Use of English

KEY WORD TRANSFORMATIONS: PAPER 1, PART 4

1 Complete the second sentence so that it has a similar meaning to the first sentence, using the word given. Do not change the word given. You must use between two and five words, including the word given. There is an example at the beginning (0).

0 It's not worth going on a diet if you don't do any exercise.
   POINT

   There ......*is no point going*....... . on a diet if you don't do any exercise.

1 Can you look after the children this afternoon?
   CARE

   Can you .... the children this afternoon?

2 I still have problems with driving on the left.
   USED

   I haven't .... on the left yet.

3 We didn't think about his inexperience before we gave him the job.
   ACCOUNT

   We didn't .... before we gave him the job.

4 Let's delay the decision until next week.
   OFF

   Let's .... the decision until next week.

5 Your mother is upset because you don't think about the work she does for you.
   GRANTED

   Your mother is upset because you
   ....

6 My grandmother would spend all day long baking cakes.
   USED

   My grandmother .... all day long baking cakes.

7 How is Martina doing at university?
   ON

   How .... at university?

8 I'd prefer to eat at home.
   WE

   I'd rather .... at home.

When learning new verbs, also take note of the prepositions that follow them. Many questions in the Cambridge English: First (FCE) exam concentrate on verb–preposition collocations.

After finishing a Reading and Use of English exercise in this book, look at all the questions and write down any verb–preposition collocations that you find. For example, in exercise 1, you can see the collocation: *go + on + a diet*.

OPEN CLOZE: PAPER 1, PART 2

2 Read the text below and think of the word which best fits each gap. Use only one word in each gap. There is an example at the beginning (0).

What is a normal price to pay for lunch? I **(0)** ....*still*........ remember the most expensive lunch of my life. It was in **(1)** .... hotel in Paris and I was entertaining a business customer. Between the two of us we spent €75!

But at a country house hotel in the UK, chefs **(2)** .... recently produced a sandwich that on its own costs £100 (€150)! The sandwich is made from corn-fed chicken, Italian ham and a topping of white truffles. It is the latter that really sends **(3)** .... cost soaring!

The white truffle, a wild fungus **(4)** .... is traditionally found with the help of pigs or dogs, sells at outrageous prices. The Alba truffle of south-eastern France can sell for as **(5)** .... as £2,500 a kilo! This delicacy is the most expensive ingredient in Europe, but not quite the world.

This is because that prize must belong to the lychee, a fruit that is prized **(6)** .... Asian cuisine. On one famous occasion, a Chinese businessman paid £45,270 **(7)** .... a single fruit from a 400-year-old tree! It was **(8)** .... valuable because the fruit of the tree was once eaten by the Qing emperors of China.

Speaking

COLLABORATIVE TASK: PAPER 4, PART 3

1 Read the sentences (1–6) below. Match the functions (a–f) to the sentences.

1 Where shall we start? ____

2 Let's turn to the next one. ____

3 I hear what you're saying, but I think this one might cause some problems. ____

4 Are there any options that we haven't talked about yet? ____

5 Well, what would you suggest? ____

6 Are you suggesting that we choose this one? ____

a asking for your partner's opinion

b changing the topic

c checking that you have completed the task

d beginning the discussion

e asking someone to confirm a decision

f adding a warning

```
a fresh salad ── Are these good options for a lunch for a group of children aged five to seven? ── hamburgers and chips

cheese sandwiches ──                                  ── orange juice

fizzy drinks              ice cream
```

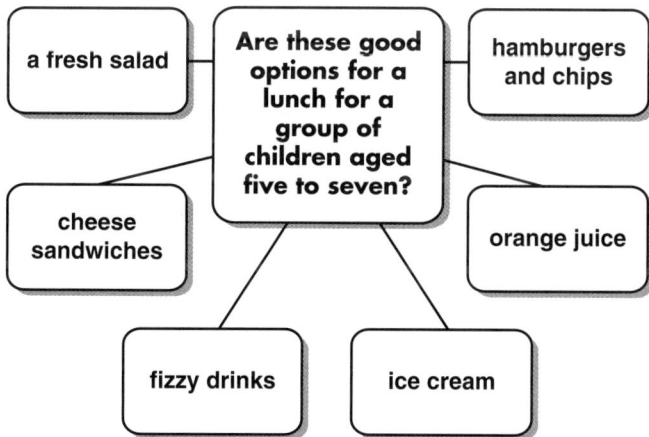

2 🎧 9.3 Listen to two students, Masa and Natalya, answering the exam question below. Who says each phrase (1–6) in exercise 1? Write *M* for Masa and *N* for Natalya.

Phrase 1 ____

Phrase 2 ____

Phrase 3 ____

Phrase 4 ____

Phrase 5 ____

Phrase 6 ____

> Imagine that you are looking after a group of children aged five to seven for the day and you have to prepare lunch for them. Decide together which things you would prepare and tell each other why.

3 If you are working with a partner, answer the exam question. When you are speaking, try to use the phrases in exercise 1 and tick (✔) each one after you have used it. Follow this order:

1 Take two minutes to discuss the question in the diagram.

2 After two minutes, the interlocutor will ask you a further question. Discuss this with your partner and make a decision. Your further question here is 'You now have about a minute to say which two options you would choose for the children.'

Shopping and money

LANGUAGE CHECKLIST

☐ I know words to describe shopping and consumerism, page 80.

☐ I know how to use some phrasal verbs for shopping, page 80.

☐ I know how to use conditionals, page 80.

☐ I know when to spell some words as one word or two words, page 81.

EXAM CHECKLIST

☐ I have practised the multiple matching question from the Reading and Use of English paper, page 78.

☐ I have practised the Part 1 extracts + multiple choice question from the Listening paper, page 82.

☐ I have practised the key word transformation question from the Reading and Use of English paper, page 83.

☐ I have practised the multiple-choice cloze question from the Reading and Use of English paper, page 83.

☐ I have practised writing an essay from the Writing paper, page 84.

☐ I have practised the individual 'long turn' from the Speaking paper, page 85.

Reading and Use of English

MULTIPLE MATCHING: PAPER 1, PART 7

1   Buying something immediately without thinking about it for a long time is called making an **impulse buy**. You are going to read an article about four people who made an impulse buy. For questions 1–10, choose from the people (A–D). The people may be chosen more than once.

Which person

1   made their impulse buy in their own country? ___

2   was disappointed by the impulse buy? ___

3   originally planned to give the impulse buy to someone else? ___

4   often makes impulse buys? ___

5   doesn't usually make impulse buys? ___

6   thought their impulse buy looked alien? ___

7   uses the impulse buy to remember a holiday? ___

8   had had an accident? ___

9   went to a shop that didn't look very new? ___

10 was visiting family abroad? ___

2   Look again at the article and find one phrase from each speaker which means *immediately* or *without waiting*.

3   Find these phrasal verbs (1–6) in the text. Then match the definitions (a–f) to the phrasal verbs.

1   I snapped one up ___

2   it really brings that trip back ___

3   The bike was completely written off. ___

4   I decided to sleep on it. ___

5   I like to think things through ___

6   I ran across this stall of fruit ___

a   to destroy something, especially a vehicle

b   to think about something overnight

c   to buy/take something very quickly

d   to consider something carefully

e   to find by chance/accident

f   to remind you of something

IMPULSE buy!

Today we talk to four people from around the world who tell us about a time when they made an impulse buy.

A Sabine, USA

My parents were both from Leipzig, but they moved to the USA in the early 1950s. I'd always wanted to visit their home country, but for many years it was impossible. I was thirty when the Berlin Wall came down and I desperately wanted to see an uncle in East Germany that I had never met.

Some time before I went there, one of my friends, Melissa, had asked me to bring her a present back. And while I was in Berlin, I saw a piece of the Berlin Wall. I thought it was perfect and I snapped one up on the spot. But when I got back, Melissa told me she already had a piece because her brother had been to Germany a couple of months earlier. So I kept it for myself as a souvenir. I'm pleased I did because it really brings that trip back to me and the emotional experience of meeting my uncle and staying with his family, who we had lost contact with for forty years.

B Dirk, Holland

I used to ride a motorbike. It was a big one too, 500 cc, but I stopped riding it after I had a crash. The bike was completely written off. After that I learnt to drive a car. But in my heart of hearts, I always wanted to be back on that bike!

About a year ago, I was online and just browsing when I found that someone was selling a bike just like my old one, and they lived about ten minutes away on the other side of Rotterdam. I would have bought it instantly, but I am married now and I thought my wife would never let me buy it. So I decided to sleep on it. But the next morning all I could think of was that machine. In the end my wife asked what was wrong and I told her. We went online together and we agreed to buy the bike. In fact, she told me it had always been her dream to ride on a motorbike too, so we got it together!

C Amandine, France

I'm not what you might call a shopaholic and I like to think things through before I make a purchase. But last year I was on holiday in Turkey and I went into a carpet shop. The shop owner was very polite and he offered me some tea. At the end I said I didn't really want to buy a rug or anything because what I was really interested in was furniture. The shopkeeper said he owned another shop across the street, so he led me over the road to that one.

At first the place seemed a bit run-down, but inside it was one of the most beautiful shops I have ever seen and at the back I saw this carved table. It was stunning. I had to have it and I agreed a price right then and there. After I bought it, I then realised that I would never get it on the plane back to Lyon, but he arranged shipping and everything too.

D Walter, Switzerland

I think in general I am quite an adventurous person and I especially like to eat new food. One of the first things I do when I arrive in a new country is go to the market to buy something completely new. I remember eating some dish in Vietnam that was the most delicious meal I have ever had in my life, but I still don't know what it was called or what the ingredients were. That's the way it is when you travel.

The last time I was abroad, I ran across this stall of fruit. One of the fruits looked extraordinary, like it had dropped out of space. In the middle it was very pink with black seeds and the outside was green but with sort of leaves. I was very excited and I bought it just like that. Unfortunately, although it looked very exciting, it was actually pretty bland and I don't think I even finished it.

Vocabulary

SHOPPING AND CONSUMERISM

1 Complete the puzzle. What is the word in grey?

1 When something is on sale for a very good price, or if it is part of a promotion like 'buy one, get one free', it is on _____ offer.

2 The amount of money you have available, or the amount of money that you allow yourself to spend.

3 Famous names of products or companies, like Nike or Coca-Cola.

4 A reduction in the normal price.

5 A symbol or picture that a company puts on all its products, like the crocodile on shirts by Lacoste.

6 When you do something for no particular reason, you do it on a _____.

7 An agreement between a buyer and seller.

8 Something that you buy for a very low price.

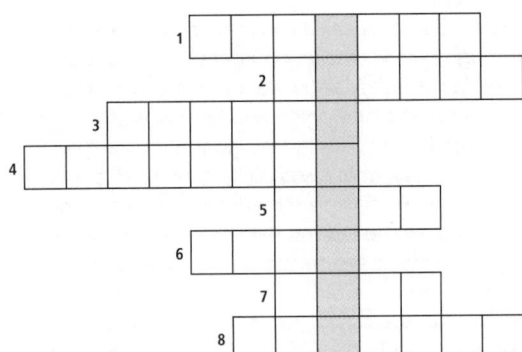

PHRASAL VERBS FOR SHOPPING

2 Choose a suitable word to complete the sentences below. Write one word only in each gap.

1 It's a good idea to pay _____ your credit card bills at the end of every month.

2 You can buy the same laptop cheaper if you go to town and shop _____ for the best price.

3 I hardly get any money in my job and I have five children. I don't know how I'm going to get _____.

4 Tim's been saving his money _____ because he wants to buy a surfboard.

5 We had a five-course meal with drinks and coffee, and in the end the bill came _____ €1,200!

6 I'm expecting a large tax bill at the end of the year, so I've set _____ some money to pay for it.

7 My dad has paid for our train trip to Sydney and he said we don't have to pay him _____.

8 Let's splash _____ and stay at this hotel right next to the beach. It's expensive, but it looks amazing!

9 If you buy both of our flights with your credit card now, I'll pay my half of the money _____ your bank account tomorrow, OK?

10 This microwave doesn't work. We'll have to take it _____ to the shop and change it.

Grammar

CONDITIONALS

1 Look at the sentences below. Five of them contain a mistake. Find and correct the mistakes.

1 I wish I study harder when I was at university.

2 If I have a million euros, I would buy a yacht and sail around the Mediterranean.

3 If it will rain tomorrow, you'll need to take an umbrella.

4 If the shop hadn't been closed, we would have bought Rob's present today.

5 If my boss didn't leave, I would still be working for the company.

6 We won't have any more of these computer problems if we get the latest software.

7 If you would work in the shop, you would be able to buy watches, rings and jewellery at half price.

2 Put the words from the box into the sentences below. Add one word to each sentence.

| had | long | provided | should | unless | were | will |

1 If the shop still has those nice earrings, I buy them.

2 I would get the DVDs online if I you. They're cheaper.

3 If I known that you can only cook this dessert in a microwave, I wouldn't have bought it.

4 Customers can return products to the store that they are not damaged in any way.

5 I'll go to the shop as as you do the washing up.

6 I see Eric, I'll ask him to call you.

7 Don't buy anything you really want to.

3 Look at the sentences. Choose the best conditional (a or b) to describe each sentence.

1 I saw a very nice jacket when I was on holiday in New York last year, but I didn't want to pay $500.

  a I would have bought it if it had been less expensive.

  b I would buy it if it were less expensive.

2 The weather says it might rain this afternoon, but don't worry – we can still play tennis.

  a If it's wet, we'll always play on one of the indoor courts.

  b If it's wet, we always play on one of the indoor courts.

3 I really want to improve my English.

  a If I spent a year living in Britain, it would get a lot better.

  b If I spend a year living in Britain, it gets a lot better.

4 There was a huge argument and I told my boss that I thought he was an idiot.

  a If I hadn't been so angry, I wouldn't have said it.

  b If I weren't so angry, I wouldn't say it.

5 I love my husband, but I sometimes dream about living a different life.

  a If I'm not married, I will travel around the world.

  b If I weren't married, I would travel around the world.

6 I'm going to look for a new TV this afternoon.

  a If I find a cheap one, I'll buy it.

  b If I find a cheap one, I buy it.

Spelling

Two words, one sound
There are a number of words in English that sound the same and are written in a very similar way. However, if you make a small spelling mistake, you will change the meaning of the word.
Example: We've **already** finished.
        Are we **all ready** to go?

1 Look at the words in bold in the sentences (1–13). Then match the full forms and meanings (a–m) to the words in bold.

1 **You're** not going to believe this! ___

2 I think **they're** leaving at three. ___

3 **Maybe** Alexis knows what to do. ___

4 The shop is open **every day**. ___

5 **It's** a really nice day today. ___

6 The sales team want to know what time **their** taxi arrives. ___

7 Does anyone know **whose** pen this is? ___

8 I saw **your** brother at the airport in Rome. ___

9 It **may be** possible to buy a cheap oven in the sales. ___

10 The department store has cut **its** prices by 50 per cent. ___

11 Mobile phones are now a part of **everyday** life. ___

12 Do you know **who's** coming to dinner tonight? ___

13 That looks like an interesting shop over **there**. ___

  a who is

  b of whom

  c it is

  d of it

  e possibly

  f might be

  g of you

  h you are

  i of them

  j not here

  k they are

  l normal, usual

  m all the time

Listening: spending money

EXTRACTS + MULTIPLE CHOICE: PAPER 3, PART 1

1 🎧 10.1 **You will hear eight people talking about money. For questions 1–8, choose the best answer (A, B or C).**

1 You hear a woman talking about her holiday plans. Why is she frustrated?

   A Her children do not want to go.

   B She cannot buy other things.

   C She has to stay with someone that she doesn't like.

2 You hear a girl talking about her job. How does she feel about the shop?

   A She thinks she receives good money.

   B She has a problem with the shop discount.

   C She would not buy anything in the shop herself.

3 You hear a man talking about a night out. How much money did he spend?

   A too much

   B more than everybody else

   C none

4 You hear a man talking about shopping at the supermarket. What happened when he had to pay?

   A He paid the full cost of the shopping.

   B He decided not to pay for any of the shopping.

   C He decided not to buy some of the shopping.

5 You hear a woman talking about clothes shopping. Why did she buy the top?

   A She needs nice clothes for her work.

   B She is addicted to shopping.

   C She bought it on a whim.

6 You hear a woman talking about her husband. What kind of things does he buy?

   A He buys lots of things that he doesn't need.

   B He only buys essential items.

   C He only does the food shopping.

7 You hear a boy describing how he spends his pocket money. What does he spend his money on?

   A toys

   B comics

   C snacks

8 You hear a woman talking about her financial plans. What does she say about her pension?

   A She hasn't made a decision about it yet.

   B She is going to take her friends' advice.

   C She has a very good pension in her current job.

Pronunciation

1 🎧 10.2 **Read and listen to seven versions of the same sentence (1–7) below. The stressed word is in capital letters. Match the reasons why the words were stressed (a–g) to the sentences.**

1 MY brother is the only person here who speaks Russian fluently. ___

2 My BROTHER is the only person here who speaks Russian fluently. ___

3 My brother IS the only person here who speaks Russian fluently. ___

4 My brother is the ONLY person here who speaks Russian fluently. ___

5 My brother is the only person HERE who speaks Russian fluently. ___

6 My brother is the only person here who speaks RUSSIAN fluently. ___

7 My brother is the only person here who speaks Russian FLUENTLY. ___

a Some people can speak other languages very well, but not Russian.

b There are people in other places who can speak Russian fluently.

c Not my sister, for example.

d Some people can speak Russian, but only my brother speaks it fluently.

e Not someone else's brother.

f There isn't anybody else.

g Believe me – this is true.

2 🎧 10.3 **Look at the sentence below. How many different places could you put the sentence stress? Listen and check your answer.**

We don't want to watch the concert tomorrow.

3 **If you are working with a partner, practise together saying the sentences in exercises 1 and 2.**

Reading and Use of English

KEY WORD TRANSFORMATIONS: PAPER 1, PART 4

1 Complete the second sentence so that it has a similar meaning to the first sentence, using the word given. Do not change the word given. You must use between two and five words, including the word given. There is an example at the beginning (0).

0 Your responsibility is to look after the money.
   RESPONSIBLE

   You *are responsible for looking* after the money.

1 I'm sorry that I didn't help Peter.
   WISH

   I .... Peter.

2 When did you borrow the money from the bank?
   LEND

   When .... the money?

3 Can I tell Ildiko the news?
   MIND

   Do .... Ildiko the news?

4 I regret telling them that I was ill.
   WISH

   I .... them I was ill.

5 If you don't phone, we'll meet outside the cinema.
   UNLESS

   We'll meet outside the cinema ....

6 I advise you not to go by train.
   WERE

   I wouldn't go by train ....

7 Petra had a clever idea for making some extra money.
   CAME

   Petra .... a clever idea for making some extra money.

8 You can borrow my racket if you give it back tomorrow.
   PROVIDED

   I'll .... that you give it back tomorrow.

MULTIPLE-CHOICE CLOZE: PAPER 1, PART 1

2 Read the text below and decide which answer (A, B, C or D) best fits each gap. There is an example at the beginning (0).

Just twenty years ago who would have (0) ....*A*......... that Russia would (1) .... a place to buy designer goods? Back then it was a country suffering from a (2) .... of major products with a limited supply of everyday items like bread and milk. Nowadays, everything has changed.

One place to see the greatest change is the GUM department store in Red Square, the heart of Moscow. Once this was (3) .... only for long queues of customers waiting outside empty shops, but now it is a shopping centre full of designer labels, jewellery and stylish cafés. With the money that rising oil prices have brought to Russia, the demand for luxury products is (4) .... all the time.

But it is a mistake to think things were always worse in the past. When I first went to Russia, caviar was incredibly cheap. But it is getting more and more expensive owing to the falling (5) .... of sturgeon, the fish that produces the caviar eggs.

For a different kind of shopping, the Izmaylovo Market on the outskirts of Moscow is popular with tourists and locals alike. It (6) .... the best location to pick up souvenirs from the country's fascinating past. Military uniforms, Soviet badges and posters are all readily (7) .... For locals, it is a popular shopping spot to pick up bargains on belts, clothes and shoes.

One final warning: don't (8) .... the cost of a visit to the capital. Prices in Moscow are high and hotel accommodation especially will make a big hole in your budget.

0 A suspected	B revealed	C learnt	D mistrusted
1 A become	B change	C adapt	D evolve
2 A hole	B minority	C collapse	D lack
3 A thought	B considered	C known	D recognised
4 A raising	B increasing	C enlarging	D towering
5 A counts	B animals	C groups	D numbers
6 A continues	B remains	C keeps	D survives
7 A found	B sale	C available	D bought
8 A underperform	B undertake	C underestimate	D undermine

Writing: an essay

1 **Complete the student's answer to the exam question below with the phrases (a–f).**

a On the other hand

b Furthermore

c So, on balance

d There are several reasons

e The most important thing

f On the one hand

In your English class, you have been talking about shopping. Now your English teacher has asked you to write an essay.

Write an essay using all the notes and give reasons for your point of view.

Should the government allow large stores to open on Sundays?

Notes

Write about:

1. the effect on small shops

2. the people who want to go shopping on Sundays

3. .... (your own idea)

Write your answer in 140–190 words in an appropriate style.

---

2 **Look again at the student's essay and answer these questions.**

1 Has the student included both points 1 and 2 from the exam question?

2 Is the style of the essay formal or informal?

3 What was the student's own idea?

---

1 _____ why stores should open on Sundays. However, this also creates several problems.

2 _____, this situation is very difficult for small shops. Many of them are family businesses and these people don't want to work every day. It's easy for a big store to open on Sunday because they have a lot of staff.

3 _____, lots of people need to go shopping on Sundays. People who work long hours don't have time to go to the shops during the week.

4 _____ if stores open every day, this will create new jobs because shops will need to employ more staff. People will also spend more money and this is good for the economy. We have a lot of unemployment in my country and it is important to have successful businesses.

5 _____ if stores open on Sunday it will be good for almost everyone.

6 _____ now is to create jobs, and Sunday opening will do that.

3 **Now write your own answer to the exam question in exercise 1.**

....

....

....

....

....

....

....

....

....

....

....

....

....

....

Speaking

1 🎧 10.4 **Look at the pictures which show people shopping. Decide whether the words and phrases below could be used for picture 1 or picture 2 – or both.**

	Picture 1	Picture 2
department store		
to try		
spices		
a special deal		
included in the price		
a guarantee		
to taste		
sacks		
special features		
shop assistant		
merchant		
to haggle		

2 🎧 10.4 **Now listen to four different students answering the exam question below. Check your answers to exercise 1.**

> I'd like you to compare the photographs, and say why you think the people have chosen to go shopping in these places.

3 🎧 10.4 **Correct each sentence (1–8) below. Then listen again to check your answers.**

1 What the pictures have by common is that they show customers talking to salesmen.

2 Both the salesman seem to be very friendly.

3 These pictures show very similarity situations.

4 One thing what is the same in the pictures is that the customers are really going to buy something.

5 We can see the same thing happens: the customers are asking questions.

6 In every picture the salesman looks very friendly.

7 There isn't a big different here: we can see people thinking about buying something.

8 The pictures show a same sort of thing.

SPOTLIGHT ON STUDY TECHNIQUES

In the first part of the 'long turn', you will be asked to compare two pictures. When preparing for the Speaking test, make sure you learn some useful phrases for discussing the differences and similarities between the pictures. You do not need to learn every phrase, but do learn at least one phrase for every situation. When you are practising for the Speaking test, try to use these phrases as much as possible.

Picture 1

Picture 2

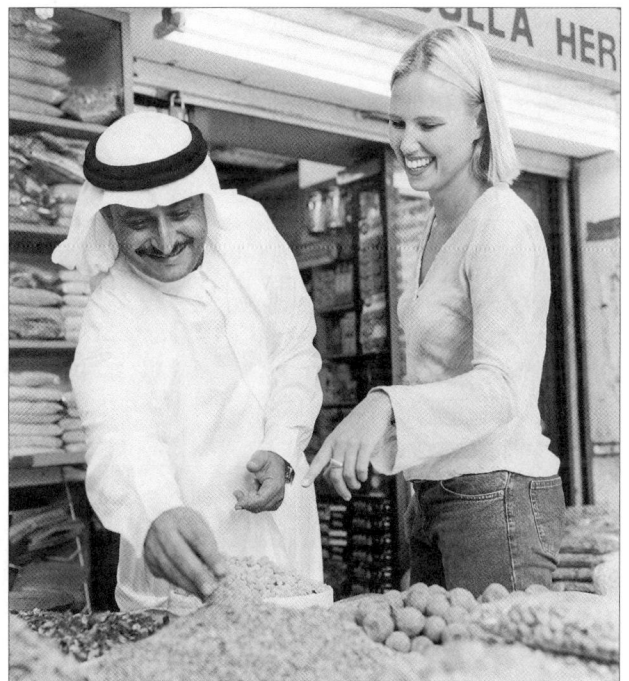

4 **If you are working with a partner, answer the exam question in exercise 2 for the pictures.**

Colours and shapes

Reading and Use of English

MULTIPLE CHOICE: PAPER 1, PART 5

1 **You are going to read an article. For questions 1–6, choose the answer (A, B, C or D) which you think fits best according to the text.**

1 From the first paragraph, we understand that Tony
   A felt disappointed when he took the test.
   B immediately understood the test.
   C thought the test was pointless.
   D was confused by the test.

2 In the third paragraph, what is Tony's purpose in mentioning gene therapy?
   A to criticise it
   B to describe how it works
   C to express positive feelings about it
   D to show he's not interested in it

3 Tony lives in
   A an area with a lot of crime.
   B an area without a lot of traffic.
   C a wealthy area.
   D an area with a lot of noise.

4 To help him use his e-reader, Tony
   A does not want any coloured lights on it.
   B wants it to make a special noise.
   C wants it to use moving lights.
   D wants two separate lights to appear on it.

5 Tony says he sometimes makes colour mistakes when
   A he's at work.
   B he gets dressed.
   C he goes shopping.
   D he makes dinner.

6 The words 'crop up' in line 64 suggests that these problems
   A happen a lot today.
   B happen very rarely.
   C occasionally happen today.
   D never happen today.

My life with CVD

by Tony Wong

I never knew there was anything different about me until I was about eleven. I had just started middle school and we all had to do a series of tests. Like everyone else, I was taken to a small room where a mysterious woman in a white coat was waiting for me. She handed me an odd-looking picture made up of dots in the shape of a long grey spiral. 'What number do you see?' she asked with a smile. I didn't know why she was smiling because there were a lot of dots to count. Once I got to about ten, she asked the same question. I didn't know what to say, so she gave me another picture which looked the same as the first. She asked me the question for the third time, and then I got frustrated. 'I don't see any numbers,' I said. 'There aren't any numbers here!' That was how I learnt that I had CVD, colour vision deficiency, or, as it's unfairly known by the general public, colour blindness.

What most people would have seen in that test was a number made of pink dots which they were expected to pick out from a circular field of green dots. I just saw lots of dots that were a sort of muddy grey.

I'm not alone. It is estimated that about eight per cent of men have some form of CVD, while it only affects less than one per cent of women. You see, CVD is a guy thing. It's all down to genes, apparently, and scientists hope to cure it one day, although I can't say that I would be keen on any gene therapy. Personally, I don't feel like I 'suffer' from CVD.

Generally speaking, people with CVD just adapt to the world around us. For example, when you get to the traffic lights, the key thing is not the colour but the order of the lights. Of course, with all the vandalism in my neighbourhood, I'm just happy if the traffic lights are working.

Unfortunately, not everything is so clear cut. When my e-reader is recharging, the light is orange when it is charging and green when it is finished. That's great, except that both colours look more or less the same to me. A much better system would be the one that my electric razor uses. It flashes when it is charging and then stops when it has finished.

Life is full of little frustrations like that. Because I see green and red as pretty similar, I do sometimes put on a top that doesn't go with my trousers. Thankfully, my wife usually spots that very quickly.

However, there are bigger problems that can occur when professionals don't take CVD into account. I once failed an exam at school because a key question related to a bar chart coloured red, green and blue. To me all of the rectangles looked almost the same. Similar problems still crop up in course books and exams today.

Moments like that aside, in my own life, CVD has been more of an inconvenience than a problem, so the term 'colour blindness' does feel like an inaccurate description of my vision. It implies a weakness or a problem. The fact is that people like me live life just like anyone else. We can continue to do so as long as people in positions of responsibility understand the condition and take steps to prevent any problems before they occur.

Vocabulary

COLOUR AND DECORATION

1 **Complete the words. Write one letter in each space.**

1 The kitchen was painted grey. It was awful: really
d _ _ _ _ y –looking.

2 This room is very c _ _ tt _ _ _ _ : there are objects
and things everywhere!

3 In British cities you see a lot of t _ r _ _ c _ _ houses,
where all the houses are connected together in a long line.

4 We get the sun all afternoon because the house is
south-f _ _ _ _ g.

5 We've painted the rooms in s _ _ _ _ g colours like
crimson and dark blue.

6 My grandmother lives in a c _ _ er _ _ _ cottage in
Cornwall. It's made of yellow bricks and it has roses
growing up the walls. It's lovely.

7 We used the wrong colour blue when we painted the
bathroom. It was so p _ l _ that you almost couldn't see it!

8 The walls are very b _ r _ . Why not put some pictures up?

2 **Complete the email with the words from the box.**

cared   cosy   impersonal   run   suburban

Hi Kiyeon!

How are you? We've finally finished moving into our
new flat. It was a lot of work. When we moved in, the flat
was really ¹_____ down because the previous
owners hadn't done any work on it. It was old and dirty.
The only good thing was the garden because it was so
well ²_____ for. There's a lovely old lady on the
ground floor and she looks after it as her hobby.

So Tom and I decorated the whole flat. In the
beginning, we had lots of arguments. Tom wanted
the living room to look cool and white, but I thought
that was too ³_____ for our home. In the end,
we agreed to use warm colours to make the room
look nice and ⁴_____. Check out the mail
attachment – doesn't it look great?

You have to come and visit next time you're in
London. Our flat is in a ⁵_____ area, but we
can get to the city centre in about 30 minutes so you
can do some sightseeing when you're here.

Speak soon.

Ali

PHRASAL VERBS

3 **Underline the correct word.**

1 I made that green by mixing *up / through* the blue
paint with the yellow, and I really like it.

2 We are *doing / making* up the house because we want
to sell it. If you decorate, you can usually get a better
price.

3 You're doing a great job working on the garden. Keep
it *on / up*!

4 They bought an old windmill and they *turned / brought*
it into a home.

5 Jennifer *picked / chose* out the colour for the kitchen.
I never know which paints look good.

6 If you have an old house, you have to keep decorating
it and repairing things or its condition worsens. You
mustn't *let / allow* it go.

7 All the furniture in the room was old and dark, so the
red plastic chair really stood *out / off*.

8 We painted the bedroom pink and put up some cheerful
new wallpaper to *brighten / lighten* it up a bit.

9 Oh no! Those curtains have horizontal strips so they
won't *combine / go* with the carpet at all. The two
designs are completely different.

Grammar

MODAL VERBS FOR GUESSING, SPECULATING AND DEDUCING

1 Eric and Jack were camping when they heard a noise and saw something moving in the forests. Complete their sentences using the words in brackets and *can't*, *must* and *might*.

E What was that noise?

J It ^{1}_____ (be) a plane. I'm sure that was it.

E No, it ^{2}_____ (be) a plane because the noise came from over there.

J Where?

E There, in the bushes.

J Rover ^{3}_____ (make) the noise when he was looking for something. That dog is always looking for rabbits or cats.

E No, look. Rover's asleep over there. What's that light in the tent?

J My mobile.

E Maybe that's the answer? Someone

^{4}_____ (sent) you a text message and then the noise woke us up. Check.

J No. There's no message on my phone. The light's on, but I don't know why. Something else

^{5}_____ (happen).

E Hey, look at our bags! Our food is all over the floor.

J That explains it. Some animal ^{6}_____ (found) our food and then it woke us up when it was

eating. It ^{7}_____ (run) away when we woke up and started talking.

E I hope it wasn't a bear that did the damage.

J Don't be ridiculous. A bear ^{8}_____ (do) that! There aren't any in these forests. It

^{9}_____ (be) a fox or something like that.

2 Put the words from the box into the sentences below. Add one word to each sentence.

> be can't could have must not

1 You should read his email right away! It be important – we don't know.

2 He have been in a hurry because he ran out of the room.

3 I know she spoke French, but she might be from France because we also have students here from Quebec.

4 It may not been the postman. We get a lot of people here delivering junk mail.

5 You have seen Diana at the station: she's in Lithuania at the moment!

6 He says he's a detective, so he must from the police.

DESCRIBING OBJECTS

3 Put the words in **bold** in the correct order to complete the sentences.

1 A parcel has arrived for you. It's a **brown cardboard big** box.

2 We saw a **pink long mysterious** light in the sky.

3 Are you going to throw that **woollen horrible old** coat away?

4 I saw these **black leather cool** boots in the shops.

5 Can you pass me that **green plastic round** thing please? It's part of this toy.

6 We have just got a **ginger little cute** kitten.

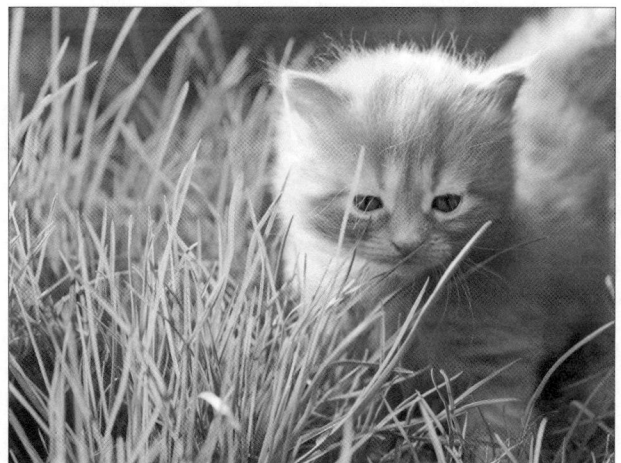

Spelling

SPOTLIGHT ON SPELLING

ei and ie

The vowel combinations *ei* and *ie* are commonly misspelt in English. English children learn the rule, 'i before e, except after c'.

Examples: bel**ie**ve rec**ei**ve

1 The words in this group all follow the rule. Complete the words with *ei* or *ie*.

1 fr _ _ nd

2 exper _ _ nce

3 rec _ _ pt

4 rev _ _ w

5 perc _ _ ve

6 dec _ _ ve

7 ch _ _ f

8 inconc _ _ vable

2 There are also a number of exceptions. All of the words below break the rule in exercise 1. Complete the words with *ei* or *ie*.

1 n _ _ ther

2 anc _ _ nt

3 effic _ _ nt

4 n _ _ ghbour

5 for _ _ gn

6 profic _ _ nt

7 w _ _ rd

8 prot _ _ n

9 spec _ _ s

10 h _ _ ght

11 sc _ _ nce

Listening: a ghost hunter

SENTENCE COMPLETION: PAPER 3, PART 2

1 🎧 11.1 You will hear David Hick talking about his experience as a ghost hunter when he was a student. For questions 1–10, complete the sentences. You will need to write a word or a short phrase in each gap.

2 Before checking your answers in the back of the book, check the spelling of the words that contain *ei* or *ie*.

David was an **(1)** .... ghost hunter.

He was studying **(2)** ....

He was told a ghost story by his
(3) ....

The person who told the ghost story had been staying in a **(4)** ....

Suddenly the **(5)** .... of her room just opened.

David investigated it with **(6)**
....

When they stayed in the same room, they saw
(7) ....

David's website was called
(8) ....

People could leave **(9)** .... on the website.

All the messages they received came from
(10) ....

Reading and Use of English

MULTIPLE-CHOICE CLOZE: PAPER 1, PART 1

1 Read the text below and decide which answer (A, B, C or D) best fits each gap. There is an example at the beginning (0).

UFO **(0)** ....*C*........ means *Unidentified Flying Object*: it refers to any object in the sky that you cannot explain. There have been increasing numbers of UFO reports from the late 1940s onwards, when a craze swept across the USA. People really started to believe that UFOs were **(1)** .... craft from alien planets.

Much of this interest was **(2)** .... by the growth of science fiction. Movies from the 1950s such as *Invasion of the Body Snatchers* (1956) were full of aliens. However, this was not a new **(3)** .... In 1938 a radio broadcast by Orson Welles included news reports of alien attacks: many people believed that what they were **(4)** .... was true!

The public's fears were fuelled by events such as the Roswell Incident in 1947. **(5)** .... to most reports of the accident, some kind of vehicle crashed in the desert. At first the US military **(6)** .... to journalists by saying it was a UFO. Then later the official story changed and it was explained **(7)** .... a weather balloon. Since then there have been countless rumours of what really happened. In 1995 a film was even produced which claimed to show the scientific examination of the spaceship's alien crew!

Although many in the scientific community may doubt the existence of extraterrestrial life, there are still experts who **(8)** .... reports of UFO sightings. Indeed, many professional pilots have seen strange fast-moving objects in the sky. So perhaps there really is something out there after all.

0	A almost	B quite	C simply	D likely
1	A presently	B actually	C completely	D increasingly
2	A sparked off	B run off	C moved off	D flown off
3	A phenomenon	B manifestation	C demonstration	D exhibition
4	A listening	B attending	C hearing	D presenting
5	A Concerning	B According	C Deciding	D Including
6	A answered	B spoke	C defended	D responded
7	A to	B as	C by	D like
8	A decide	B enter	C gather	D harvest

WORD FORMATION: PAPER 1, PART 3

2 Read the text below. Use the words given in capitals at the end of some of the lines to form a word that fits in the gap in the same line. There is an example at the beginning (0).

About five years ago my grandparents retired and moved to a **(0)** ....*cheerful*........ little house quite near Cardiff in Wales. The house is a cottage in a really friendly **(1)** .... It is decorated beautifully: it feels really **(2)** .... and I love visiting them.	**CHEER** **NEIGHBOUR** **HOME**
What is special about the house is that my grandparents have tried to make it as **(3)** .... friendly as possible. My grandfather has covered the entire roof of the building with some huge **(4)** .... solar panels. In **(5)** .... , they have put very good insulation through the whole house, so it loses very little heat.	**ENVIRONMENT** **RECTANGLE** **ADD**
In the beginning, they wanted the house to be powered by the wind, but it was too difficult to find the equipment. When my grandfather realised that wind power was not a realistic **(6)** .... to his problem, he put in the solar panels. Some people were worried that they might look strange on the roof, but my grandfather worked with a **(7)** .... to try to make all the technology work with the old building.	**SOLVE** **DESIGN**
Personally, I was worried at first because it seemed quite an **(8)** .... project for two elderly people. In the end, it has been a huge success because the house has been transformed. If I had the time and the money, I'd think about doing it myself.	**AMBITION**

Writing: an email

OPTIONAL TASK: PAPER 2, PART 2

1   In Part 2 of the Writing test, you may be asked to write an email to a friend. Read the exam question below. What information must you include in your reply?

....

....

> You have received an email from your friend, Max. Read Max's email and then write an email in 140–190 words to reply.
>
>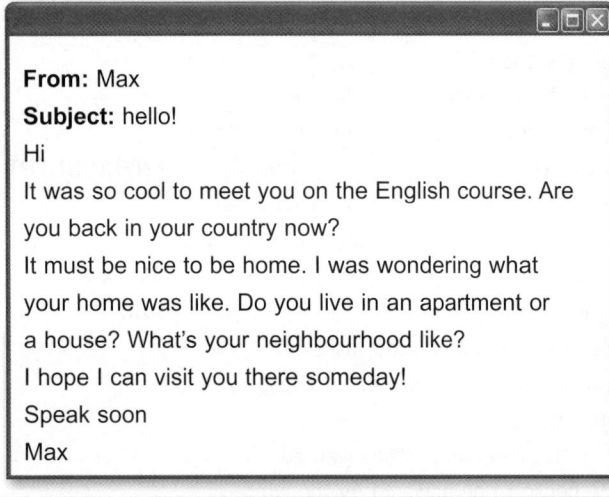
>
> **From:** Max
> **Subject:** hello!
> Hi
> It was so cool to meet you on the English course. Are you back in your country now?
> It must be nice to be home. I was wondering what your home was like. Do you live in an apartment or a house? What's your neighbourhood like?
> I hope I can visit you there someday!
> Speak soon
> Max

2   Complete the student's answer to the exam question with the words from the box.

as   asked   care   hear   looks
mentioned   there's   welcome

3   Now write your own answer to the exam question in exercise 1.

....

....

....

....

....

....

....

....

....

....

....

Hi Max

It's great to ¹_____ from you again. I hope that you can visit me here in Finland too one day.

You ²_____ me in your email about my home. I live in a village called Kivenlahti which is near Helsinki. I live in an apartment on the sixth floor of a modern apartment building.

Kivenlahti is a suburban area, but it's also near the forest. ³_____ a view of the sea from our flat and it's really beautiful in the mornings.

When we moved in, it looked a bit dreary, but my parents have done it up with wooden floors. They also painted all the walls to brighten everything up.

⁴_____ for my room, it's small but it's very nice. All the furniture is in bright colours: orange and white, so it ⁵_____ different to the rest of the house.

You ⁶_____ that you would like to come and visit one day. Well, we do have a spare room, so if you ever to come to Finland, you would be very ⁷_____ to stay with us!

Take ⁸_____.

Silka

Speaking

INDIVIDUAL 'LONG TURN': PAPER 4, PART 2

1 🎧 11.2 **Listen to the start of Part 2 of the Speaking test. What question does the student, Claudio, ask the interlocutor?**

2 🎧 11.3 **Now listen to Claudio talking about the photos below. Complete the descriptions of the pictures with the words he uses.**

> OK. Both photos show magic tricks. In the
> 1 _____ we have a magician and a girl,
> and she is above the floor. This is 2 _____
> levitation, isn't it? It looks 3 _____ he is on
> the stage in a theatre or somewhere 4 _____.
> Now, in the second picture we have another magician and
> he's doing a card trick, and everybody looks amazed.
> 5 _____ is which trick is the most
> entertaining. Well, the first picture 6 _____
> looks entertaining, but 7 _____ that the
> magician is on stage and the audience just sits and watches.
> For me it's 8 _____ boring. I
> 9 _____ prefer the second picture. This
> is a 10 _____ entertaining because the
> magician is very near and you can see what he is doing.
> You can try to see the 'trick'. I think that's definitely the
> better of 11 _____.

3 **Claudio gives a very strong opinion when he answers the question. Look again at the words he used in exercise 2. Which words does he use to show that he feels strongly about his answers?**

4 **If you are working with a partner, answer the interlocutor's question for the photographs. The question is in Listening script 11.2 on pages 155–156.**

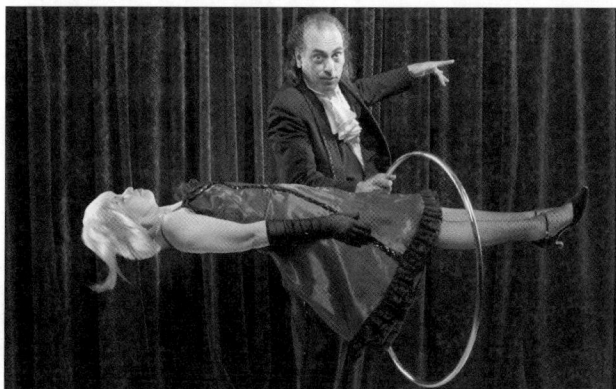

Pronunciation

SPOTLIGHT ON PRONUNCIATION

Intonation in question tags
In English, intonation of question tags goes up if the tag is a real question.
Example: Thomas won the competition yesterday, **didn't he?** I hope he did because he's telling everyone.

The intonation goes down if the tag is used to check information that the speaker believes is true.
Example: This is called levitation, **isn't it?**

1 🎧 11.4 **Listen to the two question tags.**

2 🎧 11.5 **Listen to the sentences below said twice. Write C if the speaker is checking information and Q if the speaker is asking a real question.**

1 a Sydney isn't the capital of Australia, is it? ___
  b Sydney isn't the capital of Australia, is it? ___

2 a You haven't seen Brett recently, have you? ___
  b You haven't seen Brett recently, have you? ___

3 a Matthew will be at the party, won't he? ___
  b Matthew will be at the party, won't he? ___

4 a I'm not working tomorrow, am I? ___
  b I'm not working tomorrow, am I? ___

5 a They were Irish, weren't they? ___
  b They were Irish, weren't they? ___

6 a We hadn't heard the news before, had we? ___
  b We hadn't heard the news before, had we? ___

3 **If you are working with a partner, practise saying the sentences and question tags in exercises 1 and 2.**

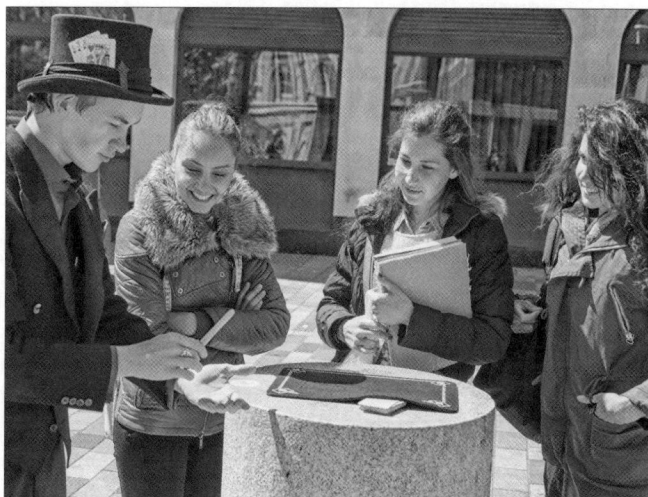

Reading and Use of English

GAPPED TEXT: PAPER 1, PART 6

1 **You are going to read an article about the history of Easter Island. Six sentences have been removed from the article. Choose from the sentences (A–G) the one which fits each gap (1–6). There is one extra sentence which you do not need to use.**

A The trees had been vital in making canoes to go fishing.

B Many of the heads were found in the island's quarry, unfinished and discarded.

C So how was it that a once green land became almost entirely deforested?

D Devastating ecological damage by rats has been recorded on other locations in the Pacific area.

E This was because they needed wood to act as rollers in transporting the giant statues.

F Rather he places the blame on another culprit: a plague of rats.

G It is possible that Europeans exaggerated the tales of horror to help destroy the islanders' original religion.

2 **Find these words and phrases (1–8) in the text. Then match the definitions (a–h) to the words and phrases.**

1 remote ___	a the process where trees and plants disappear
2 soil ___	b without knowing
3 cannibalism ___	c far away from other places
4 deforestation ___	d to support something
5 unwittingly ___	e the ground, the earth
6 to overrun ___	f the things that trees and plants grow out of
7 seeds ___	g people eating other human beings
8 to back something up ___	h to grow in numbers until an area is completely full

SPOTLIGHT ON STUDY TECHNIQUES

The best way to improve your reading and vocabulary is to read as much as possible in English. Many English language websites have extensive articles about many different issues, so it is often easy to find articles that you are interested in. The BBC website, www.bbc.co.uk, includes articles on science, entertainment, history, geography and many other issues. Try to read one web article every day.

EASTER ISLAND CATASTROPHE

Two thousand miles away from Chile, Easter Island is one of the most remote spots on Earth and yet it has fascinated visitors ever
5 since the first Europeans arrived on Easter Day, 1772. The reason at first was the mysterious giant heads that pepper the island, staring mysteriously out to sea.
10 Nowadays interest in the fate of the island has surged once more. This time it has come from new theories that the collapse of human society on the island
15 provides a warning to the modern world of ecological disaster waiting to happen.

Even when the first Europeans arrived on Easter Island, they
20 found it almost empty of trees. Yet later scientific analysis has revealed that it was once covered in palm forests. **(1)** _____ In his recent history of ancient people surviving in harsh conditions, *Collapse*, the American author Jared
25 Diamond argues that the Easter Islanders themselves were responsible for much of the devastation.

According to Diamond, the statues that so amazed those first European visitors played a part in the disaster. The population of the island began competing in constructing the stone heads and in doing so they cut down more and more of the forests. **(2)** _____

Once the forest had been cut down, serious problems emerged in the local society. **(3)** _____
30 They also kept water in the soil: with little rain on the island, this was vital to help crops grow. With agriculture and food supplies devastated, the result was war and starvation, and there is even a suggestion of cannibalism on the island.

But this is far from the only theory. The rumours of cannibalism have especially been questioned. The only real evidence for this comes from ancient stories. **(4)** _____
35 In the last few years an alternative theory has been proposed. This is the work of Dr Terry Hunt of the University of Hawaii. Like all historians of the area, Dr Hunt agrees that serious deforestation took place on Easter Island, but he does not blame the local population. **(5)** _____

Possibly unwittingly transported by the original Polynesians, the rodents would have hidden in their canoes and then escaped onto the island. With no natural predators, a rat population can
40 increase at incredible speed. Within a few years, millions of the animals would have overrun the island, eating everything in sight.

They did this not by eating the trees themselves but by eating the seeds. Instead of people cutting down the forests, the rats would have prevented any new plants from growing. This theory has strong evidence to back it up. **(6)** _____
45 Whatever did cause the final collapse of the ecosystem on Easter Island, it is clear that something terrible did happen on that small piece of rock, lying alone in the Pacific Ocean.

Vocabulary

WEATHER AND DISASTERS

1 Look at the pictures and complete the words, as in the example.

1 m e t e o r i t e

2 d _ _ _ _ _ _

3 e _ _ _ _ _ _ _ _

4 f _ _ _ _

5 t _ _ _ _ _

6 v _ _ _ _ _ _ _   e _ _ _ _ _ _

7 f _ _ _ _

8 t _ _ _ _   w _ _ _

2 Complete the crossword.

Across

4 A prediction of the weather.

7 A light kind of fog.

9 The weather conditions that a place usually has.

Down

1 Light, continuous rain.

2 Very strong wind.

3 A sort of rain made from small pieces of frozen water.

5 The sound you hear when you see lightning.

6 A time of very bad weather with strong winds and lots of rain.

8 An adjective that describes something covered in frozen water.

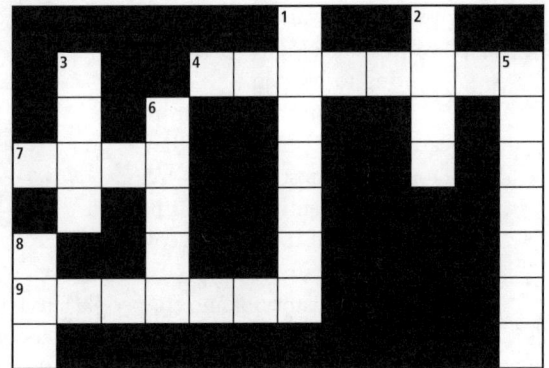

TRANSITIVE AND INTRANSITIVE VERBS

3 Complete the sentences with the words from the box.

died	disappeared	raised
rose	was killed	was lost

1 He _____ of old age. I went to the funeral.

2 The environmental campaigners _____ some serious issues at the meeting.

3 The temperature _____ by 10°C.

4 The doctors think the man _____ by an electric shock.

5 The contract _____ by my lawyer. He left it on a train.

6 After the rain came, the snowman _____.

Grammar

CONTRAST AND CONCESSION

1 Rewrite the sentences using the word in capitals, as in the example. Make any other changes necessary. You may need to write one or two sentences.

0 Dominic doesn't speak any Portuguese. He travelled all over Brazil. **DESPITE**

Despite not speaking any Portuguese, Dominic

travelled all over Brazil.

1 There was a lot of rain. We had a really good holiday in Britain. **DESPITE**

_____

2 It was warm and sunny. He was wearing a winter coat. **EVEN THOUGH**

_____

3 There was a lot of drizzle. No one was carrying an umbrella. **ALTHOUGH**

_____

4 People are buying every bottle of water in the supermarket. The government says there is no danger of drought. **NEVERTHELESS**

_____

5 People are suffering from famine throughout the country. No help has arrived from the international community. **HOWEVER**

_____

6 I have never been up the Eiffel Tower. I live in Paris. **DESPITE**

_____

THE DEFINITE ARTICLE

2 Underline the correct option. Ø means no article.

1 There was *a / the / Ø* cat in the kitchen. I had never seen it before.

2 *A / The / Ø* Aztecs came from Mexico.

3 My father is *a / the / Ø* businessman.

4 My favourite way of travelling across Spain is by *a / the / Ø* train.

5 What is *a / the / Ø* lowest temperature that has been recorded here?

6 We are expecting a visit by *a / the / Ø* President of the USA.

7 Did you read in the newspaper about the man who was struck by *a / the / Ø* lightning?

8 I don't know *a / the / Ø* reason why Karen didn't come to your party.

Spelling

Plurals of nouns ending in -o
When nouns end in -o, there are three ways of making the plural. You can add -s as in regular nouns.
Example: kilo ➡ kilos

Other nouns can only be spelt -es.
Example: torpedo ➡ torpedoes

But most nouns can either be spelt -s or -es. Both options are correct.
Example: mosquito ➡ mosquitos/mosquitoes

1 Complete the table with the words from the box. Three words go in each column.

mango	potato	radio	tomato	hero
domino	video	volcano	studio	

-os	-oes	-os/-oes
avocados	*tornadoes*	*flamingos/flamingoes*

Listening: San Francisco earthquake

DIALOGUE + MULTIPLE CHOICE, PAPER 3, PART 4

1 🎧 12.1 **You will hear an interview with an expert on earthquakes in San Francisco, Denise Wei. For questions 1–7, choose the best answer (A, B or C).**

1 Why were people surprised by the 1906 earthquake?

   A People thought there was only a very small earthquake risk.

   B At that time, nobody knew about the San Andreas Fault.

   C People thought earthquakes would only happen in other parts of California.

2 What did Liz Hickok use to make a model of the city?

   A food

   B ice

   C computer video images

3 Why did Liz Hickok make her model of San Francisco?

   A To eat it.

   B It was a work of art.

   C To make a scientific study of earthquake effects.

4 How did people react when roads and bridges were destroyed in the 1986 earthquake?

   A They expected the level of damage.

   B They thought the damage should have been much worse.

   C They expected much less damage.

5 Why were there low casualties in 1986?

   A The experts had warned everybody about the earthquake.

   B Because many people were working in their offices.

   C Because there was a major sports event on.

6 What does the Big One refer to?

   A a future earthquake

   B the 1906 earthquake

   C the 1986 earthquake

7 How likely is another earthquake in San Francisco in the next 25 years?

   A It is very unlikely.

   B It is quite probable.

   C It is almost certain.

Pronunciation

The definite article (*the*)
The definite article, *the*, can be pronounced in two ways: /ðə/ and /ðiː/. We use /ðə/ before consonant sounds. We use /ðiː/ before vowel sounds.

1 🎧 12.2 **Listen and decide if the pronunciation of *the* in these sentences is /ðə/ or /ðiː/.**

1 Do you know the answer to the question? _____

2 Have you got to the end of the book? _____

3 Do you want the orange or the banana? _____

However, many words that begin with a consonant may actually start with a vowel sound. In the same way, many words that begin with a vowel may actually start with a consonant sound.
Examples: honest ➡ /ɒnist/
unique ➡ /juniːk/

2 🎧 12.3 **Decide if the pronunciation is /ðə/ or /ðiː/ in these phrases. Then listen to check your answers.**

1 the hour	/ðə/	/ðiː/
2 the university	/ðə/	/ðiː/
3 the one	/ðə/	/ðiː/
4 the uniform	/ðə/	/ðiː/
5 the honour	/ðə/	/ðiː/
6 the European	/ðə/	/ðiː/

Reading and Use of English

OPEN CLOZE: PAPER 1, PART 2

1 Read the text below and think of the word which best fits each gap. Use only one word in each gap. There is an example at the beginning (0).

Jennifer Steele works (0) ....*as*.......... a volcanologist, an expert in volcanoes. It's an extremely dangerous occupation. Since the 1980s, over thirty experts (1) .... died whilst doing work in the field. Nevertheless, Jennifer has a huge passion for her subject. We caught up with her just before she set off for a new field trip to Papua New Guinea.

'I grew up in Washington State,' she explains. 'When I was seven, there was a huge volcanic eruption at Mount St Helens. The volcano erupted (2) .... warning. Nobody expected it. I could see the smoke from my house. I was (3) .... shocked that I just stared at it for hours. It changed my life. Later, I took a degree (4) .... Vulcanology (yes, it is a university subject) and now here I am.'

So how difficult is it to predict a volcanic eruption today? 'It's not easy,' says Jennifer. 'But we are getting better. It's difficult for me to explain the science (5) .... lies behind our forecasts. Basically, today satellite images and infrared cameras can (6) .... used to help us observe volcanic activity and predict a major eruption.'

'These innovations are also changing our lives,' she continues. 'In the past, vulcanologists (7) .... spend a lot of time actually on the volcano itself. They were in constant danger. With these infrared cameras, that is (8) .... longer the case. It's now possible to monitor a volcano from several kilometres away. Of course, our work is still dangerous, but we accept the risk because when we get a forecast right, we save hundreds of lives.'

MULTIPLE-CHOICE CLOZE: PAPER 1, PART 1

2 Read the text below and decide which answer (A, B, C or D) best fits each gap. There is an example at the beginning (0).

As global temperatures continue to (0) ....*C*............ , environmental problems are causing more and more distress for people caught up in sudden catastrophe. Summers in Europe are getting longer and hotter, and the heatwaves that result can have serious effects with many (1) .... people being hospitalised or even dying from the intense temperatures.

Along with the dangers of the heatwave, a further problem affects many Mediterranean countries: forest fires. In hot weather, fires (2) .... in the countryside causing terrifying destruction to homes, properties and lives. But what is most alarming of all is that many of these fires are not natural: they are the product (3) .... arson.

In Spain in 2007, the Canary Islands were seriously affected by fires that grew with incredible (4) .... It appears that these fires began after being deliberately (5) .... alight. The fires grew due to strong winds, making fighting the blaze an almost impossible (6) .... As a result, the government was forced to order the closure of motorways and evacuate thousands of people from their homes. (7) .... of this damage has come in spite of the best efforts of the government to educate the public about the dangers of fires in summer. The Canary Island fires came soon after the Spanish government had put up posters making people (8) .... of the dangers of fires to the environment.

0	A life	B arise	C rise	D raise
1	A antique	B aged	C ancient	D elderly
2	A break out	B cut out	C burn down	D get away
3	A from	B by	C over	D of
4	A haste	B rapid	C speed	D quick
5	A made	B took	C brought	D set
6	A trouble	B task	C work	D stage
7	A Little	B Every	C Much	D Many
8	A aware	B comprehend	C learn	D understand

Writing: an essay

COMPULSORY TASK: PAPER 2, PART 1

1 Complete the student's answer to the exam question below with the words from the box.

> even though   instead   in this case   it
> their   these places   they   this problem

In your class, you have been talking about the environment. Now, your teacher has asked you to write an essay.

Write an essay using all the notes and give reasons for your point of view. Write your answer in 140–190 words.

How can people be encouraged to recycle more?

Notes

Write about:
1. giving information about recycling
2. places where people recycle
3. .... (your own idea)

People are not recycling as much as they could because they often do not know where or how to recycle.

One way of solving [1]_____ is giving infomation to show people where they can recycle. Often [2]_____ are easy to find, but some products like bateries need to be recycled in a speshul place. Notices need to be put up to show where this can be done.

It is also important to remember that many eldrely people have trouble moving hevy objects. [3]_____ cannot always carry bottles or cans to a recycling area. [4]_____ older people should be helped by local councils who can collect rubbish from [5]_____ homes.

Finally, [6]_____ many people recycle at home, they do not recycle when they are out. [7]_____ people often throw rubbish like drink cans away in normal litter bins. To prevent this, more places need to have litter bins avalable where rubbish is seperated into cans, glass, etc.

In conclusion, it is easy to encourage people to recycle more. People will always recycle when [8]_____ is easy for them to do.

2 Look again at the student's answer. Can you find eight spelling mistakes?

3 Now write your own answer to the exam question in exercise 1.

....
....
....
....
....
....
....
....
....
....
....
....
....
....
....
....
....
....
....
....
....

Speaking

1 🎧 12.4 **You will hear two students doing the collaborative task in the Speaking test. They have to decide which of the five suggestions below would be the best way of raising money for charity. Listen and decide which suggestion (a–e) they are discussing in each extract.**

Extract 1 ___

Extract 2 ___

Extract 3 ___

Extract 4 ___

a. make and sell T-shirts

Which is the best way of raising money for charity?

e. do a sponsored sports event

b. hold a rock concert

c. have a sale of second-hand clothes

d. ask people for money in the street

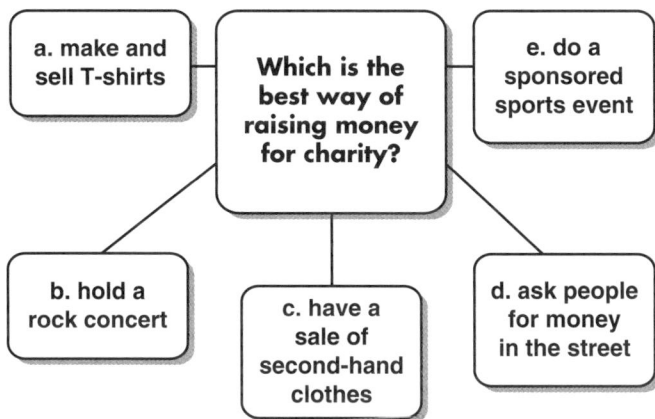

2 🎧 12.4 **Correct each sentence (1–8) below. They are all ways of rejecting a possibility or saying that a possibility may not work. Then listen to the recording again to check your answers.**

1 I don't think this is a good idea to all.

2 This doesn't work by me.

3 I don't see the point to do this.

4 This is not effective solution to the problem.

5 In this cause I don't think this is the best option.

6 I don't think it's a bad idea, but I think some of the other one are better.

7 Does this really work? I don't sure.

8 How if nobody comes to the event?

3 **If you are working with a partner, do the exam task in exercise 1 together. In the Speaking test, you will have about two minutes for this part of the test.**

Reading and Use of English

MULTIPLE CHOICE: PAPER 1, PART 5

1 You are going to read an article about Twitter. For questions 1–6, choose the answer (A, B, C or D) which you think fits best according to the text.

1 From the first paragraph, we understand that Elka
  A couldn't answer the crossword question.
  B thought the crossword question was easy.
  C wasn't interested in the crossword question.
  D was surprised by her son's crossword answer.

2 Elka believes that Twitter
  A isn't a useful place to get information.
  B is mostly used to discuss serious events.
  C is only used to gossip.
  D is a great place to talk about fashion.

3 According to Elka, the name 'Hashtag Jameson'
  A may not have been true.
  B was almost certainly illegal.
  C was absolutely shocking.
  D was an amusing name for a child.

4 IT experts used the @ symbol in emails because it
  A was easy to pronounce.
  B was already an important part of mobile phones.
  C was understood internationally.
  D wasn't used very much in the past.

5 The first message on Twitter
  A was exactly like most tweets today.
  B was the first example of a hashtag for a group.
  C was ignored by journalists.
  D was all about the use of hashtags.

6 What does the author say about Twitter in Saudi Arabia?
  A It is mostly used there to discuss current events.
  B It is the country that sends the most tweets every day.
  C It is not surprising that Twitter has been a success there.
  D It is popular there because it is user-friendly.

#Hashtag!
Elka Schmidt

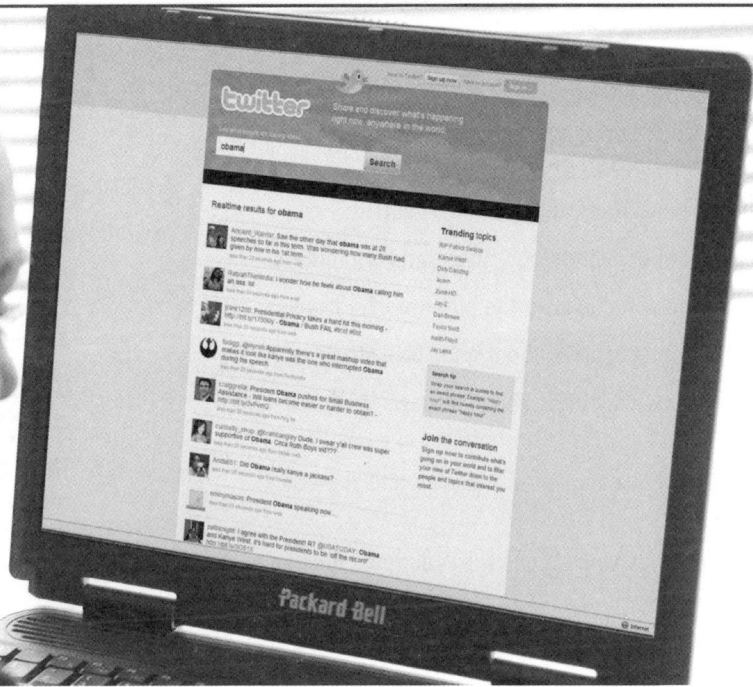

My poor father was pacing around the living room with a well-thumbed dictionary in his hands. He had spent all morning on the daily crossword and there was just one clue that he couldn't solve. It was 13 down of course, and it said 'the four
5 line square that everyone is talking about'. Even before I could open my mouth to give the obvious answer, my twelve-year-old son said, 'Hashtag, Grandpa. Like on Twitter.'

My father is decidedly old world and he must have been one of the few people left on earth who didn't know what a
10 hashtag was. For everyone else, it is probably the key that they wear out fastest on their laptops. Especially for us girls, because 60 per cent of Twitter users are female.

The whole world is tweeting like there's no tomorrow. There are now over a billion tweets sent every week. It's
15 not the case that everyone just talks about what socks they are wearing or what cereal they are having for breakfast. In fact, most Twitter activity is fired by current events, especially sports and politics. The most retweeted tweet ever was by President Barack Obama when he announced his
20 victory in the US presidential elections. Over 800,000 people retweeted it. Now that is 'hashtag amazing' as my son might say.

That is the strangest thing. Teenagers and young people are starting to say the word 'hashtag' in the middle of a
25 normal conversation. This completely mystifies my father, even when he isn't fretting over the crossword. As far as he was concerned, the hashtag was a pointless little button at the bottom of his phone. Now thanks to Twitter, it's a part of everyday speech. There was even a case last year of a pair
30 of British parents who named their baby 'Hashtag Jameson'.

Even though it was there in the headlines, the news left many people incredulous (including me). It just smacked of a hoax.

Rather like the '@' that we now use for emails, the hashtag used to be a symbol looking for a meaning. @ was
35 originally an abbreviation for 'about', for example 'the price will be about $12'. It was internet pioneer Ray Tomlinson who gave the symbol its new meaning. Tomlinson was looking for a simple way of separating a user's name from an internet domain like 'hotmail' in an email. @ was perfect because it
40 was on every keyboard, but no one really used it. There isn't even a word for it in English, unlike 'hashtag'.

In the beginning, our friend # wasn't actually a part of Twitter's plans. It didn't appear in the very first tweet, which was sent on 21 March 2006 when Jack Dorsey, one of
45 the company's founders told the few early followers that he was 'just setting up my twttr'. That simple message failed to attract any particular notice on business pages at the time. Nevertheless, the company grew, and so did the need to link conversations. It was a year later when Twitter user Chris
50 Messina suggested using the hashtag to connect tweets on the same topic. The company never looked back.

Now it's the essential tool for gossip and showbiz. The average user has posted 307 messages, and while that's about right for me, my son has almost three times that amount. It's
55 not just a phenomenon in the English-speaking world either. Twitter supports over 25 different languages including many scripts that are written right to left. That may well be one of the reasons why the country with the fastest growing number of users on Twitter is Saudi Arabia, with over three million
60 tweeters hard at work. Now tell me that isn't hashtag news.

Vocabulary

NEWS AND NEWSPAPERS

1 **Complete the puzzle with sections from a newspaper. What is the word in grey?**

1 All the big stories about world events.

2 Stories about technology, space and computers.

3 An article which shows the opinion of a newspaper.

4 All the latest stories about golf, basketball, etc.

5 A section with stories about disease, medicine and diet.

6 Stories about companies, industry and the stock market.

7 A puzzle that you complete by reading clues and writing words.

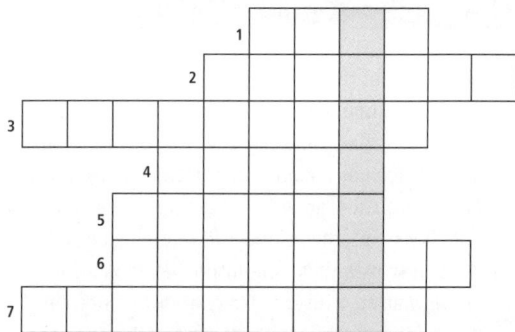

2 **Complete the words. Write one letter in each space.**

1 My grandmother was a famous dancer and she had an o _ _ _ u _ _ y in the paper when she died.

2 My parents met after my dad put a p _ _ s _ _ _ l ad in the paper and my mother replied to it.

3 If you want to sell your car, don't put an ad in the c _ _ s _ _ _ _ _ d section. Put an advert online.

4 I haven't followed the election on the news because I'm not interested in p _ _ _ t _ _ s .

5 Do you have the TV l _ _ t _ _ g _ there? I want to check what time my favourite programme is on.

6 There are six pages of s _ _ w _ _ z news in the paper today. Why? I'm not interested in the lives of actors and pop stars!

7 I know the h _ _ o _ _ _ _ _ s are silly, but I check them every day. I'm a Libra. What star sign are you?

PHRASAL VERBS

3 <u>Underline</u> the correct option.

1 The situation looks good. Our wages are *going / coming* up by five per cent next month.

2 The politicians had a furious argument and they *took / broke* off the talks with the protesters.

3 I was going to enter the tennis competition, but I hurt my arm and I had to pull *out / away*.

4 On the third day of the golf tournament Tiger Woods pulled *out / ahead* of the other players and started to lead the competition.

5 Tara was going out with her boyfriend for years, but then they broke *up / over* last week.

6 Sam and Ian were good friends for years, but they fell *off / out* about a month ago. Now they're not talking to each other at all.

7 The Mayor tried to cover *up / over* the fact that he had stolen money, but a journalist discovered what had happened.

8 We told everyone that this information was secret! How did it *flood / leak* out to the press?

Grammar

REPORTED SPEECH

1 Write the sentences in reported speech.

1 Cathy: 'We're not making any progress!'

Cathy said that we weren't making any progress.

2 Rich: 'I didn't see Tina.'

_____

3 Maria: 'Are you going to buy a newspaper?'

_____

4 School teacher: 'It'll be a nice day tomorrow.'

_____

5 Policeman: 'No one can go in the building.'

_____

6 Katy asked: 'Has Simon heard the news?'

_____

7 Joe: 'They have been asking me questions.'

_____

REPORTING VERBS

2 Put the words from the box into the sentences below. Add one word to each sentence.

for	he	him	to	us	we	who

1 When we left, our parents warned not to speak to people who seem too friendly.

2 Gemma advised me compare prices on the Internet.

3 His sister reminded to post the letter.

4 He didn't apologise arriving late.

5 When the teacher spoke to Jim and me, he suggested do an exam preparation course.

6 They criticised the people didn't do the work.

7 I recommended ask for some help from our teacher.

Spelling

1 Look at the adjectives below and circle the correct spelling.

1 a breakable   b breakible

2 a adaptable   b adaptible

3 a edable   b edible

4 a visable   b visible

5 a flexable   b flexible

6 a inevitable   b inevitible

7 a capable   b capible

8 a invincable   b invincible

9 a countable   b countible

10 a predictable   b predictible

2 Complete the table with the verbs from the box. Three words go in each column.

advise	believe	change
knowledge	manage	note

-able	-eable
excusable	noticeable

105

Listening: a journalist

1 🎧 13.1 **You will hear a journalist, Linda Bridgestone, talking about her early career. For questions 1–10, complete the sentences. You will need to write a word or a short phrase in each gap.**

When she was younger, Linda says she wanted to be Britain's first female **(1)** ....

She mentioned that she became a journalist because she was interested in **(2)** ....

Linda says she was the editor of her

(3) ....

Linda explains that she was paid

(4) .... for her work experience.

While she was doing her work experience, Linda felt like the **(5)** ....

Linda says her first job was typing

(6) ....

On one occasion, Linda says she misspelt

(7) .... Sherborne.

Linda describes a time when she and another journalist went to interview **(8)** ....

The other journalist did not go into work because he had to go to **(9)** ....

Linda says her first paid job was on

(10) ....

Pronunciation

Place names

In the interview in *Listening*, Linda Bridgestone said that she had problems spelling *Sherborne*. Many place names in the English language have a very different pronunciation from their spelling. It is important to learn the correct spelling of the more common places in English-speaking countries.

1 🎧 13.2 **Listen to the place names below and circle the correct pronunciation.**

1	Norwich	a /nɔːrwɪtʃ/	b /nɒrɪtʃ/
2	Greenwich	a /griːnwitʃ/	b /grenitʃ/
3	Leicester Square	a /lɪsestə skweə/	b /lestə skweə/
4	Gloucester	a /glɒstə/	b /glaʊsestə/
5	The Thames	a /ðə θeɪmz/	b /ðə temz/
6	Birmingham	a /bɜːmiŋəm/	b /bɜːmiŋhæm/
7	Nottingham	a /nɒtiŋam/	b /nɒtiŋəm/
8	Edinburgh	a /edinbrə/	b /edinbɜːg/
9	Melbourne	a /melbɔːn/	b /melbən/
10	Brisbane	a /brisbən/	b /brisbein/
11	Connecticut	a /kənektikʊt/	b /kənetikət/
12	Eire	a /eərə/	b /eəriː/

2 **If you are working with a partner, practise saying the words in exercise 1.**

Reading and Use of English

OPEN CLOZE: PAPER 1, PART 2

1 Read the text below and think of the word which best fits each gap. Use only one word in each gap. There is an example at the beginning (0).

They built straight roads (0) ...._that_........ still exist today and huge cities and temples. One other thing that the Romans did was to invent the newspaper. The *Acta Diurna*, which means 'events of the day', was founded (1) .... Julius Caesar. It was a newssheet, written by hand. The *Acta Diurna* was available in the capital city and all over the Roman Empire. Astonishingly the *Acta Diurna* survived for some three centuries, as long as many of the oldest newspapers today. Many of the ancient writers used the *Acta Diurna* (2) .... the basis for their historical works. Through them we are able to read about daily life in Ancient Rome as written in their (3) .... words.

The purpose of the *Acta Diurna* was to publish official news about Roman political life and the empire's inevitable victories in war. However, like most newspapers before and since, it also included lots of other general interest sections which were probably much (4) .... popular, including sports reports (gladiator fights) and predictions of the future – using omens! No doubt the obituaries section was particularly busy during the reign (5) .... the murderous emperor Caligula.

Needless (6) .... say, not all the news was printed in the *Acta Diurna*. Under the emperors (7) .... succeeded Caesar, democracy in Rome collapsed. And while the *Acta Diurna* printed the main news, a secret newssheet was prepared in (8) .... the records of government business were kept. This was known by a different name: the *Acta Publica*.

Hold the front page!

MULTIPLE-CHOICE CLOZE: PAPER 1, PART 1

2 Read the text below and decide which answer (A, B, C or D) best fits each gap. There is an example at the beginning (0).

For many young people journalism seems to be a career full of (0) ...._C_......... and adventure. However, if you are thinking of (1) .... journalism, it is important to ask yourself whether this is really for you. There is another side to the world of the journalist.

Today news is everywhere: news (2) .... are providing 24-hour coverage online while readers are clamouring for the latest headlines. However, working as a journalist is more dangerous than ever. The BBC reported that 121 journalists were killed in 2012 alone. It is well (3) .... that many of them were deliberately murdered to stop their stories reaching the public and it is essential to do more to bring their killers to justice. Furthermore, journalists are also at (4) .... risk of physical attacks, intimidation and being taken hostage.

Press photographers too must travel to some of the most violent and lawless places in the (5) .... and their lives are very different from the celebrity-chasing antics of the paparazzi. To get the picture that tells a thousand words, they have to get closer to the action than anyone else. Sometimes it is impossible to (6) .... placing themselves in danger. One can only (7) .... the courage of these men and women and it is worth remembering their bravery when flicking through the various (8) .... in the morning paper.

0	A exploration	B imagination	C excitement	D reality
1	A bringing up	B taking up	C making up	D going up
2	A sites	B headlines	C agents	D places
3	A decided	B spoken	C known	D thought
4	A considerable	B expanded	C countless	D sizable
5	A planet	B earth	C world	D globe
6	A avoid	B skip	C deny	D protest
7	A notice	B celebrate	C enjoy	D admire
8	A additions	B sections	C departments	D supplements

Writing: punctuation

SPOTLIGHT ON PUNCTUATION

Apostrophes

We use 's to show possession by one owner.
Examples: the soldier's orders (= one soldier)
the boss's seat   the man's office

We use an apostrophe after the plural ending *s* to show possession by more than one owner.
Examples: the soldiers' orders (= more than one soldier)
the bosses' seats

We also use 's with irregular plural nouns.
Examples: the men's office   the children's games

If someone's name ends in *s*, you can either simply add an apostrophe or 's.
Example: Anders' house / Anders's house

---

1 Read the Spotlight on Punctuation box on apostrophes and then correct the sentences below. There are two correct sentences.

1 I think that's Gary's wifes car.

2 Eight students answers were right.

3 Tina's brother's go to the same school as me.

4 Where can I find ladies' shoes?

5 I couldn't find Charles phone anywhere.

6 We were surprised by peoples' response to the questionnaire.

7 The pasta was made with sheep's cheese.

8 Everybodys answer is wrong.

2 In Part 2 of the Writing test, you may be asked to write a report. Look at the exam question below and the student's report to the right. Add six apostrophes to the text. Then organise the report into five separate paragraphs.

Your English teacher has asked you to write a report on sports facilities in your area. You should explain what the most popular sports facilities are and say why they are popular. Write between 140 and 190 words.

---

3 Now write your own answer to the exam question in exercise 2.

....

....

....

....

....

....

....

....

....

....

....

....

....

....

Sports in Zagreb

Zagrebs sports facilities are the best in Croatia. There are plenty of opportunities for playing sports all over the city. One of the most popular facilities is the Mladost Sports Park. This contains two of the countrys largest swimming pools. The park is enormous and there are also clay courts for tennis. It is popular both with locals and tourists because you can buy a visitors ticket to use in any part of the park. For people who like winter sports, there is the Sljeme ski resort. This is incredibly popular because it is only a 20-minute drive from the city centre. The resorts pistes are enormous and several thousand people can ski there at the same time. There are also childrens slopes and areas for beginners. When the weather is hotter, many people like to go to the Jarun Sports Centre. The lakes at the centre are a great place to go sailing. It is also a lovely place to go running and cycling, because there are no cars and there are lots of green spaces. Zagreb is a sports city and you can play almost any sport here. The probably explains our national teams success in several sports like football, handball and basketball.

Speaking

TOPIC DISCUSSION: PAPER 4, PART 4

1 At the end of the Speaking test, the interlocutor will ask you some general questions. These questions are usually on the same general topic that you talked about in Part 3. Read the interlocutor's questions (1–6) on the right. Match the students' answers (a–f) to the questions.

2 🎧 13.3 Now listen to six people answering the questions. Check your answers in exercise 1.

3 🎧 13.3 Listen again. Complete the answers (a–f) in exercise 1 with phrases that are useful when answering general discussion questions.

4 If you are working with a partner, ask and answer the exam questions in exercise 1.

1 What do you think is the best way of getting news? ___

2 Do you often read newspapers or watch the news on TV? ___

3 Is it important for people to watch the news? ___

4 What are the advantages and disadvantages of getting news over the Internet? ___

5 Do you like reading about celebrities in newspapers and magazines? ___

6 What part of the newspaper is most interesting to you? ___

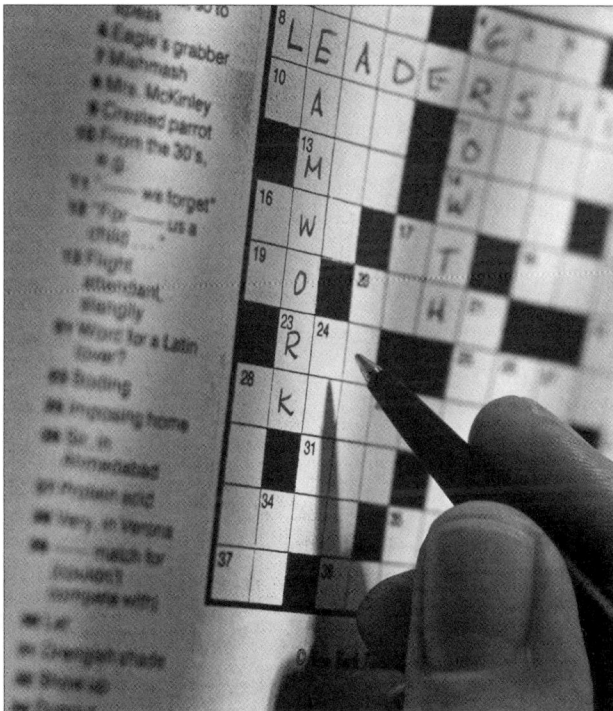

a _____ I think if there is a big story, then it's important that the public know what's going on: if there is a weather problem or something like that. But often there isn't really any big news, so it's not necessary to find out what's going on all the time.

b _____ I read a free newspaper if there's one in the station. And I sometimes watch the news when I'm cooking because we have a TV in the kitchen. But I don't think I'm very interested in the news.

c _____ it's the crossword. I love doing it in my coffee break when I'm at work. Sometimes I work on it all day and I always have to buy the next day's newspaper to see what answers I didn't get.

d _____ I can't get enough gossip to be honest. I think everyone really likes to read about that sort of thing. I buy two or three gossip magazines each week. I think I'm a bit addicted!

e _____ Er … it's a very quick way of getting information, of course, and you can get a lot of different opinions too. I think it's good as long as you use the sites from serious newspapers or news services. Otherwise you don't know who wrote the news that you're reading.

f _____ I have to say the radio. On TV they don't really have enough time to discuss all the complicated issues. On the radio they have a lot of time to talk and you can hear experts speak.

LANGUAGE CHECKLIST

☐ I know words to describe fashion, page 112.

☐ I know some phrasal verbs for using with clothes, page 112.

☐ I know how to use *have something done*, page 113.

☐ I know how to use the passive, page 113.

☐ I know how to use *make, let* and *allow*, page 113.

☐ I know how to pronounce some homographs, page 117.

LANGUAGE CHECKLIST

☐ I know words to describe fashion, page 112.

☐ I know some phrasal verbs for using with clothes, page 112.

☐ I know how to use *have something done*, page 113.

☐ I know how to use the passive, page 113.

☐ I know how to use *make, let* and *allow*, page 113.

☐ I know how to pronounce some homographs, page 117.

EXAM CHECKLIST

☐ I have practised the multiple choice question from the Reading and Use of English paper, page 110.

☐ I have practised the Part 1 extracts + multiple choice question from the Listening paper, page 114.

☐ I have practised the topic discussion from the Speaking paper, page 114.

☐ I have practised the key word transformation question from the Reading and Use of English paper, page 115.

☐ I have practised the word formation question from the Reading and Use of English paper, page 115.

☐ I have practised writing a description of a person for the Writing paper, page 116.

Reading and Use of English

MULTIPLE CHOICE: PAPER 1, PART 5

1 **You are going to read an article about the latest handbag craze. For questions 1–6, choose the answer (A, B, C or D) which you think fits best according to the text.**

1 How does the writer feel about women's obsession with handbags?

A He thinks men need to carry them too.

B He thinks they contain a lot of non-essential objects.

C He thinks they are too expensive.

D He thinks it's a short-term craze.

2 What is the problem with the Dior Gaucho bag?

A There are not enough of them on sale.

B It is the most expensive bag on the market.

C It is not popular any more.

D You have to be a member of a special club to buy one.

3 Most handbag sales in the UK are

A only from a few famous shops.

B generated only by a small number of designers.

C only made in one season of the year.

D from selling bags that look like more famous ones.

4 How does Tamara Mellon feel about handbags?

A Any handbag will look good.

B You have to match your clothes very carefully with your handbag.

C What you wear on your feet is as important as your handbag.

D Handbags aren't really very important.

5 What does 'it' in line 55 refer to?

A the typical handbag

B annual sales of handbags

C a report on handbag ownership

D the number of handbags people have

6 What do women's handbags typically contain?

A some cosmetic items

B mainly cheap objects

C no objects that are useful for work

D nothing relating to their home

HOW HANDBAGS BECAME A GIRL'S BEST FRIEND

By David Derbyshire

Of all the subjects that divide men and women, it is probably the female love of accessories – and handbags in particular – that baffles men the most. For women, a handbag is a statement of personality

5 and attitude. It is an indicator of status, a weapon in a crowd and a home on the move.

For men, it seems to be little more than an expensive device for carrying around unwanted receipts and other useless items. It is certainly no

10 substitute for a really good trouser pocket.

The gap between the sexes looks likely to grow deeper with a study suggesting that women's love affair with handbags has reached a new level of intensity. Between 2000 and last year sales of

15 handbags in the UK soared by 146 per cent to a record £350 million.

Claire Birks, the author of the study, believes that the phenomenal growth is being fuelled in part by the must-have celebrity handbag. 'The rising number of

20 working women has played a key role in this market as they not only have the money but also the need for stylish, well-accessorised outfits and handbags. It is now commonplace for women to have a wide variety of bags for a whole host of occasions — from smart

25 evenings out to a night in the pub and from a day in the office to a day's shopping.'

Top of the range designer bags with price labels of £1,000 are not uncommon and their popularity has never been greater. Any woman wanting one of

30 this season's must-have handbags, the Dior Gaucho, should be prepared to fork out £815 and join a month-long waiting list.

It takes just a glimpse of a new Gucci or Chloé bag on the arm of Kate Moss or Paris Hilton in *Heat*

35 magazine for that model to fly off the shelves at Selfridges and Harrods. But while designer brands have played a part, the rising sales have mostly been driven by cheaper imported handbags and own-label imitation designs. Supermarkets are also branching

40 out into the lucrative accessories market.

Tamara Mellon, the owner of the Jimmy Choo label, said she had seen a major change in the accessory market. 'It doesn't matter what you are wearing – if you have good shoes and a good bag, you will look right,' she said. 'Handbags are a status symbol, the 45 perfect accessory to dress up your day and your outfit. For women of all ages and from all walks of life, acquiring a handbag is an enjoyable experience.'

Last year a study found that 60 per cent of women own at least ten handbags, while three per cent have 50 at least 25. In addition to this, it also suggests that the demand for handbags has yet to be sated.

'There is no reason to believe that sales will not continue to increase over the next five years,' Miss Birks said. 55

While men may remain baffled by the attraction of handbags, some light has been shed on what they contain. A survey of 1,700 women carried out by Prudential discovered that alongside the old train tickets, receipts and pens, the average 60 handbag contains around £550 worth of personal possessions. Typically, they include a mobile phone, a purse, a hairbrush, perfume, a make-up bag, a leather diary or personal organiser, and house and car keys. In summer months, a pair 65 of sunglasses usually joins the collection. Most women questioned assumed that their handbags and contents were worth only £150.

Vocabulary

FASHION

1 Complete the puzzle. What is the word in grey?

1 To lose colour and become paler.

2 A time when everybody is excited about doing or buying the same thing.

3 Something which is very fashionable, especially among young people.

4 Another word for *fashionable*.

5 Things which are fashionable for a short time.

6 When two colours or styles look awful together, they _____.

7 Something that used to be fashionable and is now fashionable again.

8 This is what people have when they stand out from a crowd and are exciting to look at.

9 This is an adjective that describes someone who dresses very well and looks good.

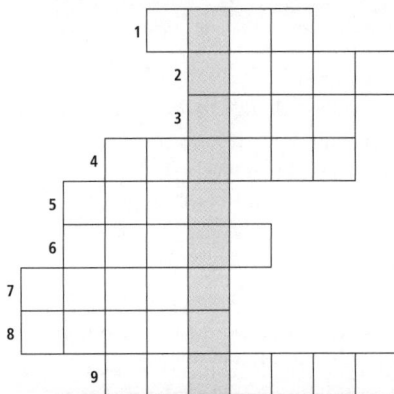

2 Complete the words in the blog. Write one letter in each space.

Blast from the past!

We moved house last week and I had to clear out my old [1] w _ _ dr _ _ _ . It was full of clothes that I hadn't worn in years and I found some clothes that I had forgotten about. There was a leather jacket: that's a design [2] c _ _ _ _ _ c , so it'll never go out of fashion. I also came across some [3] d _ _ _ g _ _ _ sunglasses which I had left in an old suitcase. My daughter Miranda wants those, but she just laughed when she saw some of my other clothes. I mean, I must have been her age when I wore these things. Back then I was really [4] i _ _ _ the Spice Girls and I have clothes like one member of the band. You know, tracksuits and trainers with all the [5] l _ g _ s on them. The clothes are good quality and they have famous [6] b _ _ _ d names. Unfortunately, Miranda thinks I can't even give them to the charity shop now because they are so 'uncool' (her words, not mine). Personally, I think they'll make a [7] c _ _ _ b _ _ k and be fashionable again, but she just laughed. Mind you, she wears retro clothes herself. Her look is 1990s 'grunge' with ripped jeans and other [8] s _ _ _ f _ y clothes. My husband hates it. They look so different. She has blue hair, and he's usually in a grey business [9] s _ _ _ !

PHRASAL VERBS FOR USING WITH CLOTHES

3 Underline the correct word.

1 It's getting a bit cold. I'm going to *put / take* a jumper on.

2 If the trousers are too long, I can *send / turn* them up for you.

3 If you would like to *place / try* the suit on, there is a fitting room behind you.

4 I'm getting a bit fat. I can't *do / make* up these trousers any more.

5 It's getting hot. I think I'll *put / take* my coat off.

6 This is your costume for the play, but I think we need to *let / make* the jacket out a bit so that it will fit you.

7 It's a black-tie event, so we're going to *dress / wear* up for the occasion.

8 These trousers are too large. Can you *take / put* them in for me?

Grammar

HAVE SOMETHING DONE

1 Look at the pictures. Complete the sentences using the words in brackets and the correct form of *have something done*.

1 Before they joined the army, the soldiers

_____ (their heads / shave).

2 Annie _____ yesterday (her windows / clean).

3 My grandmother always _____ (her shopping / deliver).

4 The house looks terrible, but we

_____ next week (the walls / paint).

5 My computer broke down last year and I

_____ (it / repair). It cost €200.

6 Grandad isn't here because he is at the optician's.

He _____ (his eyes / test).

THE PASSIVE

2 Look at the sentences below. Six of them contain a mistake. Find and correct the mistakes.

1 The city destroyed by a volcanic eruption.

2 I couldn't believe that he was being question by the police.

3 They hadn't been told about the fashion show.

4 Many synthetic fibres, like nylon and polyester, are use in clothes manufacture.

5 *The Name of the Rose* was written for Umberto Eco.

6 The window had been opened from a screwdriver.

7 The washing machine has been ruined my new shirt!

MAKE, LET AND ALLOW

3 Complete the email with the correct form of *make, let* and *allow*.

Hi Mick

I had such a terrible flight last week. I am never flying through that airport again! First of all, lots of flights had been cancelled so there were thousands of people waiting in the airport. They ¹_____ everyone queue outside. We weren't even ²_____ into the airport to get a drink of water.

Finally, after two hours, they ³_____ us go inside. Check in was easy but when we got to Departures, they took my bag off the X-ray machine. Then I was ⁴_____ to take everything out of it. It was so annoying and there was no reason for it.

They were so rude too. These days they don't ⁵_____ you to go on the plane unless you put all your toothpaste and stuff in a special plastic bag. Well, guess what? They wouldn't ⁶_____ me use my own plastic bag. Oh no. The woman there ⁷_____ me buy a 'special' plastic bag from a machine at the airport. It was a pathetic way to get €1 from every passenger. They say it's for our security, but I don't feel safer when they ⁸_____ me do all these stupid things. People should just be ⁹_____ to take any bottles on the plane, if they are under 100 cl. That plastic bag is a rip off. And of course, they don't ¹⁰_____ you to complain. No, you just have to keep quiet and accept it. Personally, it ruined my holiday!

Anyway, I hope you're OK!

See you

Katja

Listening: clothes and fashion

EXTRACTS + MULTIPLE CHOICE: PAPER 3, PART 1

1 🎧 14.1 **You will hear eight people talking about clothes and fashion. For questions 1–8, choose the best answer (A, B or C).**

1 You hear a woman talking about a present she bought for her husband. Why did he not wear the shorts?

   A He thought they were not fashionable.

   B He did not like the colour.

   C He did not like the design.

2 You hear a father talking to his son. Why does he tell the son to change his clothes?

   A The colours clash.

   B He is wearing the wrong clothes for the weather.

   C He does not look smart enough.

3 You hear a daughter talking to her mother. Why does the daughter want to have the dress?

   A She wants to wear it in a play.

   B It is now back in fashion.

   C She needs some new clothes.

4 You hear a man talking about buying a shirt. Why did he buy the wrong size?

   A He was not able to try it on.

   B He ordered it on the Internet and the size was wrong.

   C He didn't look at the label.

5 You hear a woman shopping with a friend. Why does her friend convince her to buy the necklace?

   A It has a classic look.

   B It matches her new earrings.

   C It looks good on her.

6 You hear a mother talking to her son. Why does she stop him throwing the shirt away?

   A She can repair it.

   B It was very expensive.

   C It is almost new.

7 You hear a man talking about a clothes shop. What does he complain about?

   A Their clothes are boring.

   B Their clothes are not good quality.

   C Their clothes are expensive.

8 You hear two people talking about clothes. Where are they?

   A at a party

   B at work

   C at a wedding

Speaking

TOPIC DISCUSSION: PAPER 4, PART 4

1 🎧 14.2 **Listen to two students discussing the exam question below. Why do they disagree about the answer?**

....

....

> Do you think young people spend too much money on clothes and fashion?

2 🎧 14.2 **Listen again. Complete the phrases that Claudio and Eleni use to disagree with and challenge each other's opinion.**

1 But _____ that sometimes you have to go to the expensive shops?

2 But do you really need the brand name?

   _____, if clothes look good, the name is not important.

3 What _____ that if you want to look good, you need to buy quality clothes, designer clothes, big brands.

4 Yes, _____ speaking about young people.

5 I _____. But if your friends have the best clothes, you want them too.

6 All _____, I think there are better things to spend your money on when you're young.

7 I _____ so. But I still think they spend too much money on clothes.

3 **Look at the extract from the conversation and choose the best definition (a or b) of *Not necessarily*.**

   a That is never true. The situation is impossible.

   b That is not always true. There are other possibilities.

Eleni	So their parents have to spend money on these clothes.
Claudio	Not necessarily. Many of my friends have jobs, and they study and work. So they can buy their own clothes.

4 **If you are working with a partner, discuss the exam question in exercise 1 together.**

Reading and Use of English

KEY WORD TRANSFORMATIONS: PAPER 1, PART 4

1 Complete the second sentence so that it has a similar meaning to the first sentence, using the word given. Do not change the word given. You must use between two and five words, including the word given. There is an example at the beginning (0).

0 My shoe has got a hole in it.

THERE

............*There is a hole in*.......... my shoe.

1 He had to wear a uniform.

MADE

They .... a uniform.

2 The teacher said I couldn't leave early.

LET

The teacher didn't .... early.

3 We are not permitted to wear jewellery.

ALLOW

They don't .... jewellery.

4 Someone should water the plants.

NEED

The plants ....

5 We have to give these tickets to Jane immediately.

GIVEN

Jane .... these tickets immediately.

6 I have a hire car because they are repairing mine.

HAVING

I have a hire car because I

....

7 Someone cleans Steve's house once a week.

CLEANED

Steve .... once a week.

8 Two famous artists were designing the new clothes.

DESIGNED

The new clothes .... two famous artists.

WORD FORMATION: PAPER 1, PART 3

2 Use the word given in capitals at the end of each sentence to form a word that fits in the gap. The words in each pair of sentences have the same endings. There is an example at the beginning (0).

0 a You will get a wide ....*variety*.......... of different customers. **VARY**

 b He gave me back my wallet with all my money and credit cards, and I thanked him for his
 ....*honesty*.......... . **HONEST**

1 a I cannot believe that there is still famine and .... in the world. **HUNGRY**

 b There was a lot of .... because of the price of the team's new football shirts. **ANGRY**

2 a This haircut is really .... at the moment. **FASHION**

 b After they had heard the bad news, they looked .... **MISERY**

3 a These jeans were .... last year, but they've gone out of fashion already. **TREND**

 b These trousers have a special pocket for my mobile phone, which is really .... **HAND**

4 a What is the .... of the carpet? **WIDE**

 b We are going to study this subject in .... **DEEP**

5 a Everyone should know about the .... of many workers in this industry. They work in terrible conditions. **EXPLOIT**

 b You need a lot of .... to be a successful clothes designer. **IMAGINE**

Writing: a description of a person

1 In Part 2 of the Writing test, you may be asked to write a description of people or places as part of a story, a review or an article. Look at the exam question below and the extracts from two students' answers. Which genre are the students writing about (history, romance, etc.)?

1 _____   2 _____

Book reviews wanted

You see this announcement in an online magazine.

> Have you read a book in which a character changed in an interesting way?
>
> Write us a review of the book, explaining what the main character did and how he or she changed. Tell us whether or not you would recommend this book to other people.
>
> The best reviews will be published in the magazine.

1

Dorian Gray is the hero of The Picture of Dorian Gray by Oscar Wilde. At the beginning of the story, he is a handsome young man who wears the latest fashionable clothes. He is sociable with plenty of friends, but as the story develops his life changes. Dorian's friend, the worldly aristocrat Lord Henry Wotton, encourages him to enjoy the dark side of life. Slowly, Dorian becomes a cruel murderer. His face remains young but upstairs in the attic of his house, a painting of him is changing all the time. It is becoming very, very ugly.

2

Angela Tramelo, the hero of *Great North Road* by Peter F. Hamilton, is a 'one in ten'. As a baby, she was genetically engineered to be a perfect human and to live for centuries. While other people become plump and get wrinkles, she still looks like a beautiful young woman. She seems fun and lively, but Angela has had a difficult life. At the beginning of the book, she is released after 20 years in prison for a murder that she did not commit. Angela becomes more and more determined as she goes on a mission to find the real murderer. Only she knows that it is an alien.

2 Look again at the students' answers. Find adjectives to describe appearance and personality. Use them to complete the table below.

Appearance	Personality
handsome	sociable

3 Before you start writing a description, it is a good idea to think of as many words as you can to use in your answer. Read the sentences (1–8) and think of other words to replace those in bold.

1 She was **a little bit fat.** _____plump_____

2 She was an elderly lady with lots of **lines in her face.**

_____

3 She was **too thin and it looked unhealthy.**

_____

4 He was **a person who was lots of fun and talked to everyone at parties.** _____

5 She had lots of **brown dots on her face** because she had been out in the sun. _____

6 Her hair was **very untidy.** _____

7 Her hair was **not its natural colour.**

_____

8 She was **a person who never gave up. Nothing stopped her.** _____

4 Now write your own answer to the exam question in exercise 1. Write your answer in 140–190 words.

....
....
....
....
....
....
....
....
....
....
....
....
....
....
....
....
....
....

Pronunciation

SPOTLIGHT ON PRONUNCIATION

Homographs
There are many words in English that are spelt in an identical way, although the words actually have a different meaning and a different pronunciation.
Examples: close = near ➡ /kləʊs/
The hotel isn't close to the beach.
close = shut ➡ /kləʊz/
Close the door please.

1 Look at the sentences below. In each group of sentences, one word in bold is pronounced differently to the other two. (Circle) the word which is pronounced differently.

1 a He always wears a **bow** tie.

   b You use a **bow** in archery.

   c Give a **bow** at the end of the performance.

2 a We employed a guide to **lead** us through the forests.

   b They use **lead** to protect the body from radiation when they take X-rays.

   c Where is the dog's **lead**?

3 a Don't worry – this job will only take a **minute**.

   b There is a **minute** difference between the results: a difference of 0.001 per cent.

   c Who is going to **minute** what is said in the meeting?

4 a Everyone disagreed and there was a terrible **row**!

   b There is a **row** of chairs on the stage.

   c I don't know how to **row** a boat.

5 a The road **winds** through the valley.

   b The clock is very accurate because an engineer **winds** it every day.

   c It was a real hurricane, with **winds** of 150 kph.

2 🎧 14.3 **Listen and check your answers.**

3 **If you are working with a partner, practise saying the words in exercise 1.**

LANGUAGE CHECKLIST

- [ ] I know words to describe culture and heritage, page 120.
- [ ] I know some more phrasal verbs, page 121.
- [ ] I know how to use *so*, *such*, *too* and *enough*, page 121.
- [ ] I know how to pronounce some adverbs in conversation, page 122.

EXAM CHECKLIST

- [ ] I have practised the gapped text question from the Reading and Use of English paper, page 118.
- [ ] I have practised the multiple matching question from the Listening paper, page 122.
- [ ] I have practised the key word transformation question from the Reading and Use of English paper, page 123.
- [ ] I have practised the word formation question from the Reading and Use of English paper, page 123.
- [ ] I have practised writing an article from the Writing paper, page 124.
- [ ] I have practised the individual 'long turn' from the Speaking paper, page 125.

Reading and Use of English

GAPPED TEXT: PAPER 1, PART 6

1 **You are going to read an article about the Mongolian emperor Ghengis Khan. Six sentences have been removed from the article. Choose from the sentences (A–G) the one which fits each gap (1–6). There is one extra sentence which you do not need to use.**

A But the reverence in which he is held by mainstream Mongolians comes as a shock to visitors.

B During this event Mongolian men and boys compete in the three 'manly sports' of wrestling, archery and horse-racing.

C Historians also point to the introduction to the West of inventions such as gunpowder and paper that his empire made possible.

D Throughout his lifetime he extended his rule to the south and west.

E The Mongolian president was formerly a student at Leeds University in the UK.

F This is because of disputes over building contracts.

G This is presumed to be Genghis himself.

2 **Find these words and phrases (1–8) in the text. Then match the definitions (a–h) to the words and phrases.**

1	clan ___	a	ignored, did not notice
2	rituals ___	b	a large area with open grass and no forests
3	overlooked ___	c	using a large number of something
4	an advocate ___	d	religious ceremonies
5	the steppe ___	e	give energy to
6	hordes ___	f	a supporter
7	reinvigorate ___	g	a large family group
8	mass ___	h	a large group of people

GENGHIS KHAN IS BACK –

WITH A NEW IMAGE

The Mongolian capital has been covered with images of its former leader, Genghis Khan, for the anniversary of his unification of the nation in 1206. A crowd of onlookers including visiting royalty gathered in the city for the event. At the climax of celebrations in Ulan Bator yesterday, soldiers in traditional uniform heralded the unveiling of an enormous statue of the Great Khan in the main Sukhbaatar Square. The monument contains earth and stones from the holy and historic places in Mongolia associated with his rule.

Ghenghis Khan was born in 1162, the son of a murdered clan chief. After a childhood spent mostly on the run from family enemies, he was elected the tribes' Great Khan in 1189. **(1)** _____ Finally his reign came to an end when he fell from his horse and died in 1227.

Genghis has always had a cult of admirers. **(2)** _____ After all, in the West his name is associated with bloodshed and terror.

To those who still think of themselves as his people, he is a unifying symbol. 'People know his military side, but they do not know his philosophy,' said Nomch P. Davaanyam, a thirtieth-generation descendant who is trying to revive the sky-worshipping rituals Genghis performed.

Mr Davaanyam is not alone in his assessment. In a radical reshaping of Genghis's popular reputation, historians are increasingly taking the Mongolian side. 'The West was blinded by his conquests,' said Jack Weatherford, the American author of _Genghis Khan and the Making of the Modern World_. 'They overlooked his great impact on law and commerce. He outlawed the kidnapping of women, guaranteed diplomatic immunity to ambassadors and granted religious freedom to all people.' **(3)** _____ 'He was an advocate of free trade and a flat tax system,' Mongolian President Enkhbayar told a gathering of journalists. 'He changed the whole world.'

Unfortunately, the monument of Genghis Khan remains half-finished. **(4)** _____ Mr Enkhbayar unveiled it beneath scaffolding.

The ceremony was timed to match the beginning of the annual festival of Naadam. **(5)** _____ Visitors can also watch _Genghis Khan – the Rock Opera_ in the state theatre. On the steppe outside Ulan Bator, 500 members of the armed forces are re-enacting the campaigns of the Khan's hordes.

Despite the money being spent on the monument and the celebrations, most Mongolians seem to appreciate the effort to reinvigorate the memory of Ghengis Khan. Tumurbat Altanmur, 16, said: 'I think he was very cruel and tough. But without cruelty his kingdom would not have stood.'

Recent studies based on mass DNA testing have suggested that 16 million men living in Eurasia are descended from one person in the early thirteenth century. **(6)** _____ President Enkhbayar said: 'That shows he is not just Mongolia's; he is the world's.'

Vocabulary

CULTURE AND HERITAGE

1 Complete the crossword.

Across

1 A formal event such as a wedding or a funeral.

3 A painting or drawing of a person.

7 A painting or drawing of nature or the countryside.

9 These are places where the public can look at paintings and other works of art.

Down

1 A tradition, such as eating a particular food to celebrate a special day.

2 A work of art or a structure that is built to remember people who have died.

4 A special event or day when everybody in a place or country has a party and celebrates together.

5 A public building where you can see important objects, especially from history.

6 An artwork made of stone or metal that represents a person or animal, for example *David* by Michelangelo.

8 Tourist _____ are places where tourists can see famous and important buildings.

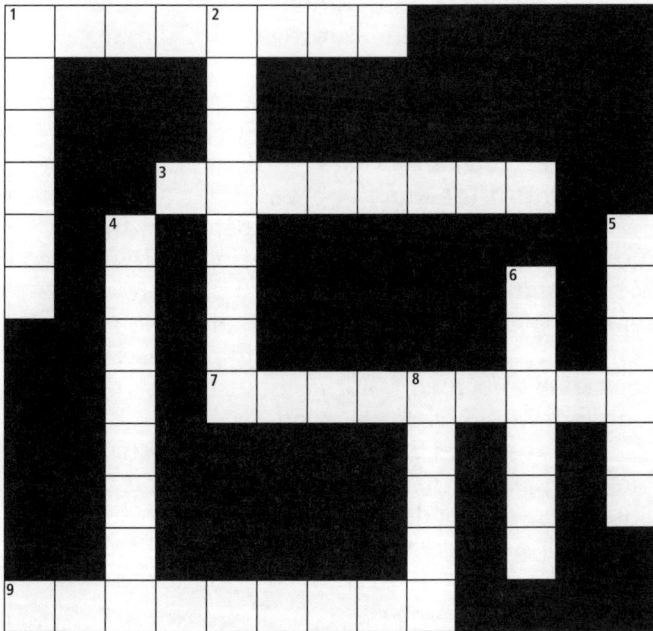

2 Complete the words in the news article. Write one letter in each space.

Lost masterpieces

If you are short of money, stop looking for change down the back of the sofa and go to the attic. You may have a ¹ pr _ _ _ l _ _ s masterpiece up there that nobody knows about.

It really does happen. In 2011, a Swedish man kindly donated an old painting to his local charity shop, thinking it was ² w _ _ th _ _ _ s . It was only when the experts examined it that they realised it was a lost classic, The Battle of Bomarsund, by Russian painter Aivazovsky. The painting shows a ³ h _ st _ _ _ c _ _ scene from the Crimean War. In the end, the painting was sold for $21 million.

In this case, the charity and the seller got some ⁴ i _ v _ _ u _ b _ _ advice before the sale. Many people are not so lucky and they sell some old family ⁵ h e _ _ l _ _ m without ever knowing its true value.

It's even easier to make this mistake with pottery. ⁶ A _ c _ _ n _ Chinese dishes are now very collectable in Asia. Lots of European families have some from the travels of their ancestors. Many of these people have no idea that they have items that are of importance to the national ⁷ h _ _ it _ g _ of another country. The collectors do know this, and they are quickly buying up this old pottery and making millions when these objects come up for auction. One minute a plate is at the back of a dusty cupboard, and the next it's the centrepiece of a major ⁸ ex _ _ _ it _ _ _ .

However, it is always important for the buyer to beware. You might think you are about to snap up a forgotten masterpiece in a market, but these are ⁹ n _ t _ _ io _ _ places for fakes. That vase may not be quite as old as you think it is. There are many ¹⁰ i _ f _ _ o _ s examples of people being tricked in this way.

PHRASAL VERBS

3 Choose a suitable word to complete the phrasal verbs below. Write one word only in each gap.

1 I set _____ to be a serious artist, but my whole career has been drawing comics.

2 They tried to pass the painting _____ as a genuine Picasso, but an expert realised it was a fake.

3 Have you found a babysitter yet to look _____ the children?

4 I hadn't seen my nephew for five years and then he turned _____ at my front door one day. It was completely unexpected.

5 The factory is turning _____ 100 cars a week.

6 The family had had the painting for 50 years before they found _____ that it was by Raphael. They were all amazed.

7 He's going _____ a bad time at the moment. He failed an important exam and he's lost his job.

8 Have you ever heard Tony when he's taking _____ the boss? His impression is hysterical!

9 He spent €500,000 on a fake vase. He was completely taken _____ by the fraudsters.

10 They offered us $1,000 for our silver mirror, but we turned them _____. We didn't want to sell because it's a family heirloom.

Grammar

SO, SUCH, TOO AND ENOUGH

1 Complete the sentences with so, such, too or enough. Use each word twice.

1 It was _____ a gorgeous house! I wanted to buy it as soon as I saw it.

2 We liked the flat, but it was _____ expensive for us. We couldn't afford it.

3 We couldn't get our chairs into the living room. The door wasn't wide _____.

4 Those are _____ lovely paintings. They look great!

5 I was _____ tired after I'd finished decorating the kitchen.

6 The painting is _____ big to fit in the car.

7 The garden isn't big _____ for a swimming pool.

8 We're _____ happy here that we don't want to move.

2 Read the sentences (1–6) below. Match the pictures (a–f) to the sentences.

1 We've got such a lot of things to recycle! ____

2 The recycling bank is too far for me to carry my bags there! ____

3 I've got too much work to do. ____

4 I haven't got enough work at the moment. ____

5 I'm working on such a complicated project. ____

6 There are so many meetings in my job that I never have time to do any work! ____

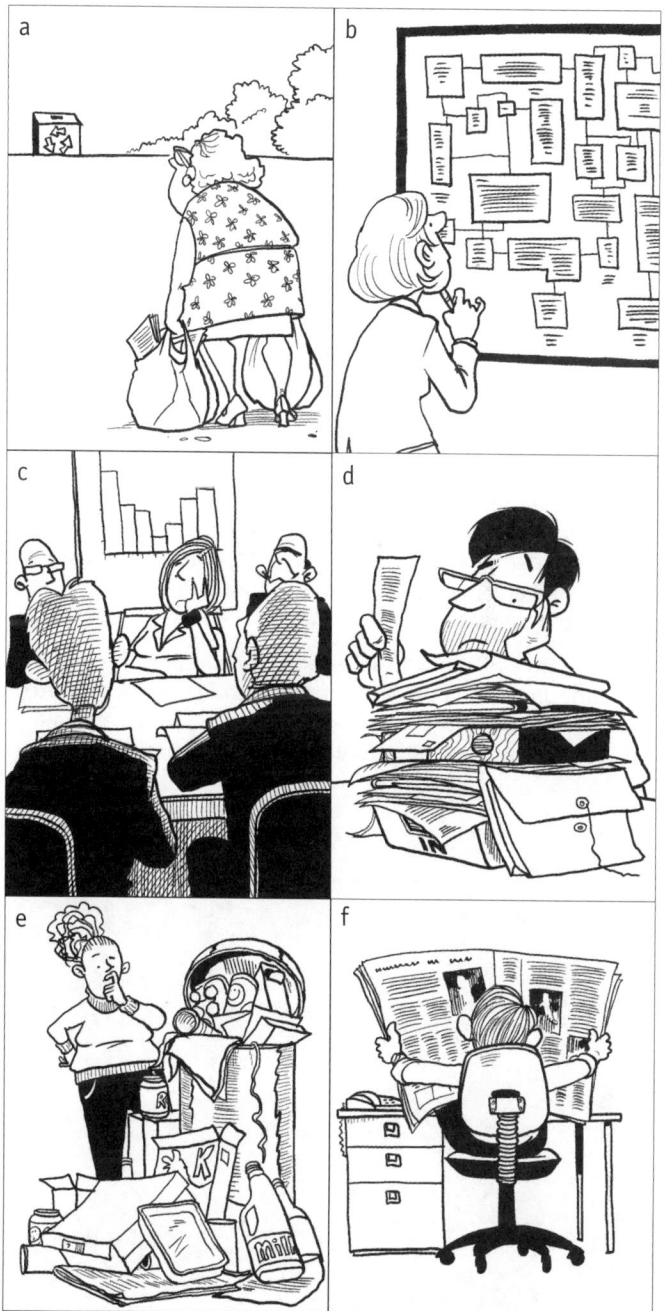

Listening: works of art

MULTIPLE MATCHING: PAPER 3, PART 3

1 🎧 15.1 **You will hear five people talking about works of art that are important for them. For questions 1–5, choose from the list (A–H) the work of art that each person is talking about. Use the letters once only. There are three extra letters which you do not need to use.**

Which work of art

A was discovered underground?

B was made from wood? Speaker 1 ___

C was not by a famous artist? Speaker 2 ___

D was damaged by contact with cars? Speaker 3 ___

E is an abstract work of art? Speaker 4 ___

F was based by the artist on his own body? Speaker 5 ___

G is an illustration of a bird?

H is not as famous as it should be?

SPOTLIGHT ON STUDY TECHNIQUES

Listening is one of the most difficult skills to practise if you do not live in an English-speaking country. It is also difficult to listen to English-language films and television programmes. If you get English-language films on DVD, it is a good idea to watch the film in your own language first and then to watch the original version in English. This will help you to understand the story and characters, making it easier to concentrate on the English language when you watch the second time around.

You may also have the option of changing the language on your TV remote control so you can watch programmes in the original language. This is also a good way of practising your English at home.

Pronunciation

1 🎧 15.1 **Listen again to the extracts in exercise 1 and complete the sentences with adverbs.**

1 _____, it's not there any more.

2 _____, the experts think that it will be easier to preserve there.

3 _____, most of the tourists who come to London don't know it's there.

4 _____, there is only one Michelangelo sculpture in the UK.

5 It's not easy to find even when you're in the museum, _____.

6 _____, it still has the original glass eyes that bronze statues used to have.

7 _____, it's a miracle that the sculpture survives at all.

8 _____, it's by Antony Gormley, who is one of Britain's most important living artists.

9 You know, _____, Picasso liked children's art.

2 **Where do the speakers make pauses in sentences 1–9 in exercise 1?**

3 🎧 15.2 **Now mark the pauses in these sentences using the symbol /, as in the example. Then listen and check your answers.**

1 Luckily, / the portrait wasn't damaged.

2 He didn't tell anyone the bad news, surprisingly.

3 They did not ask the cost of the painting, however, because they weren't interested in buying it.

4 This is a very dangerous expedition. Nevertheless, I want to be involved in it.

5 Basically, they weren't really interested in art.

6 Actually, I have a degree in History of Art.

4 **If you are working with a partner, practise saying the sentences in exercises 1 and 3.**

SPOTLIGHT ON PRONUNCIATION

Adverbs in conversation
Adverbs such as *actually*, *however* and *unfortunately* add to the whole meaning of a sentence. When they are used in speaking, it is usual to separate them from the rest of the sentence with a short pause before or after the adverb.

Reading and Use of English

1 Complete the second sentence so that it has a similar meaning to the first sentence, using the word given. Do not change the word given. You must use between two and five words, including the word given. There is an example at the beginning (0).

0 Can you explain why you decided to hold the exhibition in Liverpool?
   REASON

   Can you .... *give the reason* .... why you decided to hold the exhibition in Liverpool?

1 You can borrow my bike.
   MIND

   I .... you borrow my bike.

2 You have to make a decision!
   MIND

   You have to .... !

3 Could you work on Saturday this week?
   MIND

   Do .... on Saturday this week?

4 He completely fooled me: I believed everything he said.
   IN

   He completely .... :
   I believed everything he said.

5 Poor Mike! He's having a terrible time at the moment.
   THROUGH

   Poor Mike! He's .... a terrible time at the moment.

6 I want everyone to be involved in the school play.
   PART

   I want everyone to .... the school play.

SPOTLIGHT ON STUDY TECHNIQUES

Paper 1 of the Cambridge English: First (FCE) exam is Reading and Use of English. You have only one hour and fifteen minutes to complete this paper. When you are doing practice exams and practice papers, decide how much time you want to spend on each section. Some questions are worth more marks than others.

In Parts 1–3 of the exam, each question is worth one mark.

In Part 4, the key word transformation, there are six questions. Each one is worth two marks.

In Parts 5–6, the questions are worth two marks each.

In Part 7, each question is worth one mark.

If you find something is too difficult, just move onto the next section. Don't spend too long worrying about a question if it is only worth a single mark.

2 Read the text below. Use the words given in capitals at the end of some of the lines to form a word that fits in the gap in the same line. There is an example at the beginning (0).

In 2003 the Dutch (0) .... *artist* .... **ART**
Vermeer was the subject of the film
Girl with a Pearl Earring, which showed
a fictional (1) .... **RELATION**
between the painter and his maid.
Since then, Vermeer's work has become
more and more popular for his
(2) .... ability to **REMARK**
capture light and colour. However,
Vermeer died in 1675 when he was only
43 and he left only 35 paintings behind.
The fact that he painted so little has led
to (3) .... cases of **FAMOUS**
fraudsters making counterfeit versions of
his works. These have been sold for huge
prices, and only afterwards the discovery
was made that they were fakes.

The cost of a new exhibition means it
is now (4) .... that all **LIKELY**
of the real 35 pictures will ever appear
together in one place. Because of this,
a new museum in Vermeer's home city
of Delft has (5) .... **RECENT**
opened, which aims to show all of
the artist's works – in the form of
reproductions.

Also in the (6) .... **BUILD**
there are models of the houses where
Vermeer worked and the equipment that
he used. There is also information on
the (7) .... background **HISTORY**
to his work and a 3D animation which
provides an (8) .... **EXPLAIN**
of the complicated process used by
Vermeer in creating his small number of
masterpieces.

Writing: an article

1 Look at the exam question below and the student's answer. Complete the answer with the phrases (a–f).

a afterwards

b At first

c Before

d eventually

e First of all

f Once

You have seen the following announcement in an international travel magazine.

Calling all travellers!

Write an **article** about the best festival that you have ever been to, explaining why you liked it so much. We will publish the most interesting articles next month.

Write your answer in 140–190 words.

The best festival that I have ever been to was Carnival in Cologne in Germany. The whole city goes crazy. ¹_____ I was quite shocked, but I soon started enjoying it.

²_____ everyone puts on fancy dress. ³_____ going out, the men also all put on ties. I didn't know why until a girl cut my tie off – and she was a stranger! It's a tradition on women's day.

There were crowds everywhere. ⁴_____ we got into a restaurant, we saw that there were no tables and chairs. They do this all over the city because there isn't enough room for people as well as furniture! We stayed there for a while and ⁵_____ we went to a friend's house because we'd been invited to his party.

Everyone was singing carnival songs. I didn't know any of the words in the beginning, but ⁶_____ I learnt them and I was singing with everybody else. I really enjoyed the procession through the city too, which came at the end of the celebrations.

There was a fantastic atmosphere throughout Carnival. It was an incredible festival. It was like the whole city became one big party.

2 Look at the sentences below. They all contain a mistake. Find and correct the mistakes.

1 We all put on fancy clothes: I was dressed as a pirate.

2 There was crowded everywhere: it was difficult to move.

3 The best part of Carnival is when a huge manifestation walks though the main street of the city.

4 Several people have been invited at our party tomorrow.

5 It's a traditional in Carnival that women can cut off men's ties.

6 The whole city makes crazy during Carnival.

3 Now write your own answer to the exam question in exercise 1. Use words and phrases from exercise 2.

....

....

....

....

....

....

....

....

....

....

....

Speaking

INDIVIDUAL 'LONG TURN': PAPER 4, PART 2

1 🎧 15.3 **Listen to two different students talking about similarities between the pictures below. Decide which question (a–c) the interlocutor asked them.**

Student 1 ___

Student 2 ___

---

a Say which of these activities you would enjoy most.

b Say how you think the people are feeling in these photographs.

c Say what sort of person would enjoy these activities.

---

2 🎧 15.3 **Complete the sentences the students used to describe the pictures. Write one word in each gap. Then listen again to check your answers.**

1 Well, _____ me see.

2 In the _____ a girl is looking at some abstract art, I think it is, and er ... in the _____ a man is looking at some very small pictures.

3 _____ the second picture, I think perhaps this is more for party people.

4 They are celebrating something, _____ in the other photo the people are looking at art.

5 So _____ photos show people doing something in their free time.

6 But _____ back to the other picture, I think this looks like a lot of fun.

3 **If you are working with a partner, answer the exam questions in exercise 1 together.**

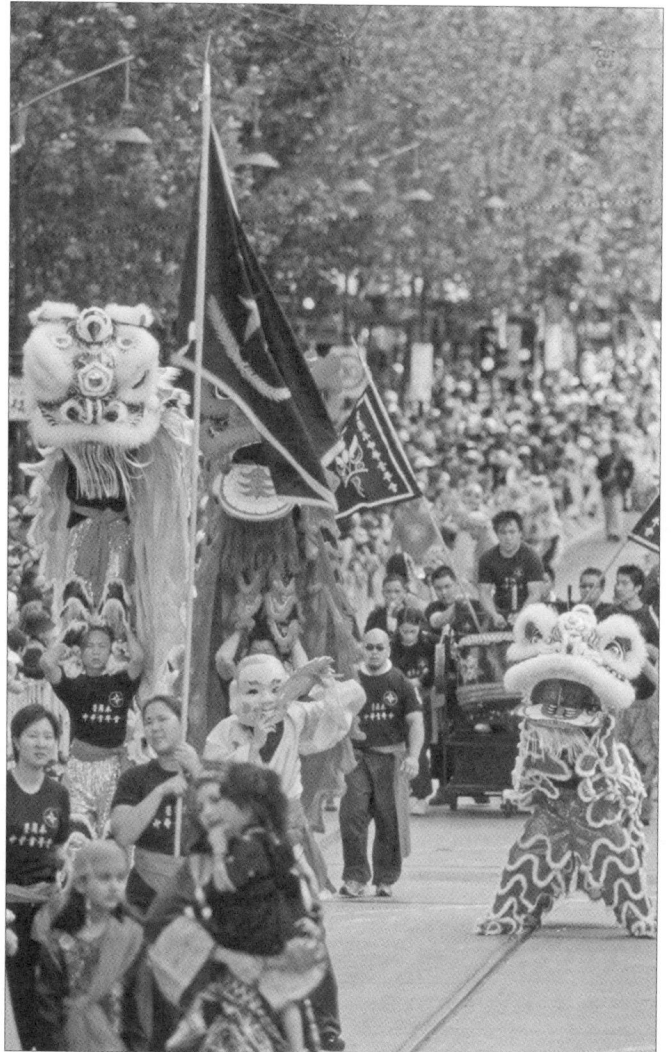

Practice Test

PAPER 1: READING AND USE OF ENGLISH Part 1 (Questions 1–8)

Part 1

For questions **1–8**, read the text below and decide which answer **(A, B, C** or **D)** best fits each gap. There is an example at the beginning **(0)**.

Mark your answers **on a separate answer sheet.**

Example:

0 **A** obsession **B** interest **C** enthusiasm **D** attraction

0	A	B	C	D
	▭	▬	▭	▭

Voluntary conservation work

For those of you with an **(0)** ...... in conservation, what could be a better experience than voluntary work? Volunteers UK are currently running several projects focusing on **(1)** ...... data in South American mountain regions.

Conservation projects often attract science students; by volunteering, young people can **(2)** ...... valuable experience in the field. But anyone can apply to be a voluntary worker as **(3)** ...... skills aren't required. Instead we try to **(4)** ...... the best use of the abilities and knowledge each voluntary worker has to offer. It is, however, necessary for you to be **(5)** ...... of doing demanding physical work.

On arrival, you will attend a **(6)** ...... of lectures on the local culture. You will also be given basic training that may come in **(7)** ...... out in the field.

Naturally, it is up to you how much you are prepared to **(8)** ...... into a project, but most volunteers come away with experiences that will stay with them for a lifetime.

1	**A** saving	**B** keeping	**C** gathering	**D** selecting
2	**A** achieve	**B** make	**C** earn	**D** gain
3	**A** specific	**B** exact	**C** definite	**D** detailed
4	**A** take	**B** do	**C** give	**D** make
5	**A** able	**B** capable	**C** possible	**D** suitable
6	**A** series	**B** path	**C** group	**D** chain
7	**A** practical	**B** handy	**C** sensible	**D** necessary
8	**A** insert	**B** contribute	**C** put	**D** go

Part 2

For questions **9–16**, read the text below and think of the word which best fits each gap. Use only **one** word in each gap. There is an example at the beginning **(0)**.

Write your answers **IN CAPITAL LETTERS on a separate answer sheet.**

Example: | 0 | A | S | | | | | | | | | | | | | | | | |

Grow your own herbs

I've been growing herbs for over forty years. **(0)** .... a matter of fact, I cultivate over sixty different kinds. Some are aromatic and **(9)** .... few are medicinal, but the majority are for use in cooking. I grow others simply **(10)** .... they're so pretty to look at!

I'd recommend anyone with even a small patch of land to grow herbs. You don't need a garden **(11)** .... get started because herbs can survive in a plant pot. Nothing's more satisfying **(12)** .... watching plants grow, and by using fresh herbs, you'll improve the flavour of your cooking. Finding out about herbs is fascinating: the more you learn about these wonderful plants, the **(13)** .... you want to know!

I live in Crete, **(14)** .... the climate is warm and the soil allows me to grow virtually anything. In a cooler, wetter climate, you **(15)** .... to take local conditions into account. Wherever you live, you'll find growing **(16)** .... own herbs a worthwhile experience.

Part 3

For questions **17–24**, read the text below. Use the word given in capitals at the end of some of the lines to form a word that fits in the space **in the same line**. There is an example at the beginning **(0)**.

Write your answers **IN CAPITAL LETTERS on a separate answer sheet**.

Example:

0	I	M	P	O	R	T	A	N	T							

Beethoven: a great composer

Beethoven was one of the most **(0)** .... composers in the history of Western classical music.   **IMPORTANCE**

Born in 1770, he was the son of a **(17)** .... , and he moved to Vienna in 1792, where he gained a reputation as a piano **MUSIC**
virtuoso. He acquired **(18)** .... patrons, and earned money **WEALTH**
from giving concerts and lessons, and from selling his works. He
wanted to be financially **(19)** .... so he would have the **DEPEND**
freedom to compose whatever he wanted.

Beethoven began to suffer from hearing **(20)** .... in his **LOSE**
twenties, and by 1814 he couldn't hear at all, but this didn't affect
his **(21)** .... to compose music. **ABLE**

As a result of his **(22)** .... , he began to keep **DEAF**
'conversation books': he and his friends would 'talk' by writing to
each other in them.

Consequently, we have a unique **(23)** .... record of many **HISTORY**
of Beethoven's conversations. They provide us with
(24) .... insights into how he wanted his works to be **VALUE**
performed.

Part 4

For questions **25–30**, complete the second sentence so that it has a similar meaning to the first sentence, using the word given. **Do not change the word given.** You must use between **two** and **five** words, including the word given. Here is an example **(0)**.

Example:

0 It might be cold tonight, so you'd better take a coat with you.

CASE

You'd better take a coat with you .... tonight.

The gap can be filled by the words 'in case it is cold', so you write:

Example: | 0 | | IN CASE IT IS COLD |

Write **only** the missing words **IN CAPITAL LETTERS on the separate answer sheet.**

---

25 Despite the traffic, the courier wasn't late delivering the package.

TIME

The courier .... despite the traffic.

26 The detective interviewed the suspect this afternoon.

BY

The suspect .... this afternoon.

27 'It isn't necessary for you to drive me home,' Francesca told him.

NEED

Francesca told him .... to drive her home.

28 There are very few places left on the web design course.

HARDLY

There .... places left on the web design course.

29   Students are not allowed to turn on their mobile phones in class.

MUST

All mobile phones .... before class.

30   If it doesn't start to rain soon, there will be a water shortage.

UNLESS

There will be a water shortage .... soon.

Part 5

You are going to read an article about animal intelligence. For questions **31–36**, choose the answer **(A, B, C or D)** which you think fits best according to the text.

Mark your answers **on a separate answer sheet**.

Animal intelligence

For centuries humans considered themselves unique in their ability to walk upright, use language and be creative. But as we studied and gained a greater understanding of the world around us, so too did we develop important insights into the animal kingdom. We discovered that some of our characteristics were not at all unique, that certain species were able to stand up on their hind legs, use tools, communicate and show emotion, just like humans.

Researchers working with great apes such as gorillas and chimpanzees claim to have taught them to recognise language, respond to it and use it themselves. Scientists argue amongst themselves about whether these animals demonstrate 'real' language in the way humans do, but we cannot deny that the great apes are more intelligent than previously believed. Of all the apes, it is chimpanzees which are considered the smartest of all, with their human-like ability to manipulate their environment in order to accomplish important tasks.

Elephants are known for their complex social interactions, and are amongst the most empathetic of our planet's creatures. To my mind, this charming characteristic makes them one of our closest friends. Like us, they form close familial bonds and have been observed to greet each other with fondness after separation, and even revisit the bones of deceased group members.

Some species of parrot are also highly intelligent creatures, and have been reported to count, identify colours and build an impressive vocabulary with which they are apparently able to communicate with humans – though some experts agree that they do little more than mimic, or copy, what humans say, without any actual ability to string words together to make meaningful utterances. Parrots aren't the only intelligent feathered creature, however. A species of crow found in Japan has discovered a cunning way to obtain food: in certain areas, they pick up walnuts left lying under trees that grow at the side of roads. Then they take them to junctions where they wait until the traffic lights change and it is safe to cross the road. They drop the walnuts on the tarmac and wait for vehicles to drive over them and crack the hard outer shells. When the lights change again, the crows join the pedestrians and pick up the nuts which are now ready to eat!

A more surprising discovery though, concerns chickens. Traditionally regarded as less intelligent creatures, they have been proven to be a lot cleverer than initially thought. They have excellent memory and a demonstrated ability to recognise other chickens. They employ a range of about twenty different cries to communicate with each other, and are good at solving a problem. If you show a chicken an object and then hide it, it will look for it – provided that it is a desirable object, such as a piece of food. In other words, the chicken is capable of understanding that the object has not stopped existing simply because it is out of sight. This only develops in a human baby between the ages of four and six months. *line 62*

Several species of animals have also demonstrated self- (and therefore global) knowledge by passing what is known as the mirror test, a fascinating experiment where the animal is placed in front of a mirror with, for example, a marking in dye on its fur. If the animal appears to react to the marking by turning round, trying to touch it and so on, scientists are satisfied that they recognise themselves. The significance of this is that it shows the animal clearly understands its environment and its place within it. Such animals include not only humans, elephants, and all of the great apes, but also certain species of dolphin, whale and bird.

Our awareness of animal intelligence has led to a conscious improvement in our treatment of animals fairly and an interest in the conservation of habitats and species.

31   What does the writer do in the opening paragraph?

    A   describe details of research that was carried out
    B   say how he thinks animals and humans differ
    C   explain how studies have changed what people think
    D   challenge his own previously-held beliefs

32   What does the writer appear to be uncertain about in the second paragraph?

    A   whether scientists have reached firm conclusions
    B   whether scientists have defined language accurately
    C   whether scientists have carried out thorough research
    D   whether apes are as clever as scientists have suggested

33   What does the writer particularly like about elephants?

    A   their well-organised family networks
    B   their highly-developed sense of understanding
    C   their similarity to humans in terms of behaviour
    D   their ability to communicate with others of their species

34   Why does the writer include the example of how crows break into nuts?

    A   to make a comparison with humans
    B   to highlight their ability to use tools
    C   to emphasise their communicative ability
    D   to demonstrate their intelligence

35   What does 'this' refer to in line 62?

    A   a desirable object
    B   an understanding
    C   a human baby
    D   a problem

36   What does the writer say about the mirror test?

    A   It is an accurate measure of an animal's heightened awareness.
    B   It is only possible to carry out on particular species of animal.
    C   It enables scientists to interact better with animals who pass it.
    D   Its success was an unexpected breakthrough in the scientific world.

Part 6

You are going to read an article about an educational television series called *Sesame Street*. Six sentences have been removed from the article. Choose from the sentences **A–G** the one which fits each gap **(37–42)**. There is one extra sentence which you do not need to use.

Mark your answers **on a separate answer sheet**.

Sesame Street

TV critic Charles Grimshaw reflects on an educational classic

It was one of the most successful television series for children ever produced. By 1999 it held the record as the longest-running American children's programme. The show? *Sesame Street*. The reasons for its success? They are almost too numerous to mention, although its educational value was, without doubt, one of its finest achievements.

The series soon became popular beyond the United States. **37** It was broadcast in 120 countries and there were numerous versions in other languages. Despite the show's emphasis on American culture, the programme appealed to a global audience and delighted children the world over, from the 1970s right through to the early 2000s.

Sesame Street aimed to teach young children letter and word recognition, simple arithmetic and life skills such as road safety and healthy eating. **38** This lively bunch of personalities inhabited a fictional part of New York City in the USA. The area, with its traditional houses, was inspired by the real-life neighbourhoods of Brooklyn Heights, where some of the show's producers were living at the time of the programme's production.

The puppet characters – known as Muppets – were created by puppeteer Jim Henson. Some Muppets looked like people while others resembled animals or monsters. **39** The idea behind including this broad range of characters in the series was to encourage children to be tolerant and inclusive towards others.

One of the best-loved 'animal' Muppets in *Sesame Street* was Big Bird, an enormously tall yellow bird who could roller-skate, ice-skate, dance, sing, write poetry and draw. **40** Big Bird's enquiring approach to life helped him to seek answers to things young viewers might also have been asking themselves, albeit on a subconscious level.

One of the most well-loved 'monster' puppets included the ever-popular Cookie Monster. This lovable puppet is covered with blue fur, has huge, globular, protruding eyes. **41** Concerns expressed by some parents that the Cookie Monster might be demonstrating poor eating habits to their children led to a change in the character's behaviour, and he became the series' greatest promoter of the importance of eating a healthy, balanced diet.

Other favourites were Bert and Ernie, two of the 'human' Muppets. They shared the basement apartment of number 123 Sesame Street, and the comic situations they acted out formed one of the staples of the series. But they, too, stood the test of time. **42** The fact that these actors agreed to appear on *Sesame Street* spoke for the affection which generations of viewers held for this remarkable show.

A They varied enormously in appearance and personality.

B One of the factors which led to this was its wide appeal – not only to pre-school children but to their older siblings and parents, too.

C Like the other characters, they were a culturally diverse set and embraced the differences between people from widely-varied backgrounds.

D It did so through a cast that consisted of puppet characters and human actors.

E However, the audience was excited by this and were grateful for the programme's emphasis on diversity.

F Much to the audience's delight, this lovable character consumed anything and everything in his way – although he had a particular fondness for biscuits, hence his name.

G He questioned the world around him as a child might as his awareness of the environment in which he finds himself grows

Part 7

You are going to read an article about four people who have started their own businesses. For questions **43–52**, choose from the people **(A–D)**. The people may be chosen more than once.

Mark your answers **on a separate answer sheet.**

Which person

felt nervous about becoming self-employed?	**43** ☐
believes it is necessary to behave fairly towards clients?	**44** ☐
had held a mistaken belief about certain workers?	**45** ☐
started working in an unfamiliar environment?	**46** ☐
hadn't expected the work to be as challenging as it was?	**47** ☐
acknowledges that setbacks happen during the learning process?	**48** ☐
emphasises the importance of communication?	**49** ☐
suggests requesting advice from a specialist?	**50** ☐
was persuaded to start a business after receiving praise?	**51** ☐
now has more freedom in the business than previously?	**52** ☐

'I've never looked back'

Benjamin Carlisle interviews four people who decided to quit their jobs and set up their own businesses.

A

Bob Jenkins

I decided to go into the gym business when I saw an advertisement for the sale of a small local gym. If you knew me, you'd probably have already burst out laughing by now – I'm not exactly a keen exerciser and had never even set foot in a gym before I went to look round. You might ask why I entered a world I appeared to have little interest in and if I answered honestly, I'd have to say it was the challenge of trying something so alien. I badly needed a change of direction in my professional life and thought, why not give it a go? I can be very determined to succeed and I threw myself into making it work – and it did. My tip for anyone thinking of starting their own business is to enlist the help of an expert, especially if it's a field that's completely new to you.

B

Jane Krauser

My catering business has been up and running for a year now and I'm really pleased with its success. I'd always enjoyed putting together delicious treats for family parties and so many people encouraged me to go professional with my ideas that in the end I thought I might as well follow their advice. Not that I wasn't apprehensive about giving up my well-paid job and starting from nothing! But I'm pleased to report that the work soon started flooding in and I started getting so many requests that I had to take on an assistant. You have to be prepared to make a few mistakes along the way when you start your own business – you get ahead by trial and error really, but I'm so glad I took the risk as there's nothing I'd rather do now and I haven't looked back.

C

Ted Turnbull

I run a small employment agency in my home town. I'd been working in recruitment for years, won several awards and to be honest I was fairly confident about going into business on my own. I don't regret making the decision to go it alone but boy, it was harder work than I'd imagined! I'd always assumed people who 'work for themselves' had a bit of an easy time of things – you know, getting someone in to manage things while they go off and enjoy a life of leisure. The reality is far from that idea, though now things are ticking along nicely, I am able to leave senior staff in charge if I need to go and do something like look after one of my kids or something. I certainly don't take advantage of my position though – you can't have one rule for employees and one for yourself, and you've got to be prepared to do the dirty work, too.

D

Victoria Michaels

I've started up an accountancy firm in the city. We aren't the biggest but I certainly hope we're one of the best! One of my personal annoyances is when smaller customers are overlooked because they don't bring in as much revenue as larger ones – this is the wrong way to go about things in my opinion. You've got to treat everyone equally, not just because one day they might put more business your way, but because it's the right way to behave towards others. I think the most challenging aspect of setting up your own company is bringing in business. It doesn't just come to you – you've got to get out there and find it. So, it helps if you're good at talking to people. It's been hard work but I don't regret giving up my job at a larger firm because now I've got much more control.

Part 1

You **must** answer this question. Write your answer in **140–190** words in an appropriate style **on a separate answer sheet.**

---

1   In your English class you have been talking about wearing a uniform for school. Now, your English teacher has asked you to write an essay.

Write your essay using **all** the notes and give reasons for your point of view.

All school and college students should wear a uniform.

Notes

Write about:

1. cost
2. style
3. .... (your own idea)

Part 2

Write an answer to **one** of the questions **2–4** in this part. Write your answer in **140–190** words in an appropriate style **on a separate answer sheet**. Put the question number in a box at the top of the answer sheet.

---

2   You have received this email from your English-speaking friend Jo.

> **From:** Jo
> **Subject:** Open day
>
> ---
>
> We're having an 'open day' at college, where students who are thinking of studying English here can come to look around. Our teacher has asked us for ideas to make the college look interesting. Do you think we should display students' work, for example? What should we display? Do you think we should offer refreshments? Can you think of anything else we could do?
>
> Thanks for your help!
> Jo

Write your **email**.

3   You see this announcement on an English-language website.

> **Articles wanted!**
>
> We are looking for articles on places of interest. Have you visited anywhere interesting recently, either in your own country or abroad? If so, why not write an article about the place and send it to us? Include information about what there is to see and do there, and whether you'd recommend the place to other people of your age.
>
> The best articles will be uploaded onto the website next month!

Write your **article**.

4   You see this notice in an English-language magazine.

> **Reviews of useful websites needed!**
>
> Do you know of a website which helps you with an area of study or work? Why not share what you've found with others? Write a review telling us what you find helpful about the site and saying who you think might benefit from using it.
>
> We'll print the best reviews in our magazine!

Write your **review**.

PAPER 3: LISTENING Part 1 (Questions 1–8)

Part 1

🎧 PT.1 You will hear people talking in eight different situations. For questions **1–8**, choose the best answer **(A, B or C)**.

---

1   You hear a young woman talking about her work.
     Why does she want to change her job?
     A   She would like a more competitive salary.
     B   She is in need of a new kind of challenge.
     C   She's been offered a role that interests her.

2   You hear a woman talking about the benefits of musical education.
     How does she feel about it?
     A   grateful she learnt an instrument as a child
     B   uncertain about how valid the scientists' claims are
     C   surprised that her own children enjoy music so much

3   You hear a man talking to his friend about taking his car to be fixed.
     What is he complaining about?
     A   the length of time he waited for the work to be carried out
     B   the unprofessional attitude of the staff at the garage
     C   the amount he had to pay for the repairs that were made

4   You hear two friends talking about different ways of travelling.
     How does the woman suggest her friend should travel?
     A   by car
     B   by plane
     C   by boat

5   You hear two friends talking about a film they have seen.
     What do they agree about?
     A   how disappointing the ending was
     B   how much better than the book the film was
     C   how poor the choice of leading actor was

6   You hear a man talking on the radio about a cinema.
     Why is the cinema going to be pulled down?
     A   It is no longer profitable.
     B   It is in a poor location.
     C   It is unsafe.

7   You hear a woman leaving a phone message.
     Why will she be late for her meeting?
     A   She's had to return home for some documents.
     B   She's had to wait in for an important delivery.
     C   She's had to take a longer route to work.

8   You hear a skydiving instructor talking about his job.
     What does he say about it?
     A   He is constantly amazed by people's reactions to jumping.
     B   He loves seeing the reactions of people who have jumped.
     C   He understands why people change their minds about jumping.

Part 2

🎧 PT.2 You will hear an interview with a man called Bob Sanders, who runs a shelter for horses. For questions **9–18**, complete the sentences with a word or a short phrase.

Penfold Horse Shelter

Bob compares the shelter to a **(9)** .... home for animals.

According to Bob, horses are **(10)** .... and sociable creatures.

Bob is currently looking for more **(11)** .... to look after the animals.

Penfold Sanctuary is looking for young people from the **(12)** .... to take part in its summer programme.

'Buddies' will get the chance to learn to **(13)** .... in addition to looking after the horses.

Participants in the programme will be provided with **(14)** .... without charge.

One successful youngster will be offered the chance to work as what Bob calls a **(15)** .... at the end of the summer.

Bob hopes to employ someone with a **(16)** .... personality to work with the horses.

Applicants to the summer programme need to send in a **(17)** .... explaining their reasons for wishing to join.

Bob will interview applicants by **(18)** ....

Part 3

PT.3 You will hear five short extracts in which people are talking about studying at university. For questions **19–23**, choose from the list **(A–H)** what each speaker says they found particularly useful. Use the letters only once. There are three extra letters which you do not need to use.

A questioning what you hear and read

B meeting people from different backgrounds

Speaker 1   **19**

C becoming responsible for your own learning

Speaker 2   **20**

D managing time effectively

Speaker 3   **21**

E learning to respond positively to feedback

Speaker 4   **22**

F having to deal with complex concepts

Speaker 5   **23**

G making valuable personal contacts

H getting used to presenting ideas to people

Part 4

🎧 PT.4 You will hear a radio interview with a woman called Tessa Hartley, who is the owner of an art gallery. For questions **24–30**, choose the best answer **(A, B or C)**.

24   What led Tessa to choosing 'Galimoto' as the name of her gallery?
   A   It represents the kind of work she displays there.
   B   It refers to a particular process relevant to artwork.
   C   It was something that the children she met suggested.

25   When Tessa saw toys children had made, she was
   A   impressed by the toys' simplicity.
   B   fascinated by the children's ability to recycle.
   C   surprised by how quickly the children produced toys.

26   What did Tessa think when she saw the bicycle a boy had made?
   A   how original the boy's idea was
   B   how tricky it was to make
   C   how attractive the end result was

27   What does Tessa aim to do in her gallery?
   A   reach a worldwide audience
   B   draw attention to individual artists
   C   attract sponsorship for its development

28   Why does Tessa believe visitors will enjoy upcoming events at the gallery?
   A   They will be able to observe certain toys being made.
   B   They will gain practical experience of making toys.
   C   They will be able to display toys they have made themselves.

29   The documentary that Tessa is working on will
   A   include an interview with Tessa about her business.
   B   be shown as part of a series on creativity.
   C   focus on the personal lives of toy-makers.

30   When asked what makes children creative Tessa says she believes that
   A   adults can be to blame for holding back children's creative skills.
   B   adults and children would both benefit from visiting her gallery.
   C   all children are capable of making toys worthy of display.

PAPER 4: SPEAKING Part 1

Part 1 (2 minutes)

The examiner (interlocutor) will introduce him or herself, ask you your names and where you are from. He or she will then ask each of you to speak briefly in turn and to give personal information about yourselves. You can expect a variety of questions, such as:

Likes and dislikes
- Do you prefer staying in or going out? (Why?)
- Do you like music? What sort of music do you listen to?
- Do you prefer listening to recorded music, or going to concerts?
- Tell me about a concert or show you went to or have seen on TV.

Education and work
- Are you studying or working at the moment?
- What are you studying? Do you like it? (Why? / Why not?)
- Do you work on your own or with other people? Do you like it? (Why? / Why not?)
- What would your ideal career be? (Why?)

Free time
- How much free time do you have? Is it enough for you? (Why? / Why not?)
- What do you like to do in your free time?
- Do you have any plans for this weekend? What are they?
- Do you have a hobby or pastime? What do you do?

Holidays and travel
- What kind of holidays do you prefer? Relaxing or exciting? (Why?)
- What kinds of activities do you like to do when you have a holiday?
- Do you take photos on holiday? (Why? / Why not?)
- What would your perfect holiday be?

PAPER 4: SPEAKING Part 2

Part 2 (4 minutes)

You will each be asked to talk for a minute without interruption. You will each be given two different photographs in turn to talk about. After your partner has finished speaking, you will be asked a brief question connected with your partner's photographs.

Interlocutor: In this part of the test, I'm going to give each of you two photographs. I'd like you to talk about your photographs on your own for about a minute, and also to answer a question about your partner's photographs.

(*Candidate A*), it's your turn first. Here are your photographs. They show **people working in different environments.**

I'd like you to compare the photographs, and say **what you think the advantages of working in each environment are.** You have a minute to do this. All right?

Candidate A: .... *(1 minute)*

Interlocutor: Thank you.

Now, (*Candidate B*), which environment would you prefer to work in? (Why?)

Candidate B: .... *(approximately 30 seconds)*

Interlocutor: Thank you.

Now, (*Candidate B*), here are your photographs. They show **people on different kinds of excursions.**

I'd like you to compare the photographs, and say **what you think the people will enjoy about these different excursions.** You have a minute to do this. All right?

Candidate B: .... *(1 minute)*

Interlocutor: Thank you.

(*Candidate A*), **which of these excursions would you prefer to go on? (Why?)**

Candidate A: .... *(approximately 30 seconds)*

Interlocutor: Thank you.

1 | Candidate A

What are the advantages of working in each environment?

2 | Candidate B

What do you think people will enjoy about these different excursions?

Parts 3 and 4 (7 minutes)

Part 3 (4 minutes)

The examiner (interlocutor) will ask you to discuss something together with your partner. You will have a page of prompts (pictures or words) and questions to help you. The examiner will not take part in the conversation.

Imagine that someone wants to open a new hotel for business travellers. Here are some of the features they are thinking of including in the hotel.

First, talk to each other about how useful each feature might be for business travellers.

Then decide which two would attract the most people to the hotel.

Part 4 (4 minutes)

The examiner (interlocutor) will ask you some questions related to the Part 3 task. You should discuss these together with your partner. The examiner will not take part in the conversation, other than to ask you the questions.

These are some examples of the kinds of questions you may be asked:

- Would you like to spend time in a hotel like this? (Why? / Why not?)

- What kind of people travel for business in your country?

- Would you like to/Do you like travelling for business? (Why / Why not?)

- Would you like to work in a hotel? (Why? / Why not?)

- What sort of things might business people complain about in hotels?

- Do you think younger business people might choose a different kind of hotel to older travellers? (Why? / Why not?)

- Some people say that travelling for business is boring. Do you agree? (Why? / Why not?)

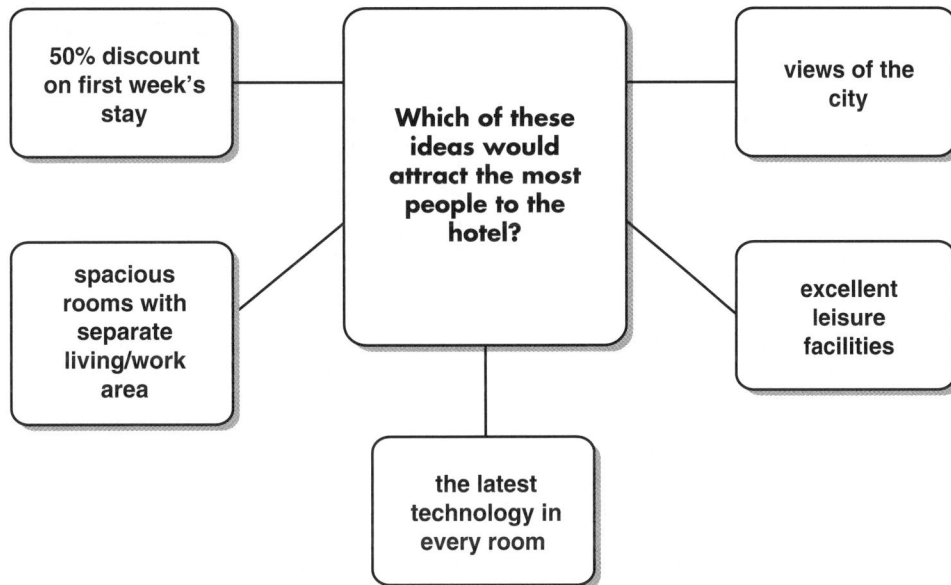

Listening scripts

Unit 1

🎧 1.1 **Listening: friends and family** (page 10)

1 *M = Mark, T = Tony*

M Hi, Tony. How are things?

T Hi, Mark. Everything's fine, thanks. I didn't expect to run into you here.

M No, it's not really my sort of thing. But my wife has read the book and she wanted to see it on the big screen.

T Oh, Sandra's here too. Where is she?

M She's just getting some popcorn. I'm starving.

2 I'm babysitting tonight. I quite like it because I'm an only child, so it's good fun to look after Roger and Tom for an evening. The only problem is that the two brothers are always fighting. My aunt said that if I have any problem with them, then I should call her, and she and my uncle will come back home. But they'll be really angry if they have to come home because their children are misbehaving.

3 I've really fallen out with Liam. We used to be great friends, but one day we were on the beach. He was laughing about something and then he stepped on my sunglasses. They just snapped and they were really expensive. He didn't apologise or anything. He just said it was an accident. We had a big argument then and I haven't spoken to him since. He's always calling me on my mobile, but I don't answer the call.

4 Practically everything is finished now. We've made all the arrangements. Unfortunately, we have to get married in winter. My fiancé, Pete, is in the army and we've found out that the only time we can get married is January. That's what life is: if I were marrying an accountant or something, it would be different. The other problem is that my brother can't come because he's working in a hospital in India at the moment.

5 *C = Clara, G = Gary*

C What's wrong, Gary?

G Oh evening, Clara. I'm locked out! I was running around today because I was so busy and I must have dropped my keys somewhere. So, I've fixed all my work problems, and now I have something else to worry about! It could have been worse. I mean luckily it wasn't my wallet or credit cards or anything like that.

C Well, come and wait in my house.

G OK, thanks.

6 This is a picture of my brother. It's so strange that he's a redhead when all of our relatives are quite dark. I remember when we lived in Japan, everyone used to look at him because of it and they thought it was fascinating. He really stuck out. No one was interested in me or my sister, though.

7 Ian and Eric are really alike and people often think they are twins, which isn't true. I look very different to them because they're actually my stepbrothers. Our father was married twice and so Ian and Eric are the children from his first marriage. At the moment they are at university, so I don't see them very much. But if I pass all my school exams, I might go to the same college as Ian next year.

8 I fell in love with her as soon as I met her. It was at my grandfather's house. We were celebrating his retirement with a barbecue and some drinks. There were about 100 people there. He's a teacher and he invited lots of colleagues from his school, including Rachel. We got talking and later, you know, we started going out. That was how we met.

🎧 1.2 **Speaking** (page 13)

I = Interlocutor, J = Julieta, P = Philippe

I Good morning.

J Good morning.

P Morning.

I Could I have your mark sheets, please?

J Here you are.

P Yes.

I Thank you. My name is Robert Smith and this is my colleague, Sarah Jones. She's just going to be listening to us. So, what's your name?

J Julieta.

I And?

P My name is Philippe.

I Fine. First of all, I'd like to know something about you. Julieta, where are you from?

J I'm from Zaragoza. In Spain.

I And, do you live alone or do you live with your family?

J I live with my parents. In Zaragoza.

I Do you come from a large family or a small family?

J Er ... normal? We are four in my family. I have one older sister, Ana, who has twenty-four years.

I OK. And what about you, Philippe? Where are you from?

P Lille.

I Do you come from a large family or a small family?

P Small. I don't have some brothers and sisters.

I What do your parents do?

P My father is teacher and my mother works as doctor.

I Thank you.

Unit 2

🎧 2.1 **Listening: Do you like your job?** (page 18)

1 I never wanted to work in an office at all. It's all the office politics that I hate. I feel relieved when I get home because I can close the door and forget all the arguments and all the stress. I come here two or three times a day because I need a coffee when I'm at work. I have to have a break from sitting at my desk.

2 When I finally got the letter, I couldn't believe it. The local newspaper had accepted me for their trainee journalist position. I never thought I would get the job. Today was my first day and I was thrilled to be in the office. We print the newspaper on Mondays, and everyone was running around and shouting. I can't wait to see what happens in the rest of the week!

3 W = Woman, M = Man

W I always wanted to work with the team here in Boston and most of the time it's great. I mean we have the flexitime system and that was Chris's idea. He is a good boss sometimes.

M Yeah, he's always talking to everyone, giving encouragement.

W But there's just one problem. He got the job because he's friends with the company owner, but he doesn't really know anything about the business. He never studied it. He hasn't got a diploma. He doesn't have anything!

M I know. It is a problem.

4 So, Stefan Jung came to the office for an interview yesterday. I wanted you to meet him too. He was excellent and I asked Rachel to send a letter to him offering him the job. I know that I should have asked your opinion too, but if I don't offer him the job now, someone else will. I know we agreed to share all our decisions, but this one time I had to work on my own. We're interviewing again next week. Why don't you do those ones?

5

M I like the company and everything, but I want to do something else for a while.

W Me too. I'm thinking of asking Francis for a sabbatical. I saw a project in Nicaragua where you do voluntary work, protecting the forests and the wildlife.

M That would be great for me too. I studied languages and I'd love to improve my Spanish.

W Would you like me to give you the information? I can send you the weblink if you like.

M Could you? That'd be great.

6 There are over a thousand people working here, so we are a large company. People come from all over the world because these are the headquarters, so it was important to make a space that everyone felt comfortable in. We brought in architects and designers from many different countries, and they all had very interesting ideas. They used a lot of glass, so there's a lot of light. The furniture is very modern and it's a very nice place to work. I think everyone says that they are happy to be in our offices.

7 What a day! This morning a major client asked us to change a delivery at the last minute. It was a delivery of plastic toys and we needed to change the contents of the shipment. There was no one else in the office and it was crucial that we made the change today. Anyway, I managed it. I can laugh about it now, but it was very stressful. I'm sure my boss will be delighted too when he comes back next week.

8 People forget that looking for a job is a full-time job itself. You really have to sell yourself and that's not easy for a lot of people. It takes a lot of time to prepare a CV and to write a letter so it doesn't have any mistakes. It's terrible! One mistake can ruin everything. Personally, I can't wait to start work again and do something useful rather than putting bits of paper in the post and waiting for a reply.

2.5 Speaking (page 21)

I = Interlocutor, V = Victoria, B = Bastien

I Now I'd like you to talk about something together for about two minutes. I'd like you to imagine that you are a student at university and you want to do a part-time job while you are studying. Here are some ideas that you are thinking about. First, you have some time to look at the task. Now talk to each other about which is the best summer job for a student.

V OK, Bastien. Which one should we start with?

B The waiter?

V OK. What do you think about it?

B Working as a waiter or waitress is much better than working in an office.

V Do you think so?

B Yes, because you can work at different times. If you work in an office, you work at the same time as classes at university.

V That's true. But the money you get isn't anything like as good as you get in an office.

B Right! OK. So how does the office job compare to the ... the lifeguard?

V Lifeguard. Uhm ... Is it much different from working in an office, or as a waiter?

B Yes. I think so. I think it's boring if you work as a lifeguard. You sit down, you watch people. I don't think I like it.

V I see your point. But for me this lifeguard seems like the best job.

B Why do you think that?

V I like swimming! And lifeguards ... you don't have to think a lot. You can watch the people swim and think about your university subject. That's very good if you have to study and work at the same time.

B That's a good point.

V Which job would you go for? The lifeguard too?

B No. I think the tourist information job is the best one.

V Really? It looks fairly similar to working in an office.

B That's right. But if you work in tourist information, you speak to people from many different countries. You can use your languages. And that's good for me because I am a student and I study French and English.

V I see!

I Thank you.

Unit 3

3.1 Listening: footvolley (page 26)

V = Vera

V So I'm going to talk about the sport of footvolley. So, what is it exactly? Well, footvolley is a combination of volleyball and football. Usually, it's a game played with four players, two on each side. The game is played just like volleyball with one big difference. In footvolley, you're not allowed to touch the ball with your hands. You have to try and kick it back and forwards over the net.

It's quite a difficult game. In footvolley you have to kick the ball over the net, but you're only allowed to kick the ball three times before it goes over. You have to be careful too because if you accidentally touch the ball with any part of your body, that counts as a kick.

Now, there are lots of ways that you can lose points. For example, uhm ... if you touch the ball more than three times, you lose the point. Also, no player can touch the ball two consecutive times. You can also lose points if you kick the ball out of the court or if you don't get it over the net.

Those are the rules. Footvolley is very popular here in Rio because the sport is from my country, Brazil. If you go there, you'll see people playing this on all the beaches. No one is sure exactly which city started footvolley, but it is played all over the country.

Apparently, footvolley started as a warm up for a football game – a chance for the players to get ready before the match. Now it's a sport too!

It's also spreading to other countries. I was recently working in the States, where the sport is becoming very popular. I was training a team over there. There are also footvolley groups starting in many countries including some in Europe. Last month, I was part of a big tournament in Birmingham in the UK.

That was very strange for me because they had to have the tournament indoors. There's no beach in Birmingham! I think footvolley will soon be everywhere.

Personally, I love it and I do everything I can to tell people about the sport. For example, I'm also a photographer and I take lots of pictures of people playing the game. In fact, I had an exhibition in São Paulo last year. That was wonderful for me. Lots of people came to see it so there is a lot of interest in footvolley at the moment.

That makes me optimistic for the future of the sport. Personally, I think that one day footvolley will be in the Olympic Games. Why not? It's a wonderful game that you can play on the beach with your friends. It's competitive, but there's always a good atmosphere and that's what a game should be like.

🎧 3.4 **Speaking** (page 29)

1 *I = Interlocutor, J = Julieta*

I In this part of the test I'm going to give each of you two photographs. I'd like you to talk about your photographs on your own for about a minute. OK? Julieta, here are your photographs. They show people competing in activities. I want you to compare the two photographs and say which activity is the most difficult.

J Sí ... I mean yes. In both photographs we can see people competing. In the first photograph they are playing a board game. This is a big room and lots of people are playing the same game. So the first picture is indoors whereas the second picture is outdoors. OK. And they are riding bicycles, in a race. They look very hot and I think you have to practise a long time to do this ... activity. Although I like chess, I prefer the second activity. Because I like to be outdoors and I like cycling very much. Er ... Also, to play chess you must study a lot at home and practise, and it's not very exciting. If you want to go biking, you can go to ... you can go in the countryside and see different places. That is why I prefer the second picture.

2 *I = Interlocutor, P = Philippe*

I In this part of the test I'm going to give each of you two photographs. I'd like you to talk about your photographs on your own for about a minute. OK? Philippe, here are your photographs. They show people competing in activities. I want you to compare the two photographs and say which activity is the most difficult.

P This is very nice. This is a chess competition and lots of people are playing the game. In the second picture we can see a cycle race on the ... road. Both pictures show people in competitions. In each picture there's a different type of competition. In chess you have to use your brain and in cycling fitness is very important. Er ... I think chess is the most difficult activity. Cycling is hard and difficult, but anyone can ride a bike and it's not important to win. In chess you have to think very hard. I think you need a special brain and many people don't understand ... how to play the game. So cycling looks harder, but I think chess is the most difficult activity.

Unit 4

🎧 4.1 **Listening: special animals** (page 35)

1 We used to go there all the time because it didn't cost very much in those days. We used to watch the tigers in their enclosure. They were my favourites. One of my earliest memories is watching them eat an enormous piece of meat that the keepers had thrown into their cage. I remember watching them and imagining what they would do to their prey. Although I think it's cruel to keep animals in captivity like that, I think it does help people understand that animals are important and we need to protect them.

2 We were stupid really. There'd been a film about turtles on TV and I said to my parents that I really wanted one. So my father went to the exotic pet shop and bought a turtle. We were all really excited. Unfortunately, we hadn't done much research on the animals. As it grew up, it became larger and larger. In the end it was so big that we had nowhere to put it. Turtles need a lot of water to live in, you see. So we had to take it to a special sanctuary and they looked after it after that.

3 When we lived in the countryside, there was this really skinny cat that used to come into our garden. He was a stray. He wasn't tame at all. If anyone went near him, he would run away, terrified. But we loved him anyway and we called him Scraggy, which means 'not healthy' or 'messy'. Anyway, my mother was determined to look after him, and although he never trusted us, he did use to eat the food that we left for him. But he'd only eat the food if no one was nearby.

4 The kingfisher is a beautiful bird. It has bright blue feathers and it looks like it should come from Brazil or somewhere in South America. But they live here in Britain. I've only seen one once in my life and it came as a complete surprise. I was eight years old and I was eating breakfast in my kitchen when I saw this bright blue colour outside ... and there it was! A kingfisher. You don't often see a kingfisher in the wild, so it was a special memory for me.

5 Digger was special for me because although I can hear perfectly well, both of my parents are deaf. They were lucky though because there are charities which provide special dogs, hearing dogs, for the deaf. They teach the dogs to listen for particular noises and they can help deaf people in their everyday lives. My parents had Digger, who was one of these dogs, and he was the first pet that we had when I was growing up. I used to take him for long walks before school and after school, and at the weekends. Yeah. I still miss him today, actually.

🎧 4.5 **Speaking** (page 36)

T = Teacher, J = Julieta

T I'd like you to talk about your photographs for about a minute. OK? Julieta, here are your photographs. They show people interacting with animals. I want you to compare the two photographs and say which experience is the most memorable.

J Well, let me see. In the first photo there's a lion and people are on safari. I think they are on holidays. I don't think these people are scientists. There are too many. They are tourists. OK. The second photo shows two girls, riding a white horse. Maybe the young girl is learning to ride a horse. Yes. Both photos show people who interact with animals and I think you remember both ... experiences. But I think the second one is the most memorable because you remember things very strongly when you are very young. I too learnt to ride a horse when I was six or seven and I remember it very well. Er ... returning to the first picture, I don't think this is so memorable because people have a lot of holidays nowadays and these experiences are not so important, so special, today.

T Thank you.

Unit 5

🎧 5.1 **Listening: a ghostwriter** (page 42)

I = Interviewer, G = George

I George Moore, thank you for coming in to chat with us today.

G It's my pleasure.

I So we're going to talk about your work as a ghostwriter. First of all, what exactly is a ghostwriter?

G The answer to that question very much depends on who you talk with and what genre the ghostwriter is working in. I can only speak for myself. I write 'autobiographies' for singers, celebrities and people like that. Basically, the public wants to know about the lives of famous people and the fans want to know what the stars really think. So it's a big publishing industry. The problem is that the stars themselves are often very busy or often are not very experienced writers. So the publisher asks a ghostwriter to help them write the book.

I What do you mean by 'help'?

G It depends on who I'm working with. Actors in the theatre often write very well and they write most of the book themselves. I just correct things or change the order of chapters, that kind of thing. If the person is, for example, a teenage rock star, I would write every word of the book, and the teen star would just read it and make suggestions afterwards.

I How do you write a biography of a teenager?

G Well, a teen rock star has already lived a life that most people can only dream of, and they have had special experiences that they can talk about. Often people like grandparents and parents save news stories from the local newspaper or have videos of early TV appearances and I can use that too to build up the story.

I But it must be really difficult to write the biography of a teenager?

G Not necessarily. I once wrote the history of the music festivals in the 1960s. That was a lot more work because I needed to speak to a huge amount of people and there was a lot to read. That was much harder. I loved the subject though.

I Now, how do ghostwriters get paid?

G Often you get a fee. So the star would get royalties from the book, maybe 10 per cent of every book sold, but the ghostwriter would get a one-off fee. The problem is that people are not buying the book for the ghostwriter's name, so it's difficult to negotiate more money. Sometimes ghostwriters do get royalties. But I never have.

I For many people this would be a dream job. How did you get into ghostwriting?

G When I was a student, I used to write articles for pop music newspapers. After I graduated, I got a job as a reporter on a music magazine – it's not published any more. The editor of the magazine used to write biographies of bands. One year he had too much work on and he had to give up one of his writing projects. He suggested to the publisher that I do the work instead.

I It's not what you know, it's who you know.

G Always.

I One more question. I've looked at your books and you almost never get your name on the cover. Does it hurt you that you don't get recognition for your work?

G Not really because I am very well paid. You have to remember that there are lots of writers out there who write books and don't get their name on the cover: the writers of dictionaries, encyclopedias, etc.

I The world of publishing is quite a confusing world, isn't it?

G It certainly is.

🎧 5.5 **Speaking** (page 45)

N = Natalya, M = Masa

N So we have to decide on two options to encourage children to read.

M Right, and there are options which appeal to different people.

N Let's go through the options one by one. OK?

M Yes. Er ... comics. This is a good idea because children like comics and picture books.

N But comics are not proper books.

M Kids start reading comics and then they read other books. No?

N Children read comics anyway. Let's move on to the second suggestion and come back to this one.

M Introduce silent reading in school?

N When I was at school, we had silent reading once a week.

M Yes? I think it's very boring. I can't stand reading in the classroom.

N That's true. It's not an obvious choice, is it?

M Something that would appeal to me is to invite famous authors to schools.

N Yes! This is exciting! I remember a famous author coming to us in Russia.

M Uhm ... but maybe it is difficult. It can be difficult to find writers.

N Yes, you're right. Uhm ... A national competition for a book review is a good idea. Children like competitions.

M Maybe. But I think it is good for children who read a lot now. Will children start reading books just for a competition?

N I think this is a good idea. I think we should go for it.

M OK, if you think so. But we have two more possibilities. Give every child a free book. Personally, I think this is difficult because it is expensive for the government.

N Yes, I quite agree.

M And the book exchange? I think this is a good idea. Children don't have a lot of money and so if they exchange books, then they can read many more books.

N Yes, I quite agree. So to sum up, we have chosen the national competition. Er ... and we need one more. I'm weighing up two possibilities: the famous authors and the book exchange.

M Let's try the famous authors. It can be exciting for the children.

N OK. We choose the book review competition and visits by famous authors.

Unit 6

🎧 6.1 **Listening: travel and visits** (page 50)

M = Man, W = Woman

1

M So my plan is that I'll arrive in New York City and then travel by car through Pennsylvania, Maryland, Virginia, right the way down the east coast to Florida. It's a journey that I've always wanted to do.

W That's terrific, Dennis. It sounds really exciting. Can I help you at all?

M Actually, yes. I was wondering if you could put me up for a couple of nights?

W Of course! That's no trouble at all.

2 Well, of course, in the brochure it looked perfect. The hotel was right next to the beach, there was a swimming pool and the rooms looked beautiful. But, when we arrived, things were a little bit different. Don't get me wrong. It was a very high quality hotel and it was nice to be there, but it was nowhere near the beach. Why do they put these things in the brochure if they're not true? It's all quite frustrating.

3 Our Interrail trip around Europe was great fun. The transport ticket was a bit expensive, but that was no problem really. We saw loads of cities and had a great time. There was only one really bad moment. We had to get a train in the morning from Frankfurt to Hamburg and the only train we could get was at 7 a.m. We got there OK, but it was full of commuters and it was packed! We had to stand almost the whole way and it's a long journey. That was the worst thing.

4 That was a marvellous trip to Crete. I knew I had to find something to take back with me. In the end I decided to get a print of one of the pictures at the palace of Knossos. The image is about 3,000 years old. It shows a man leaping over a bull. It's really nice and I've hung it in my living room. Every time I look at it, it reminds me of the fabulous two weeks we spent there.

5
W Come on! You must have the tickets somewhere.
M Er … yes. They're in my bag. Here.
W Look at the queue for check in! I told you we should have got here earlier.
M It's OK. We're here now.
W How long is it before we take off?
M An hour and a half. Don't worry. Everything is on track.
W I just hope I have time to do some shopping. Oh well.

6
M What about this one? It's a package holiday on a coach that travels through the Alps.
W But look, they take you somewhere every day: castles, museums. I want some time to do other things too. A bit of skiing perhaps. Let's just book our own flights and hotels over the Internet.
M I think the package holiday will be cheaper.
W I'd rather make all the decisions and spend more.

7 The thing that I really wanted to do on the trip was to go diving. The weather had been bad for days and the boats weren't going anywhere. Eventually, though, it cleared up and the sea was calm. I'd already paid up and I was all set to go. Unfortunately, I'd cut my foot a week before and it hadn't healed, so I wasn't able to go on the excursion. It was so frustrating!

8 I don't think it's a job for everyone. I take large groups and show them round the historic centre of the city. I do this about three or four times a day. Some people might think that it's quite boring doing the same thing all the time, but I really enjoy it and you get to meet different people all the time. I also get to use my foreign languages and that's important to me too.

6.4 Speaking (page 53)
I = Interlocutor
I Now I'd like you to talk about something together for about two minutes. I'd like you to imagine that you are in charge of organising a one-day school trip for teenagers aged 14 to 15. Here are some of the places that you could go. Talk to each other about what the students could learn by visiting these different places. You now have some time to look at the task. All right? Could you start now, please?
Thank you. Now you have a minute to decide which two places would be most interesting for the students to visit.

6.5 Speaking (page 53)
I = Interlocutor, B = Bastien, V = Victoria
I Now I'd like you to talk about something together for about two minutes. I'd like you to imagine that you are in charge of organising a one-day school trip for teenagers aged 14 to 15. Here are some of the places that you could go. Talk to each other about what the students could learn by visiting these

different places. You now have some time to look at the task. All right? Could you start now, please?
B What do you think, Victoria? What could the students learn at the ancient ruins?
V It depends on the ruins. Sometimes there is not a lot to see.
B It could be very interesting. The teenagers would learn about how people lived in the past.
V Yes, that's true, Bastien. I think it's a good option. It's a better one than the Museum of Modern Art.
B Do you think so?
V I think teenagers wouldn't learn anything in the Museum of Modern Art. They would just look at pictures and photos and things.
B Yes, I see. What do you think about the Car and Motor Vehicle Museum? They would learn all about cars and motorbikes there.
V Absolutely. It would be educational but personally, I'm not really interested in cars.
B That's true for a lot of people. Surely, the most interesting option is the dairy farm. Many students have never seen a cow!
V I agree … but these are teenagers and maybe farming wouldn't interest them. I mean, walking in the mountains is a good idea, isn't it?
B I can't see why the trip to the mountains is a good option.
V The students would learn about nature and their countryside. That's really important.
I Thank you.

6.6 Speaking (page 53)
I = Interlocutor, B = Bastien, V = Victoria
I Thank you. Now you have a minute to decide which two places would be most interesting for the students to visit.
V Hmm … two places. As I say, I think the trip to the mountains would be very educational. Also, teenagers would enjoy it because it's outside and it's an active trip. You, know it's different to school.
B Yes, that's a very good point, Victoria. I think I agree.
V Now we have to choose one more. What do you think, Bastien? You said the farm.
B That's right. I think this will be interesting. Teenagers need to know where their food comes from. Many people have never been to a farm.
V I've never been to one.
B Are you happy with that?
V That sounds good to me. So we think the most interesting school trips are the trip to the mountains and the trip to the farm.
I Thank you. Can I have the booklet please?

Unit 7

7.1 Listening: Yume (page 58)
O = Oliver
O It's now time for Bits and Bytes with me, Oliver Feldmann. Every week I bring you the latest in technology news from around the world. Today, we're travelling to Japan to meet Yume.

Yume is not your typical Japanese girl. For a start, she's made of metal, plastic and wires. Because Yume is an android, a real-life robot. Yes, we're all familiar now with those little robots that people use to clean their homes. Yume is another step entirely. She is designed to look and act human, and that is not an easy thing to achieve, even for the world's best scientists. Maybe that's how they came up with her name. You see, Yume means 'dream' in Japanese.

The project has been something of a dream for Yume's developers, and unfortunately, it's been rather an expensive one. So far, over $250,000 have been spent on the robot, and she is still only a prototype. Although she can talk and respond to people, Yume is not working at 100 per cent yet. For example, she cannot always recognise faces. Mind you, I have that problem myself.

More strangely, the robot cannot completely close her mouth, which gives her a slightly unreal appearance. The scientists on the team have done what they can to disguise this drawback. One trick is to use dark lipstick around the mouth, which helps to hide the problem.

The other strategy is to use clever programming. Sometimes people get angry or frustrated with the machine if it doesn't recognise them or it responds wrongly. The researchers have learnt that people are friendlier to the robots if the robot tells them it makes mistakes. So Yume always warns people that she makes mistakes from time to time. As you might expect, Yume is not the only robot that her developers are working on. Yume's inventor Hiroshi Ishiguro has also invented another robot called Geminoid, which looks like Ishiguro's twin brother.

Geminoid is very similar to Yume, although I don't know if he wears the same colour lipstick. Hiroshi certainly has big plans for his tin twin. Hiroshi wants to put Geminoid in his mother's house. He can't be there in person all the time because he lives a long way away, but he hopes that the robot can help her at home.

This is actually a prime objective of the project. One of the main motivations for the scientists was the need to develop a robot to help elderly people. The elderly could then continue living an independent life in their own homes with a robot like Geminoid to help them. We're still some years away from that, but Hiroshi is optimistic.

Other developers are more pessimistic about innovations in robotics. There are ethical fears that the robots could be used as soldiers to fight wars. Many scientists are fundamentally opposed to this so let's hope that in the future, robots stay friendly like Yume and Geminoid. It would be very sad if all this development work just created killing machines.

🎧 7.4 Speaking (page 61)

1 *P = Philippe, J = Julieta*
P I think this would be very useful for people learning English. I like the idea of a list of classic mistakes. For example, I know that I shouldn't say 'Last year I studied in England during three weeks', and that it's correct to say 'Last year I studied in England for three weeks'. Lots of French speakers make the same error.
J I know what you mean, but I don't think you can have a list for every language. So this helps some people but not everyone.
2 *C = Claudio, E = Eleni*
C I don't know about this. I mean, if you use the Internet, it's easy to find an article in English. And if the article is difficult, you can print it and then look up new words in a dictionary.
E Yes, but this does have some questions as well as the text. They can really help you understand a text.
3 *P = Philippe, J = Julieta*
P That's a good idea. I never get the opportunity to see English as it's used in real life. I would really like to watch this, especially if they have the words – what they say – written down on the website too.
J Yes, I think so too. You need to see the words because British people can speak very fast when they speak together.
4 *E = Eleni, C = Claudio*
E For me, this is the best one. When you are preparing for an exam, it's really useful to see what people write. I think it's the hardest part of the language.

C And we could also highlight useful words and phrases that students can learn. Then they can use these in their own writing.
E Good idea. We'll choose this one, shall we?
5 *P = Philippe, J = Julieta*
P I don't think this is a good idea at all.
J Why not?
P This kind of thing never works. Language is just too difficult for a computer program. You can read books which have been changed into English like this and they are ridiculous! Are you happy if we say no and move on to something else on the list?
J Sure. I think it's a bad idea too.

Unit 8

🎧 8.1 Listening: victims of crime (page 66)

1 We'd been away on holiday and we'd had a lovely time, so we weren't expecting it at all. But I knew as soon as I came through the front door that something was wrong. The house was very cold and the dining room door was open. We never leave that door open when we're out. Anyway, they'd broken in through the back window. They'd taken everything: the rugs, TV, fridge, everything. It was awful.

2 In the movies it's all very open. Someone comes up to you with a knife and they say they want your bag or your wallet or something like that. In fact what happened to me was that I was walking home one night. It was very late because I'd been to a nightclub with some friends and someone hit me very hard on the back of the head. They knocked me unconscious and I woke up in hospital. I never saw them. But the joke was on the thief. I didn't have any money left. I think they stole about five cents.

3 It happens all the time, doesn't it? I'm a big football fan and I drove down to see an away match. In my car I have a sticker which says 'I support Manchester United', which is my team. Anyway, I think a fan from the other team saw this and while we were at the game, they scratched my car with a key and they broke my wing mirror. Some people say it was my fault, but that's rubbish. It's just football and no one has the right to do something like that to my car.

4 I lost money, but I still think the story is pretty funny. I run a toy store and one day I was counting the money in the till and I noticed something was wrong. I sell these game cards which are very popular with the children and I noticed that an entire shelf was empty. Someone had stolen three boxes of the game cards! I can only imagine it was a child because, to be honest, the cards are almost worthless.

5 You have to be so careful. There I was on holiday and I went to a cocktail bar with my boyfriend. We'd had a lovely day and I was treating him because it was his birthday, so I paid for everything with my credit card. Well, imagine, when I got my bank statement that month, I couldn't believe it. Someone had bought over £1,000 of goods with my card. They'd cloned the card or stolen the number or something, and I'm sure they did it in that cocktail bar. I didn't use my card anywhere else.

🎧 8.3 Speaking (page 69)

B = Bastien, N = Natalya, V = Victoria

1
B What do you think about this one, Natalya?
N I don't think it's a good idea. The problem is that you hear these alarms all the time.
V That's right.
N So if you hear one, you don't think, 'Oh no, someone's stealing a car'. You think, 'Oh, there's another alarm. How noisy!'

V I'm completely with you on that.

2

V Where are you on this one, Bastien?

B I think this is a very good idea. We have a lot of problems with speeding in my home town. I think that drivers don't care if they drive very fast.

N Exactly.

B You know, the drivers, they don't really care, so you have to do something else. To er …

V Absolutely. You have to force them to drive with more care.

B Yes. That's it. To force. If the police can give instant fines, drivers will be careful. I'm sure about that.

3

V In my country this is very common.

N Is it, Victoria?

V Sure. Every time you buy with your credit card, they ask to see your identity card. It's normal.

B Right.

V This is not a new idea, but I think it's a good one. If you don't have an identity card, the police don't know who you are, who anyone is.

N I see, but I don't think that they are very useful.

4

B Posters? I don't think this is a very good idea.

N No, this is important. Pickpockets generally work in the same areas, you know, on trains or buses. Local people know that, but tourists don't, so this is a very quick way to tell people to look out.

B I see what you mean, but I really don't agree. Posters won't stop pickpockets. It's just a waste of money.

N That's true, but it is important to say to people, 'Be careful'.

V OK, so do we think this is a good idea or not?

5

N We haven't talked about this one yet, have we?

B No, we haven't. Victoria?

V Hmm … cameras in public places? I don't know if these really work. The problem is that they are everywhere, so people don't think, 'Oh no, there's a camera'.

N I see what you mean.

V And also you can cover your face so nobody sees you.

B Good point. Anyway, the pictures you get from these cameras are often not very clear.

N Maybe. But sometimes they are useful after a crime. The police have caught lots of criminals by using these cameras.

V True.

Unit 9

🎧 9.2 **Listening: favourite dish** (page 75)

1 I've been living in London for a long time now, but I still love going home to Napoli, to Naples, to see my family. It's very special, of course. And because my parents run a pizzeria, I grew up in the kitchen, and I love going back and making a real Margarita pizza in the restaurant. We always eat together too after we've made the pizzas. In some countries people don't eat lunch on Sundays together any more because the traditional family is breaking up, but my family always eat together.

2 Normally, if I have visitors round, I just look in the fridge to see what I can rustle up. But sometimes I do something special. One thing that I always enjoy preparing is trout with boiled potatoes and some fennel. You just slice the fennel and put it in the trout. Then you heat up the oven, and bake it for ten minutes or so, something like that. I suppose what's special for me is not the cooking, but the fact that I often go and catch the trout myself in the river near my house.

3 I'm a vegan, so I don't eat meat, cheese, eggs or anything. I've become a pretty good vegan chef. My favourite is a recipe that a friend of mine gave me for a casserole with tomatoes and three kinds of beans. You need to chop all the vegetables up and put them in a saucepan. I always add extra chilli to spice it up and it's delicious. Even my friends who eat meat think it tastes great.

4 I love to prepare … in my language, it's *tête de veau*. I suppose you say 'cow's head' in English. Perfectly good food, but nowadays butchers don't often sell it. This stuff goes straight in the bin. But people have been eating this for hundreds of years and I think it's important to keep the old traditions up. So, if I have friends round, I sometimes cook this. Admittedly, I do check with everyone beforehand, just to check that they will eat it. Most people say yes.

5 Now that I'm studying in Europe, I can go to Chinese restaurants here. But I have to say that the Chinese food in this country is not the same as the food we eat in my country, especially where I come from, north of Beijing. So I often invite friends to my house to cook real Chinese food for them. Although the food tastes different, they always eat everything up. What I love to prepare most of all is very simple: fried rice. It's easy, it's delicious, and if you use the right rice, it always reminds me of home.

🎧 9.3 **Speaking** (page 77)

I = Interlocutor, M = Masa, N = Natalya

I Imagine that you are looking after a group of children aged five to seven for the day and you have to prepare lunch for them. First you have some time to look at the task. Now, talk to each other. Decide if these are good options for a lunch for a group of children aged five to seven.

M OK, Natalya, where shall we start?

N How about with the salad, Masa? I think this is a good option because it is very healthy with lots of vegetables, tomatoes, lettuce.

M Hmm … In my opinion this is very healthy, but sometimes children don't like to eat salad. If they don't like it, they won't eat it. And then you could have lots of hungry children. That would be terrible! How about the hamburgers and chips?

N Yes but burgers and chips have lots of fatty … no, lots of fat.

M Er … OK.

N Let's turn to the next one. I think this is OK, some ice cream. I mean … if the children eat the salad first, then it's OK to have the ice cream.

M OK. I agree.

N Now, what about to drink?

M Fizzy drinks. Children love them. It'll be like a party.

N I hear what you're saying, but I think this one might cause some problems.

M Oh, why?

N The children are very young. I have a little cousin and when he drinks sodas, he gets very excited …

M Hyperactive.

N He runs around everywhere. This could be a problem if we give them fizzy drinks. I think orange juice is a better idea.

M I see. Are there any options that we haven't talked about yet?

N Yes. This one. The cheese sandwiches. Everyone likes cheese.

M Yes, it's a safe option.

I Thank you. You now have about a minute to say which two options you would choose for the children.

M OK. I think we should choose the burgers and chips. Kids love eating them.

N Masa, do you really think that's a good idea? Burgers and chips are so unhealthy.

M Well, Natalya, what would you suggest?

N I think cheese sandwiches are healthier.

M OK.

N Yes, and I think we should choose a healthy drink too.

M Are you suggesting that we choose this one? The orange juice?

N I think so.

M I would prefer the fizzy drinks ...

N Really? The kids get very hyperactive.

M OK. You're right. So let's choose the cheese sandwiches and the orange juice.

I Thank you.

Unit 10

🎧 10.1 **Listening: spending money** (page 82)

1 At the moment we're saving up to go on holiday. This year we really want to go to Australia and it's difficult taking the kids, because you have to buy five tickets for the flight. That's really expensive. We are staying with my husband's brother, so the accommodation is sorted. The thing is that there are so many other things I want to buy, but I can't because of this.

2 On Saturdays I work at the local pet shop. They don't pay me very much, but I do get a 20 per cent discount on everything in the shop. But I think it would be better if I didn't get the discount because I buy so many things in the shop for my dog and my cat. Some weeks I spend more there than I earn.

3 I don't normally splash out like that. But we'd all finished our exams and we wanted to celebrate in style, so we all went to this really posh restaurant in the centre of town. The food was delicious and it was great fun, but I got through my month's allowance in one night. It was the same for us all. I wish I hadn't done that.

4 We had just moved into a new house, our first home, and so we were having a housewarming party. My wife and I went to the supermarket and we put all this expensive food in the trolley: lobster, champagne, everything. Well, when we got to the check-out, it came to something like £300. So we actually went back around the shop putting things back on the shelves!

5 I saw this beautiful top in a department store and it was perfect for me, so I had to have it. It cost me a lot of money, but for media professionals there's tremendous pressure on women to look good. I don't buy expensive clothes on a whim or because I'm vain or anything. Expensive clothes are an essential purchase.

6 My husband is driving me mad. He'll go to the shops to buy bread and come back with a new set of golf clubs. He's constantly doing things like that and it's impossible! I mean, take the golf clubs: he already had a set in the garage! And another thing, he never discusses anything with me. I'm very careful and I always pay off my credit card at the end of the month. I think very hard before I buy something expensive, but nothing seems to stop him.

7 My parents give me quite a lot of pocket money. In fact if I ask my dad for some money for a comic or something, he usually gives it to me. But actually I don't really buy anything except crisps and sweets. We don't get them at home and I love them, so that's where all my money goes. I'm lucky because I've got loads of uncles and aunts, and they're always buying me toys and games. So I don't have to buy those either.

8 There are so many options and I haven't made my mind up. In my last job everyone paid into a really good pension scheme, but now I have to arrange one for myself and I don't really know what to do. Some people have told me not to pay into a pension scheme and to put my money in the stock market instead, but I don't think that's very sensible.

🎧 10.4 **Speaking** (page 85)

1 What the pictures have in common is that they show customers talking to salesmen. Some people are in the department store and the woman is in a market or a shop. Er ... Both the salesmen seem to be very friendly. In the second picture the girl is asking to try some of the spices. I think she probably saw the shop while she was on holiday and is interested in trying something new.

2 These pictures show very similar situations. One thing that is the same in the pictures is that the customers are really going to buy something. I think that in the first picture that they are going to buy a TV. Maybe they went there to get a special deal. They might want to know if the DVD player is included in the price. In these big shops you always get a guarantee too so that's another reason to shop there.

3 We can see the same thing happening: the customers are asking questions. The girl is asking if she can taste some of the food in the sacks. In the other picture they are asking the salesman some questions about the special features of the TV. In each picture the salesman looks very friendly and that's very good. Maybe they went to each place because they don't know a lot about technology or local ingredients so they want the salespeople to help them.

4 There isn't a big difference here: we can see people thinking about buying something. They are talking to the shop assistant in one picture and a merchant in another one. The pictures show the same sort of thing. The people are shopping there because they are trying to get a good price, I think. With the merchant sometimes you can haggle to get a good price, but sometimes you can get a special deal in department stores too. They look different, but they are very similar really.

Unit 11

🎧 11.1 **Listening: a ghost hunter** (page 90)

D = David

D I was very much an amateur ghost hunter. I never did it professionally or anything like that. What happened was that I was a student of computer science at university in Scotland. One day, when I was on vacation, my neighbour told me about a strange experience that she'd had. Apparently, she'd been staying in a bed and breakfast in the Scottish Highlands. One night when she was getting ready for bed, suddenly the room felt very cold, and all of a sudden the curtains just opened. Then they closed. But there was no one else there.

Well four friends and I decided to investigate this. We stayed at the same place in the same room, and we stayed up all night. Of course, we saw nothing at all.

Nevertheless, I was interested in the story, so I set up a website called *Your Weird Events*. The idea was that people could log on to the site and leave their own ghost stories there. If there were any interesting stories, we would go and investigate them. Unfortunately, we only got messages from foreign countries. And you know, we were students and we couldn't afford to go to any of them. So it all came to nothing really. And to be honest, nowadays, I don't really believe in ghosts anyway.

🎧 11.2 **Speaking** (page 93)

I = Interlocutor, C = Claudio

I In this part of the test I'm going to give each of you two photographs. I'd like you to talk about your photographs for about a minute. OK? Claudio, here are your photographs. They show people performing magic tricks. I want you to compare the two photographs and say which trick is the most entertaining.

C Er ... I'm sorry. Could you repeat the question please?

I Of course. Here are your photographs. They show people performing magic tricks. I want you to compare the two photographs and say which trick is the most entertaining.

🎧 11.3 **Speaking** (page 93)

C = Claudio

C OK. Both photos show magic tricks. In the first one we have a magician and a girl, and she is above the floor. This is called levitation, isn't it? It looks like he is on the stage in a theatre or somewhere like that. Now, in the second picture we have another magician and he's doing a card trick, and everybody looks amazed. The question is which trick is the most entertaining. Well, the first picture certainly looks entertaining, but the thing is that the magician is on stage and the audience just sits and watches. For me it's really boring. I much prefer the second picture. This is a lot more entertaining because the magician is very near and you can see what he is doing. You can try to see the 'trick'. I think that's definitely the better of the two.

Unit 12

🎧 12.1 **Listening: San Francisco earthquake** (page 98)

P = Presenter, D = Denise

P On April 18 1906 San Francisco was devastated by an earthquake that destroyed almost 30,000 buildings and left 3,000 people dead. Denise Wei is here today to talk about the legacy of that event. Denise, what happened after the earthquake hit?

D The problem was that before this earthquake, people didn't know anything about the San Andreas Fault: that's the line along California where earthquakes can take place. It was this earthquake that revealed that the fault existed and so when the earthquake struck, the city of San Francisco wasn't very prepared at all.

P Was the centenary of the event marked in any way? What did people do to remember what happened?

D Lots of things. Firstly, they built a memorial to the earthquake victims and there was an exhibition of what happened. There were some other more unusual events too.

P Such as?

D The artist Liz Hickok made a model of the city out of jello. She lit the sculpture from underneath and even made videos of parts of the city shaking to represent what might happen in an earthquake.

P And can we still see this sculpture?

D Unfortunately, you can't see it any more. They disposed of it after it started to go mouldy. You couldn't even eat it.

P Extraordinary. Now, returning to more serious matters. San Francisco was hit by another earthquake a few years ago, wasn't it?

D That's right. On 17 October 1986 an earthquake measuring 6.9 on the Richter scale hit San Francisco. That's a very large quake and in the end some 63 people lost their lives.

P But 3,000 people died in 1906. Why were the casualties so few in 1986?

D Because people knew the city was in danger from earthquakes, buildings and roads were built to survive an incident like this. Having said that, people were still surprised by how much damage there was. Many roads and bridges collapsed, and they were built to survive. But the main reason why there were so few casualties was the San Francisco Giants baseball team were playing a big match in the baseball World Series and lots of people had left work early to watch the game.

P Thank goodness for that. So two earthquakes have hit San Francisco. Are people worried about the future?

D In a word, yes. People in California talk about the Big One, a huge earthquake that might hit in the future with enormous damage.

P How probable is that?

D Seismologists estimate that in the next 25 years there is a 60 per cent chance of San Francisco being hit by an earthquake greater than 6.7 on the Richter Scale.

P That is terrifying!

🎧 12.4 **Speaking** (page 101)

1 *B = Bastien, V = Victoria*

B Hmm ... this is where you do an event like a marathon, and people pay you some money, like five cents for every kilometre.

V Yeah, that's right.

B Personally, I don't think this is a good idea at all.

V Why not?

B If people want to give money for charity, then they can just give you the money. I'm not interested in a sponsored run.

V I agree. This doesn't work for me. People don't do this in my country.

2

V What about this idea, Bastien? So you ask people to bring their old clothes to a sale, and people buy them. Then all the money goes to charity.

B Really? I don't see the point of doing this. I don't think you would sell a lot of clothes.

V Why is that?

B People don't want to buy old, ... second-hand clothes. They want new clothes. This is not an effective solution to the problem.

3

B How about the T-shirts?

V In this case I don't think this is the best option.

B Why not?

V Well, you need to make the T-shirts. That takes a lot of time. You also have to spend money to make them. If people don't buy the T-shirts, you will lose money! I don't think it's a bad idea, but I think some of the other ones are better.

4

B Does this really work? I'm not sure.

V What's the problem?

B If you do a show like this, you have to hope that people will come. What if nobody comes to the event? That would be a disaster.

V OK, I see your point.

Unit 13

🎧 13.1 **Listening: a journalist** (page 106)

L = Linda

L My name is Linda Bridgestone and I'm a journalist. Funnily enough, when I was little, I didn't want to be a journalist at all. I wanted to be Britain's first female prime minister. But Margaret Thatcher beat me to that. I don't think I would have been a very good leader anyway. But I was always interested in politics and news. And I think when I was 15, I decided I would be a journalist because of that.

It wasn't until I went to university that things started happening for me. At university I was the editor of the college newspaper and I wrote some of the stories too. At the end of my degree, I wrote to my local newspaper and asked them for some work experience. They took me on for six months.

Of course, I got paid nothing. I did it to learn about the job and it was hard work. It was very different after being the boss on the student paper to being the office junior.

I didn't enjoy my first week at all. My first job was typing editorials: my boss dictated them to me and I remember I spelt the town name Sherborne incorrectly. My boss really shouted at me for that mistake, and I wasn't being paid anything! I remember how to spell it now though: S–H–E–R–B–O–R–N–E!

That was just the first week though and afterwards, things got better. For example, the first story I wrote was a showbiz one. There was a famous singer living locally and I went with another reporter to interview her. He asked the questions and I just took notes. But the next day the other reporter didn't come into work because he had to go to hospital to have an emergency operation. So I wrote the story from my notes. I used that story to apply for jobs later on and that was how I got my first paid job on a music magazine.

🎧 13.3 Speaking (page 109)

1 I = *Interlocutor*, J = *Julieta*
I What do you think is the best way of getting news?
J Hmm ... That's an interesting question. I have to say the radio. On TV they don't really have enough time to discuss all the complicated issues. On the radio they have a lot of time to talk and you can hear experts speak.

2 I = *Interlocutor*, P = *Philippe*
I Do you often read newspapers or watch the news on TV?
P I have to think about this one. I read a free newspaper if there's one in the station. And I sometimes watch the news when I'm cooking because we have a TV in the kitchen. But I don't think I'm very interested in the news.

3 I = *Interlocutor*, C = *Claudio*
I Is it important for people to watch the news?
C It really depends. I think if there is a big story, then it's important that the public know what's going on: if there is a weather problem or something like that. But often there isn't really any big news, so it's not necessary to find out what's going on all the time.

4 I = *Interlocutor*, P = *Philippe*
I What are the advantages and disadvantages of getting news over the Internet?
P I've not really thought about this before. Er ... it's a very quick way of getting information, of course, and you can get a lot of different opinions too. I think it's good as long as you use the sites from serious newspapers or news services. Otherwise you don't know who wrote the news that you're reading.

5 I = *Interlocutor*, J = *Julieta*
I Do you like reading about celebrities in newspapers and magazines?
J I absolutely love it. I can't get enough gossip to be honest. I think everyone really likes to read about that sort of thing. I buy two or three gossip magazines each week. I think I'm a bit addicted!

6 I = *Interlocutor*, C = *Claudio*
I What part of the newspaper is most interesting to you?
C Personally it's the crossword. I love doing it in my coffee break when I'm at work. Sometimes I work on it all day and I always have to buy the next day's newspaper to see what answers I didn't get.

Unit 14

🎧 14.1 Listening: clothes and fashion (page 114)

1 We were going on holiday to the Maldives and I bought my husband some shorts. They were dark blue, his favourite colour, and they fitted him perfectly. They weren't too trendy or anything like that, so that was OK too. The thing was there was

a big flower on the back of the shorts and he wouldn't wear them because of that! Ridiculous!

2 S = *Son, F = Father*
S Where's my coat? It's raining.
F Hang on – you can't go looking like that!
S Why, what's wrong? This is my best shirt.
F But you can't wear jeans to a wedding. It looks too scruffy.
S I'm sixteen, not sixty! I can wear what I like.
F Go and change.

3 D = *Daughter, M = Mother*
D I love that dress! Can I have it?
M Oh, but it's so old-fashioned, darling. I bought it thirty years ago. The only place you can wear this is in the theatre.
D No, no it's really retro! That's cool now.
M But you've got a wardrobe full of clothes! Why would you want this?
D You can't get a tie-dye dress like that any more. Please?
M Well, OK. Here you are.

4 I'm so frustrated. I bought this shirt and it doesn't fit. I wanted to try it on, but it was in a market and there wasn't a fitting room. It was a great price and the label said it was my size, so I bought it anyway. And now I find it's far too big for me. Next time I'm going to order online. There's a site which has some really great clothes.

5 W = *Woman*
W1 What about this necklace?
W2 Oh yes! It suits you *perfectly*. I'd get that if I were you.
W1 I don't know. Maybe it's a bit too trendy for me.
W2 I think it's good to have some trendy jewellery. You've got quite a lot of classical rings and bracelets already.
W1 But my new earrings?
W2 I know, but you can wear it with some other earrings. Trust me, the necklace is you. It really complements the colour of your eyes.

6 M = *Mother, S = Son*
M Stop! Don't throw that shirt away!
S But there's a hole in it, and I've had it over a year.
M It's only a small one. I can sew it up and no one will notice.
S That's a lot of trouble and it didn't really cost very much anyway.
M But I like it and stripes look good on you. Come on. Give it to me.
S Oh, all right then.

7 I used to go shopping there a lot, but I don't any more. The funny thing is that when I bought clothes there it was very pricey, but now things cost the same as anywhere else on the high street. The thing is, yes the clothes look very stylish, but they don't last. Look at this shirt. When I bought it, it had a design of a football tournament. I've washed it three times and now the design is really faint. You can't see it. I don't think that's good enough.

8 W = *Woman, M = Man*
W I shouldn't have worn these high heels – they are killing me!
M Next time choose a more comfortable costume, like me.
W I don't think I would look good dressed as a tiger. I feel much better as Marilyn, but the shoes are so uncomfortable. Oh, look at Martin!
M Ooh, that shirt really clashes with those trousers!
W To be fair, the invitation did tell us to dress adventurously!

🎧 14.2 Speaking (page 114)

I = *Interlocutor*, E = *Eleni*, C = *Claudio*
I Do you think young people spend too much money on clothes and fashion?
E I think so, yes. Some of my friends always want to go to the most expensive shops and they spend a lot of money on clothes, but there are cheaper shops. I think it's a bit ridiculous.

C But don't you think that sometimes you have to go to the expensive shops? I think that brand names are very important and clothes with brand names are only sold in department stores and expensive shops.

E But do you really need the brand name? After all, if clothes look good, the name is not important.

C What I mean is that if you want to look good, you need to buy quality clothes, designer clothes, big brands. You have to pay a lot of money for that.

E Yes, but we're speaking about young people. They don't need to spend a lot of money on designer clothes.

C I suppose not. But if your friends have the best clothes, you want them too.

E So their parents have to spend money on these clothes.

C Not necessarily. Many of my friends have jobs, and they study and work. So they can buy their own clothes.

E All the same, I think there are better things to spend your money on when you're young.

C Such as?

E Er … DVDs, music, going out.

C This is the same as buying clothes. When you are young, you spend money on enjoying yourself! Buying clothes is fun.

E I suppose so. But I still think they spend too much money on clothes.

I Thank you.

Unit 15

🎧 15.1 **Listening: works of art** (page 122)

1 When I was living in Cairo, I used to see the statue of the pharaoh Rameses II all the time. It's a wonderful statue and very impressive, and it was one of my favourite things in the city. It shows the pharaoh standing with a large beard and it's made from grey stone. Unfortunately, it's not there any more. The problem was that it was being damaged by pollution from the heavy traffic in the city centre, as well as vibrations from the underground rail network. As a result, it was taken to Giza, which is one of Egypt's major archaeological sites. Basically, the experts think that it will be easier to preserve there.

2 Surprisingly, most of the tourists who come to London don't know it's there. It's ridiculous really because there are very few sculptures by Michelangelo. Actually, there is only one Michelangelo sculpture in the UK and that is a round sculpture of the Madonna and Child, which is in a gallery, the Royal Academy, in London. It's not easy to find even when you're in the museum, however. So you might need to ask someone where it is. I think that it's a wonderful work of art. I often go and look at it when I'm in town.

3 In our local museum at Delphi we have a famous statue of a charioteer, which we call *Iniochos* in Greek. It's about 2,500 years old, made of bronze and it's a wonderfully lifelike portrait. Amazingly, it still has the original glass eyes that bronze statues used to have and it seems to be looking into the distance. Its left arm is broken, which is a pity. Nevertheless, it's a miracle that the sculpture survives at all. Some archaeologists found it buried in Delphi about 100 years ago and it's thought that it's by the great sculptor Pythagoras of Rego.

4 If you go to the north of England, just outside of the city of Gateshead, you can see the Angel of the North. This is a giant statue of a man, as tall as four buses. The man's arms are actually wings, and they are huge: as long as a Boeing 767. I love it and I often drive over there to look at it. Anyway, it's by Antony Gormley, who is one of Britain's most important living artists, and he modelled it on himself – except for the wings of course.

5 It's a lovely picture that my niece did of a landscape, showing some black and white cows in a green field. The sky is very blue and the whole picture is lovely to look at. She's only eight, but I think that this is great. You know, interestingly, Picasso liked children's art. He said, 'At twelve years old I could draw like Raphael, but I needed a whole lifetime to learn to paint like a child.' When I look at this picture, I know exactly what he means.

🎧 15.3 **Speaking** (page 125)

1 *J = Julieta*

J Well, let me see. Here we can see some people in an art gallery. In the foreground a girl is looking at some abstract art, I think it is, and er … in the background a man is looking at some very small pictures. I can't see what they are … photos perhaps? The other picture shows a street festival of some kind. It looks like a procession and the person is dressed in fancy dress. Well, I think intellectual people like art galleries and it is a good place to go if you are a quiet person and you like to think a lot. Regarding the second picture, I think perhaps this is more for party people, people who like to have a good time. But everyone likes going to an art gallery sometimes and I think most people enjoy parties too.

2 *P = Philippe*

P OK. The second photo shows some people in a procession. They are waving signs and maybe there is dancing and noise. They are celebrating something, while in the other photo the people are looking at … art. They are in a gallery or a museum. I don't think these two people know each other, actually. So both photos show people doing something in their free time. I think being in a place like this, a gallery, is quite boring. I wouldn't enjoy it. But going back to the other picture, I think this looks like a lot of fun. There is a large crowd in the background and people are having a good time, so I think it would be good for me too. I like to go out and do things.

Practice Test

🎧 PT.1 **Part 1** (page 140)

1 I've been thinking about changing roles for a while. It isn't like I don't earn enough – I get by. Realistically, the pay's quite competitive. But that's not always enough, is it? The job just doesn't excite me the way it used to. I went to an agency who've found me another job which sounds good: the conditions are decent and the position's similar to the one I have now. The thing is, what if I take that job and I feel the same again six months down the line. You know, the boredom? So I said to myself, it's time to find something completely different. Let's see how it goes!

2 I've just read an article about having a musical education. I regret not taking up the opportunity to play an instrument when I was younger, so I offered my kids the chance as soon as they were old enough and fortunately they took to it. It gives me great pleasure listening to them play – it brings the whole house to life. I've read there are educational benefits to playing a musical instrument, too. Apparently it improves skills in other areas such as literacy. It's difficult to know whether this is the case for my own children – they've always done well educationally. I wonder how they go about researching these things?

3 *M = Man, W = Woman*

M That's the last time I go to that garage to get my car fixed.

F Why, what's wrong?

M Well, it isn't as though the staff aren't approachable or anything, in fact the customer service isn't bad in that respect. It's all the sitting about that gets to me – like I haven't got anywhere else to be. I always dread that part when they hand you the bill, though to be fair, they're amongst the most reasonably-priced of the mechanics around here. Still, I think I'm going to start looking around for somewhere else to go, even so.

F I'll give you the number of the garage I go to if you like.

4 *M = Man, W = Woman*

M We haven't decided how we're travelling on holiday yet.

F Well, every way has its advantages. If you go by car, you can take as much stuff as you can fit in, and you can leave and arrive when you like. Flying would definitely be quicker and cheaper if you were going on your own – with the whole gang it'd work out pretty expensive. There's the ferry, of course – great fun for the children, though at this time of year there could be delays because of the weather. It's hard work sitting at the wheel for so many hours, though that might be the wisest option. You can take it in turns.

5 *M = Man, W = Woman*

F Have you seen the film adaptation of *Silver Light*?

M Yes, I have. The book leaves you hanging at the end, doesn't it – you sort of make up your own ending to the story, don't you? I thought that was one of the cleverer aspects of it. But in the film they've invented an ending.

F It's such a let-down when they do that kind of thing. I mean, if the story's good, why change it?

M I know what you mean, though I thought it worked well in this instance. I was less sure about the choice of lead actor.

F I really like him usually – but someone more mature was needed for this role.

6 Local residents will be sad to hear that the Royal Cinema, which hasn't operated for some years, will be pulled down next month. Of course, the cinema hadn't been making a profit, and young people especially preferred the newer cinema complexes on the edge of town with their wide screens, impressive sound systems and spacious seating areas. It was hoped that the beautiful old building could be converted into an arts centre – where, in addition to other arts activities, films could be shown again. Unfortunately, there are problems with the building's structure and experts say that it has become a threat to safety. It'll be sad to see it go.

7 Hi, it's Sarah. I'm afraid I'm going to be late for the meeting this morning. I'd got all the papers in order last night and left everything in the hall ready to pick up on my way out. I got halfway to work and then suddenly realised they were still sitting where I'd left them. It took me ages to get back for them as the traffic was so heavy. I'll be there as soon as I possibly can, but in the meantime can someone take delivery of the stock that's arriving this morning? I should've been there myself for that but things have gone wrong! Anyway, see you soon.

8 As a skydiving instructor I see many different reactions from people doing a jump. Many are doing it for charity – and they tend to be the more nervous crowd because they wouldn't necessarily have chosen to do it if it hadn't been for a cause. So, I'm always especially reassuring with them. Some of those who are really excited back out at the last minute once they realise how high they are! I get that – nothing surprises me any more. Of course, anyone who completes their jump is thrilled – sometimes I think it's simply the relief of having landed safely. It's a great job and I wouldn't do anything else.

🎧 PT.2 **Part 2** (page 141)

My name's Bob Sanders and I run the Penfold Horse Sanctuary, which is a kind of shelter where we look after horses that were once working animals on farms. I'm here to tell you a bit about what we do but also ask for your help. The horse shelter is kind of like a home for retirement if you like! Some owners are no longer able to keep the animals on after they finish working, mainly through cost, so they bring them to us and we take over the role of looking after them. We usually have around fifty animals at any one time.

Of course, it takes a considerable amount of time and money to look after so many animals. Horses are intelligent and being highly sociable, they form close and special relationships with people. The bond between man and horse can be quite incredible – horses pick up on human emotions and respond to them.

It's a pity we don't have more full-time employees to give them the attention they need, though financially we can't take many more people on at the moment, which is why we're on the lookout for volunteers. This is where I'm hoping you might help out!

We need people all year round, but this summer we want to give young city dwellers the chance to come and learn about our fabulous creatures, with a view to working in animal welfare in the future, or simply to experience life in the countryside. So we're offering a unique summer programme at the shelter.

What we're aiming to do is team up youngsters with horses and ponies who need a bit of care and human company. Each individual 'buddy' as we'll call them, will have their own horse to look after – this will involve not only feeding and brushing the horses, but also taking them out for exercise – with the opportunity to ride for the first time under the watchful eye of qualified instructors based at the shelter. This is exciting for horses and people alike!

I'm aware that the shelter is quite a distance from where many of you live and so we'll put on free transport from several pick-up areas in the region on a daily basis, dropping you back home again at the end of each day. We suggest you bring a picnic for lunch and any snacks you might want, though we can provide drinks for you at a minimum cost. It'll be a long day with an early start but well worth it.

At the end of the summer, we'd like to offer the opportunity for one lucky school- or college-leaver to join us as a carer on a full-time basis. You'll join our team and benefit from learning from our vet, trainer, and so on to give you a comprehensive view of the world of horses.

What kind of person are we looking for? Well, it takes some motivation to get out of bed at six in the morning! Enthusiasm is a key quality, too. Horses are very aware of their surroundings and can 'spook'– become afraid - quite easily so a calm person with a soothing manner is what we're looking for.

So, if I've managed to spark your interest and you'd like to apply for the summer programme, please send me a composition along with your application form – which I'll hand out in a moment – telling us why you'd like to come and join us this year. You don't need any qualifications or experience, so don't let that put you off.

After that, you'll be invited for an interview – it isn't a formal affair, so don't worry about that. It's just to find out a little bit more about you as a person. You'll be sent a letter about this and then we'll talk to you by phone. I'm going to leave it there, but if you have any questions, please ask now, or we can set up a web chat via the website. I look forward to speaking to you.

🎧 PT.3 **Part 3** (page 142)

1 I enjoyed university and made some really great friends who I'm still in touch with. A few of them have gone to live in different countries, so I always have somewhere nice to go on holiday! I studied linguistics, which was far more complicated than I'd expected it to be. Not that that was necessarily a bad thing – I'm a teacher now and the ability I developed to think my way round difficult issues has been pretty valuable. We didn't do many presentations thankfully – would you believe me if I said I was shy? It isn't something you expect a teacher to be, but it doesn't hold me back.

2 I hadn't been the world's most hard-working student at school, though I always did OK. I ended up studying history because I thought it would be straightforward, but we looked at familiar things in a completely new light, which I found hard. University was a totally different experience to school, where the teachers more or less spoon-feed you – you know, they make sure you do your homework and all that kind of thing. At university you've got to develop your own discipline. No one's going to tell you off if you don't complete an essay or assignment, or if you're late – you'll just get a bad mark. You soon learn it isn't worth messing with your future.

3 I had loads of friends and we'd study together, which made the whole thing a bit more bearable. I didn't really like the subject I'd picked, even though it had sounded really interesting, but I was determined to see it through. I'm glad I did because otherwise I wouldn't have got the job I've got now. Having all those friends was actually really useful for networking and I went into business with one of them. She's got skills I don't have, like presentation skills, which come in handy when we're pitching a new idea to a potential investor. Getting a degree was worth all the hard work.

4 I've never minded studying and I went to university because I couldn't think of anything else to do at that point in my life – I knew I wasn't ready to enter the world of work. At school you accept what the teachers tell you is right, so it's a bit weird realising that you're expected to challenge things. It was hard at first – I couldn't see any reason not to believe what I was told, especially if it was a published study or something. I didn't really enjoy getting essays back with criticism, but I suppose thinking for yourself is the only way you're going to improve. I'm still not keen on getting feedback now.

5 I did question the idea of going to university, if I'm honest. It isn't that I wasn't interested in learning more or didn't see the point of the qualifications, I just wanted to get on with life, you know? Anyway, in the end I thought it would probably help me to get a better job, so I went ahead and studied maths – not my favourite subject but I've never struggled with it and enjoy getting my head round complex problems. I found meeting deadlines for assignments hard work as there were so many – it meant I had to get myself organised – useful for my current job as a newspaper editor.

🎧 PT.4 **Part 4** (page 143)

I = Interviewer, T = Tessa

I November is an exciting month for art lovers, with plenty to see, especially in the city's smaller galleries. Today on *Culture Corner*, I'm pleased to welcome gallery owner Tessa Hartley. Tessa, first of all, your gallery has an interesting name: Galimoto. For the benefit of our listeners, that's spelt G–A–L–I–M–O–T–O. Does the name mean anything?

T Yes, it does. It means 'car' in Chichewa – that's a language spoken in south central Africa. But it also refers to a type of toy.

I How come you named your art gallery after a toy?

T Well, some years ago, my husband went to southern Africa on business, and I was lucky enough to be able to go with him. It was my first time in Africa, and we were there for several months. I was fascinated by the kids' creativity there in terms of the toys they made themselves and I spent ages watching and chatting to them. That's when I got the idea of opening a gallery devoted to children's toys back home.

I Tell us about what they were doing.

T Well, they would spend hours making stuff out of the things others throw away: wire, tin cans, bits of rubber, things like that. But you mustn't imagine these toys are simple. They're lovely – made with such care and attention to detail. It was such an amazing experience.

I Can you give us an example of a toy you saw?

T Yeah, I once watched a child making a bicycle using wire. The bicycle had a rider, also made of wire. The child attached a long stick to the toy, and when he pushed the bicycle with the stick, the wheels actually turned. Even more exciting, the pedals went up and down. It isn't like you've never seen a working miniature bicycle before but I thought: these aren't just toys; they're works of art!

I Tell us more about the gallery itself.

T Well, we've now built up a collection of toys made by children from all over the world. You can view them online if you can't get to the actual gallery. We hope to discover wonderful young artists from around the world as well, and sponsor their education so they can go on to become designers, artists, architects, whatever. That's why toys are exhibited with the artist's photo, name, age and a note of where they're from. We think it's very important for people to know who made each object.

I I see that a number of events will be held at the gallery this month. Can you tell us a little about them?

T Well, three young artists whose work is on sale will be talking about the work on display – what materials they used and so on. There will also be daily morning workshops where visitors can have a go at producing toys from things they've found and brought along with them. We're sure these events will be very popular, and many schools have expressed an interest, so we advise people to book in advance.

I What else are you involved with at the moment?

T We're currently in the middle of making a one-hour documentary showing how children around the world make toys. It includes interviews with them: we learn about their daily routines, how they learnt their creative skills and so on. It will be broadcast later this year and I guarantee you'll be glued to the screen. If it goes well, you never know – we might even get to make a series of programmes.

I Tessa, time for one more question. What makes kids so creative?

T Kids everywhere are creative to some degree – though they might not produce work of the quality we display in the gallery, but that doesn't matter. In some cultures we've lost the joy that comes from making things ourselves. Adults ought to focus more on getting their kids outside and developing their imaginations, like previous generations did, rather than filling their rooms with a load of plastic stuff bought from toyshops.

I Tessa, thanks for being with us today.

T Thanks for having me.

Answer key

Unit 1

Reading and Use of English

1 1 C 2 B 3 A 4 C 5 D 6 B
       7 C 8 A 9 D 10 B

2 1 expecting   4 thrilled   7 Practically
       2 dilemma   5 overseas   8 grow up
       3 heritage   6 bullying

Vocabulary

1

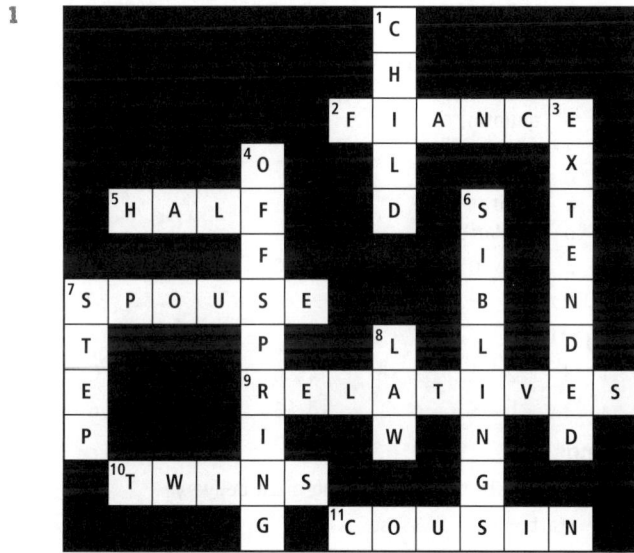

2 1 down   4 after   7 on
       2 out   5 up   8 by
       3 with   6 into   9 back

Grammar

1 1 are growing up   5 Do you usually send
       2 eats   6 she is playing
       3 is changing   7 are getting
       4 speaks

2 1 owns (state verb)
       2 are thinking (dynamic verb)
       3 doesn't believe (state verb)
       4 is having (dynamic verb)
       5 like (state verb)
       6 tastes (state verb)

3 1 She has written five letters.
       2 She has been jogging.
       3 She has been cleaning the house.
       4 She has broken a plate.
       5 She has made a cake.
       6 She has been working on the computer.

Spelling

1 1 periodically   3 logically   5 genetically
       2 Tragically   4 Economically 6 sympathetically

Listening

1 1 C 2 B 3 B 4 A 5 C 6 B
       7 A 8 C

Reading and Use of English

1 1 fitness   4 membership   7 length
       2 professional   5 eventually   8 strength
       3 sponsorship   6 personal

2 1 have   4 is   7 a
       2 at   5 for   8 When
       3 of   6 well

Writing

1 1, 5, 6

2 a 5   b 2   c 4   d 1   e 3

3 Zdeněk forgot to write about his own family life.

Speaking

1 1 Julieta says that she lives with her parents.
       2 Julieta says she comes from a normal family: four people (Julieta, her parents and her sister). Philippe says he comes from a small family. He doesn't have any brothers and sisters.
       3 Philippe's father is a teacher and his mother is a doctor.

2 1 There are four of us in my family.
       2 I have one older sister, Ana, who is 24.
       3 I don't have any brothers and sisters.
       4 My father is a teacher and my mother works as a doctor.

Pronunciation

2 Question 3 has a different pronunciation. The intonation rises at the end of the question because this is a question made without a question word. Questions made with a question word (*who*, *which*, *why*, *when*, etc.) have a falling intonation.

3 1 rises   4 falls   7 falls
       2 falls   5 rises
       3 rises   6 rises

Unit 2

Reading and Use of English

1 1 B 2 A 3 C 4 B 5 D 6 B
2 1 d 2 h 3 g 4 c 5 e 6 f
       7 b 8 a

Vocabulary

1

Crossword (across):

1. QUALITIES
2. REDUNDANT
3. WAGES
4. SALARY
5. OVERTIME
6. FLEXITIME
7. PAYRISE
8. CV
9. SACK
10. RECRUIT
11. RESIGN
12. NOTICE
13. TRAINEE
14. PERKS

2
1 look	4 send	7 take
2 fill	5 write	8 find
3 deal	6 lay	9 turn

3 1 e   2 a   3 c   4 f   5 d   6 b

4 a 1, 6   b 2   c 4, 5   d 3

Grammar

1
1 sunnier	3 most boring	5 further / farther
2 worst	4 more popular	6 bigger

2
1. The harder you work, the **quicker** you get promotion.
2. My new job isn't as interesting **as** my old one.
3. *correct*
4. We're **busier** this year than last year.
5. London is the **most** expensive city in Europe.
6. *correct*

3
1. The new program is a **bit** more complicated than the software we were using before.
2. The new office is as good **as** the old one.
3. I have to do **a** lot more overtime in my new job than in my old one.
4. My job is **far** too easy. I want a job with more responsibility.
5. The job in Berlin pays €30,000 and the one in Madrid pays €29,000. So the money is **almost** the same.
6. My new project is easy. It isn't anything **like** the project that I've just finished. That one was a nightmare!
7. I don't think working as a journalist is **any** more difficult than working as an editor.

Listening

1 1 A   2 B   3 A   4 C   5 A   6 C
     7 B   8 A

Pronunciation

2 underline = stress, *italics* = schwa
org*a*n*is*at*i*on
possessions
int*er*nat*i*onal
inf*or*mat*i*on
qualif*i*cat*i*on
powerful
cert*i*ficate
computer

3 The word in *italics* is pronounced with the schwa in the b sentences.

4
1. the first example of *to*
2. have
3. the second example of *you*
4. a

Reading and Use of English

1
1. a assessment
   b improvement
2. a application
   b communication
3. a successful
   b doubtful
4. a reference
   b existence
5. a ability
   b similarity

2 1 A   2 D   3 A   4 C   5 D   6 A
     7 B   8 D

Writing

1 1 B   2 A   3 B   4 C   5 A   6 C

2 a 2   b 5   c 1   d 3   e 4   f 6

Speaking

1 They forget to talk about doing pizza delivery.

2 1 start   3 so   5 think
     2 it   4 compare   6 for

Unit 3

Reading and Use of English

1 1 G   2 B   3 A   4 F   5 C   6 E

2
1 demanding	5 bulk up	9 sacred
2 talisman	6 stew	10 trace back
3 bout	7 soles	
4 one-sided	8 grip	

Vocabulary

1
1 karate	3 backgammon	5 bowling
2 wrestling	4 golf	

2
1 archery	5 tennis
2 volleyball	6 badminton
3 synchronised swimming	7 tenpin bowling
4 table tennis	8 snowboarding

3
1 trophy	5 let
2 fans	6 lost
3 spectators	7 supporters
4 pitch	

4
1 I like **board** games like chess and backgammon.
2 There's a gym in the city centre where people do boxing.
3 We played tennis on a grass **court**. It was really different to playing on clay.
4 We played golf yesterday and Sarah **beat** me!
5 Gareth Bale used to play **for** Tottenham Hotspur.
6 *correct*
7 We played a game of football at our local stadium, but the **pitch** was terrible.
8 *correct.*

Grammar

1 1 c   2 f   3 b   4 e   5 a   6 d

2 1 Roger **has** to go running at 5 a.m. every morning to train for his triathlon.
2 When we got to the slopes, we discovered that we needn't **have** brought our skis.
3 You **don't** need to be a member of the tennis club to use the courts. Anyone can play here.
4 You **are** supposed to wear special shoes when you play golf.
5 I **didn't** have to buy my own bowling ball but I bought one because I really wanted it.
6 You had **better** start training if you want to run the marathon in July.

3 1 managed to pack
2 wasn't able to come
3 succeeded in developing
4 couldn't drive
5 didn't succeed in making
6 was able to speak

Spelling

1

a	d	e	l	i	g	h	t	f	u	l	l	c
g	k	r	o	d	k	t	l	h	p	w	f	o
o	e	t	e	u	p	m	v	o	a	g	o	l
l	x	w	a	a	w	a	e	p	f	y	r	o
b	w	c	m	o	d	i	w	e	i	j	g	u
e	g	o	n	h	z	f	b	f	b	b	e	r
u	a	i	f	d	v	b	n	l	h	l	f	u
t	t	y	a	o	e	v	e	n	t	f	u	l
i	e	w	s	s	r	r	p	a	n	r	l	x
f	f	p	o	w	e	r	f	u	l	l	l	a
u	u	o	z	r	e	u	j	u	b	y	d	n
l	l	g	r	a	c	e	f	u	l	l	m	r

Listening

1 a 1, 2   b 3, 4, 6, 7   c 10   d 5, 8, 9
2 1 two   6 the States *or* the USA
2 three   7 beach
3 court   8 photographs *or* pictures
4 Brazil   9 the Olympic Games
5 warm up   10 competitive

Pronunciation

1 a 2   b 4   c 1   d 3
4 bending, best, bars, vote, buyer, very

Reading and Use of English

1 1 mustn't go / must not go
2 is good at
3 had better tell
4 aren't supposed to / are not supposed to *or* 're not supposed to
5 don't have to / do not have to
6 keeps beating
7 from time to time
8 spent a long time

2 1 contestants   5 patience
2 intelligence   6 expensive
3 correspondence   7 impressive
4 entrants *or* entries   8 competitive

Writing

1 1 frightening   4 boring   7 exciting
2 relaxed   5 fascinated   8 amazed
3 frustrated   6 interesting

2 Possible answers:
1 Upside-down yoga.
2 Because she had back pain.
3 It's fun. It's active and it's unusual.

Speaking

1 Julieta (candidate 1)

2 1 whereas   4 type
2 Although   5 looks
3 show

Pronunciation

1 /ɑːʒ/: camouflage, collage, espionage, garage (*US English*), massage
/eɪdʒ/: cage, enrage, stage
/ɪdʒ/: cottage, courage, damage, encourage, garage (*UK English*), heritage, image, manage, message, village

Unit 4

Reading and Use of English

1 1 D   2 C   3 A   4 D   5 B   6 B
7 A   8 A   9 D   10 C
2 1 e   2 g   3 a   4 c   5 f   6 j
7 h   8 b   9 d   10 i

Vocabulary

1 1 wild   5 endangered   9 habitat
2 tame   6 pet   10 extinction
3 breed   7 prey
4 instinct   8 train

2 1 of   4 with
2 to   5 in
3 on   6 for

Spelling

1 1 a   2 c   3 b   4 a   5 b   6 c
7 a   8 b   9 a   10 c   11 b   12 c

Grammar

1 1 Mark and Steve **get on well** together. They are great friends.
2 I was so poor that I **lived off rice**. It was all I ate.
3 Some journalists have revealed that big business is destroying wild animal habitats in Africa. I wonder how they **found it out.**

4 *correct*

5 I have some complicated instructions that I want you to **carry out.**

6 You shouldn't **look down on** environmental activists. They are trying to help all of us.

7 *correct*

8 One of the most exciting things about Indonesia is that explorers are **coming across new species** all the time.

2 1 d   2 b   3 f   4 a   5 c   6 e

Reading and Use of English

1 1 C   2 C   3 D   4 A   5 D   6 A
7 B   8 D

Writing

1 1 C   2 A   3 E   4 B   5 D

2 The student mentioned d and h.

Listening

1 1 B   2 E   3 A   4 H   5 D

Pronunciation

1 1 gr<u>ew u</u>p is linked with /w/ and larg<u>er a</u>nd larger is linked with /r/
2 s<u>ee a</u> is linked with /j/

2 1 /r/   3 /w/   5 /j/
2 /w/   4 /j/   6 /r/

3 Sentences 1, 3, and 5 make the linking sound from a letter which is already in one of the words. Sentences 2, 4, and 6 add a linking sound.

4 1 t<u>oo o</u>ld /w/, f<u>or a</u> /r/, tw<u>o-h</u>our /w/
2 th<u>ere a</u>nother /r/, w<u>ay of</u> /j/
3 t<u>ea a</u>nd /j/, Tin<u>a a</u>nd /r/

Reading and Use of English

1 1 terrifying   4 harmless   7 nervous
2 breathe   5 successful   8 attacker
3 imagination   6 mysterious

Speaking

1 a, b, c, d, f, i

Pronunciation

1 1 west   3 rail   5 red
2 rest   4 wail *or* whale   6 wed

2 1 a   2 a   3 b   4 b

Unit 5

Reading and Use of English

1 1 B   2 D   3 D   4 A   5 B   6 C

Vocabulary

1

	1					C					
1	C	L	A	S	S	I	C				
				2	C	H	A	P	T	E	R
3	V	I	L	L	A	I	N				
			4	H	E	R	O	I	N	E	
5	N	A	R	R	A	T	O	R			
				6	F	I	C	T	I	O	N
			7	P	L	O	T				
		8	S	E	R	I	E	S			
	9	S	C	E	N	E	R	Y			

2 1 serial   4 scene   7 novelists
2 novel   5 set   8 playwright
3 episodes   6 location   9 mythology

3 1 mortified   4 furious   7 delighted *or* thrilled
2 ridiculous   5 devastated
3 terrified   6 exhausted

4 1 slurp   5 gasping   9 stared
2 limping   6 sipped   10 sniggers
3 glared   7 strolled   11 staggers
4 giggling   8 sighs

Grammar

1 1 f   2 a   3 e   4 c   5 b   6 d

2 1 it had disappeared
2 the audience were clapping for ten minutes
3 had been writing all night
4 I was working in the garden
5 I was reading a novel
6 it had been stolen

Listening

1 1 C   2 A   3 A   4 C   5 B
6 A   7 B

Pronunciation

2 Words with stress on the third syllable from the end: appearances, appropriate, embarrassment, experienced, mysterious, necessarily, personality, professional, retirement
Exceptions: centimetre, characteristic, disappearance, disappointment, enthusiasm, realistic, sympathetic

3 The stress in the adjectives that end *-ic* is on the penultimate syllable (one from the end).

4 When a word ends in *-ion*, the stress is on the penultimate syllable (one from the end).

Reading and Use of English

1 1 in   4 who   7 whose
2 by   5 had   8 as
3 fact   6 not *or* never

2 1 C   2 C   3 A   4 A   5 B   6 B
7 D   8 A

Writing

1
1. 1 Yes.
   2 No.
   3 No. The story does not include the sentence 'Suddenly we realised that we were lost.'
   4 Yes.
   5 Yes.

2 Possible answer:
The text below shows a possible answer with the text in four suggested paragraphs. The eight misspelt words have been corrected and appear in bold. The text now also includes the sentence 'Suddenly we realised that we were lost'.

> Suddenly we realised that we were lost. I was with my **friend** Martin and we were staying in a **village** in the mountains. We had decided to go walking because it was a sunny day. Unfortunately, the **weather** had changed in the afternoon and it had started to snow.
>
> Suddenly, everything was white. We were worried because we only had some **sandwiches** and a bottle of water. We didn't have a map so we didn't know **which** way to go home. We wanted to phone our youth hostel to ask for help, but we had **forgotten** their phone number. It was a disaster!
>
> We were very **frightened** and we didn't know what to do. Luckily, after ten minutes, we saw a building on the road. There was a farmer outside and he was very surprised to see us. We explained what had **happened** and he agreed to help us.
>
> He was so nice because he gave us some food and then he drove us back to the youth hostel. We were lucky because it was a very dangerous situation.

Speaking

1 They choose to invite famous authors to speak to schools and to have a national competition for the best book review.

2
1 There are options which appeal **to** different people.
2 I **can't** stand reading in the classroom.
3 It's not **an** obvious choice, is it?
4 **Something** that would appeal to me is to invite famous authors to schools.
5 **Personally**, I think this is difficult because it is expensive for the government.
6 Yes, **I quite** agree.

3 1 c 2 b 3 e 4 d 5 a

Unit 6

Reading and Use of English

1 1 B 2 C 3 D 4 A 5 D 6 C
      7 B 8 A 9 A 10 D

2
1 a number of
2 all to yourself
3 The highlight
4 a treat
5 Eventually
6 even so
7 like something out of
8 nothing short of
9 nowhere more so
10 even by its standards

Vocabulary

1
1 package
2 resort
3 sightseeing
4 guidebook
5 trip
6 tourist
7 timetable
8 itinerary
9 souvenirs
10 excursion
11 heritage
12 commuters

2
1 correct
2 What time are you **checking in to** your hotel?
3 We'll **show you around** the old town this afternoon.
4 When we get to Vilnius, we're **meeting up with** some friends.
5 correct
6 We're **setting off** at 5 p.m. That's when we're leaving.
7 We were waiting for Rachel and Robert all afternoon, but they never **turned up**.
8 The match is **kicking off** in five minutes!

3
1 off   4 back
2 up   5 up
3 off   6 back

4
1 phoned … back   4 taking … out
2 drop … you   5 took off
3 travel around

Grammar

1 1 d 2 c 3 f 4 a 5 b 6 e

2
1 due
2 to receive
3 I'll just answer
4 Shall
5 will have gone
6 is driving
7 be flying … be going
8 bound

Spelling

1
2 British English
3 American English
4 American English
5 British English
6 British English
7 American English
8 British English
9 American English
10 British English
11 British English
12 American English

Listening

1 1 B 2 A 3 C 4 B 5 B 6 C
      7 A 8 C

Pronunciation

1
1 /dʒ/   3 /j/   5 /tʃ/
2 /tʃ/   4 /dʒ/   6 /j/

3 church, you'll, gin, yet, general, use, chair, jaw

Reading and Use of English

1
1 what   4 be   7 If
2 from   5 addition   8 Take
3 by   6 have

2
1 would rather go
2 time we bought *or* time to buy
3 had better book
4 could / can always go
5 the first time (that)
6 as soon as I get
7 does it take to fly / does the flight take
8 if we didn't eat

Writing

1
1 You are writing a report for tourists about a city you know.
2 To show free or cheap places to visit, cheap places where you can eat, and cheap ways to travel around the city.
3 A budget traveller (someone who doesn't have a lot of money).

2
1 However
2 all
3 instance
4 Secondly
5 Instead
6 Lastly
7 including
8 necessarily

Speaking

2
1 together
2 imagine
3 could
4 each
5 task
6 right
7 minute

3
1 The ancient ruins
2 The Museum of Modern Art
3 The Car and Motor Vehicle Museum
4 A local dairy farm
5 A trip to the mountains

4
1 It depends **on** the ruins. Sometimes there is not a lot to see.
2 Yes, that's true, Bastien. I think it's **a** good option. It's a better one than the Gallery of Modern Art.
3 I think teenagers wouldn't learn **anything** in the Museum of Modern Art.
4 It would be educational but personally, I'm not really interested **in** cars.
5 I mean, walking in the mountains is a good idea, **isn't** it?
6 I **can't** see why the trip to the mountains is a good option.

5
1 They choose a trip to the mountains and a trip to the dairy farm.
2 The interlocutor asks for the booklet (the paper with the exam questions on it).

Unit 7

Reading and Use of English

1
1 F   2 G   3 A   4 E   5 B   6 D

2
1 barely
2 warriors
3 paced
4 to hold their own
5 signed
6 narrowly
7 void
8 narrowing

Vocabulary

1
1 pioneer
2 experiments
3 setbacks
4 brainwave
5 innovation
6 breakdown
7 invention
8 breakthrough

2
1 into
2 on
3 up
4 into
5 in
6 up

3
1 obsession
2 brainchild
3 tests
4 drawback
5 prototype
6 imagination

4

	1	A	T	T	A	C	H	M	E	N	T	
	2	I	N	B	O	X						
			3	M	O	U	S	E				
			4	W	E	B	C	A	M			
5	S	E	A	R	C	H						
		6	L	I	N	K	S					
		7	S	U	B	J	E	C	T			
8	K	E	Y	B	O	A	R	D				
		9	F	O	L	D	E	R				
				10	W	E	B					
	11	O	N	L	I	N	E					

Grammar

1
1 Oh no! I've forgotten **to tell** Mika about the party!
2 I would like **to see** what the world is like in 100 years' time.
3 *correct*
4 Do you remember **visiting** the Kremlin when we were in Russia?
5 *correct*
6 Sorry, I didn't mean **to stop** you while you were working.
7 This equipment is out of date. It needs **replacing**.
8 I told them to do some work, but they went on **reading** the newspaper.

2
1 in developing
2 to look after
3 to see
4 having
5 to think
6 telling

Spelling

Note that *judgement* can also be spelt as *judgment*.

2   1 environment   2 argument

Listening

1
1. clean their homes
2. dream
3. $250,000 *or* 250,000 dollars
4. faces
5. mouth
6. makes mistakes
7. twin brother *or* twin
8. his mother's house
9. elderly people *or* the elderly
10. soldiers

Pronunciation

1 a 3   b 1   c 2   d 5   e 6   f 4

Reading and Use of English

1
1. technological
2. argument
3. security
4. criticism
5. wider
6. drawing
7. consultant
8. natural

Writing

1 1 e   2 d   3 g   4 a   5 b   6 f
7 c

Reading and Use of English

1
1. didn't remember to buy / did not remember to buy
2. went on playing
3. regret deleting
4. tried to fix
5. stopped using
6. succeeded in solving
7. looking forward to going to
8. needs checking *or* needs to be checked

Speaking

1
Pair 1   e
Pair 2   g
Pair 3   a
Pair 4   d
Pair 5   c

2
1. very useful
2. you mean
3. know about
4. That's a
5. so too
6. this is the best
7. could also
8. at all
9. of thing
10. a bad idea

Unit 8

Reading and Use of English

1 1 A   2 D   3 B   4 C   5 A   6 B
7 A   8 C   9 D   10 B

2
1. numerous
2. an institution
3. forced to
4. the state
5. colossal
6. within
7. run-down
8. bail

Vocabulary

1
1. forgery
2. shoplifting
3. kidnapping
4. arson
5. murder
6. mugging
7. hacking
8. vandalism
9. burglary
10. smuggling

1

Grammar

1
2. This is the hotel where the murderer was caught.
3. The police want to speak to the man whose car was parked outside the bank during the robbery.
4. Three people were working in the jewellery store on Wednesday when several watches and pairs of sunglasses were stolen.
5. The police interviewed five people who had reported the vandalism in the railway station.
6. No one knew the reason why the crime had taken place.
7. These are the keys which/that were stolen last night at 11 p.m.

2
1. *No commas needed.*
2. The police released the man, who then sold his story to the newspapers.
3. My father, who you met last year, is now writing a detective novel.
4. Our head office, which is being decorated at the moment, is on the top floor of this building.
5. *No commas needed.*
6. Leonardo DiCaprio starred in *The Great Gatsby*, which was directed by Baz Luhrmann.

3
1. This is the building **which** was built by Sir Norman Foster. *or* This is the building **that** was built by Sir Norman Foster.
2. That is the man **whose** dog is outside.
3. *correct*
4. *correct*
5. Denise is the woman **who** comes from France. *or* Denise is the woman **that** comes from France.
6. Do you know the name of the man **who** is working here tomorrow? *or* Do you know the name of the man **that** is working here tomorrow?
7. *correct*
8. I think 19th November is the day **when** we are having the party. *or* I think 19th November is the day **on which** we are having the party.

4 1 to   2 on   3 in   4 for

Spelling

1
1. irresponsible
2. immature
3. inaccurate
4. illogical
5. irrelevant
6. immoral
7. irregular
8. improbable
9. inappropriate
10. illiterate
11. imprecise
12. immortal
13. irresistible
14. incapable
15. impolite

Listing

Listening

1
1. the fire brigade, matches
2. a shelf, a store, a till
3. to break, to scratch
4. a bag, to hit, a knife, a wallet
5. a bank statement, to clone, a credit card, the number
6. to break in, the front door, holiday, a window

2   1 H   2 F   3 D   4 C   5 G

Pronunciation

1
	a		b	
1	a	noun	b	verb
2	a	noun	b	verb
3	a	verb	b	noun
4	a	noun	b	verb
5	a	noun	b	verb
6	a	verb	b	noun

2
2. a re<u>jects</u>   b <u>re</u>jects
3. a con<u>duct</u>   b <u>con</u>duct
4. a re<u>cord</u>   b <u>re</u>cord
5. a pro<u>duce</u>   b <u>pro</u>duce
6. a pro<u>ject</u>   b <u>pro</u>ject

Reading and Use of English

1
1	to	4	a	7	of
2	to	5	will	8	is
3	them	6	in		

2   1 B   2 A   3 B   4 C   5 C   6 D
     7 C   8 D

Writing: an article

1   1 g   2 e   3 d   4 f   5 i   6 a
     7 b   8 h   9 c

Speaking

1   Extract 1   a   Extract 2   e
     Extract 3   b   Extract 4   d
     Extract 5   c

2
1. That's right.
2. completely with you
3. Exactly ... Absolutely ... That's it
4. Is it ... Sure ... Right
5. I see
6. I see what ... That's true ... OK
7. Good point ... Maybe ... True

Unit 9

Reading and Use of English

1   1 D   2 B   3 E   4 G   5 C   6 F

2
1. originate from   4 roots
2. a wide range of   5 dominates
3. Originally   6 to domesticate

Vocabulary

1
1. hot, spicy   5 sparkling, still
2. raw, cooked   6 sour, sweet
3. well-done, rare   7 mild, cold
4. bland, salty   8 bitter, tasty

2
1	grate	4	slice	7	chop
2	boil	5	pour	8	bake
3	peel	6	fry		

Pronunciation

1
answer	island	sandwich
calm	knight	sword
castle	knitting	vegetable
chocolate	palm	Wednesday
cupboard	pneumonia	whole
guardian	psychiatrist	yacht
guess	salmon	

Grammar

1
1. used to love   4 are used to
2. can't get used to   5 have got used to
3. used to   6 aren't used to eating

2
1. My father **worked** for the post office for five years.
2. *correct*
3. I **studied** at Bristol University from 2005 to 2009.
4. *correct*
5. Bill Clinton **was** President of the USA for eight years.
6. We **travelled** across Asia from January to June 2013.

3
1. *Not possible to change.*
2. My family would always eat lunch together on a Sunday.
3. We would always go on holiday to the same seaside village.
4. *Not possible to change.*
5. *Not possible to change.*

Spelling

1

p	m	y	n	o	i	s	y	i	c
g	s	t	o	n	y	u	y	t	o
k	g	a	r	l	i	c	k	y	l
w	a	s	h	a	b	c	b	d	k
e	p	t	p	a	s	m	o	k	y
j	i	y	g	i	f	q	n	p	o
z	u	g	h	x	c	k	y	i	r
a	t	i	u	r	r	y	a	i	p
g	t	i	c	y	b	o	j	o	q
o	v	m	s	y	d	n	o	s	y

2   Garlicky. A *k* is added to the word *garlic* before the *-y* ending.

Writing

1
1. general description of the book
2. an interesting fact from historical Italy
3. food in modern Italy
4. my favourite thing in the book
5. who would enjoy it

2
1. In one interesting chapter
2. It is the perfect book for
3. What I liked best about the book
4. is a fascinating history
5. In the past
6. describes how

Listening

1   1 H   2 B   3 A   4 F   5 D

Vocabulary

1   1 e   2 a   3 c   4 b   5 d

2
1. Keep, up   3 breaking up   5 ate, up
2. spice, up   4 chop, up

Reading and Use of English

1
1 take care of
2 got used to driving
3 take his inexperience into account *or* take into account his inexperience
4 put off
5 take her for granted
6 used to spend
7 is Martina getting on
8 we ate

2
1	a *or* this	4	which *or* that	7	for
2	have	5	much	8	so
3	the	6	in		

Speaking

1 1 d 2 b 3 f 4 c 5 a 6 e
2 1 M 2 N 3 N 4 M 5 M 6 M

Unit 10

Reading and Use of English

1 1 B 2 D 3 A 4 D 5 C 6 D
7 A 8 B 9 C 10 A

2
Sabine: on the spot
Dirk: instantly
Amandine: right then and there
Walter: just like that

3 1 c 2 f 3 a 4 b 5 d 6 e

Vocabulary

1

			1	S	P	E	C	I	A	L	
					2	B	U	D	G	E	T
	3	B	R	A	N	D	S				
4	D	I	S	C	O	U	N	T			
					5	L	O	G	O		
			6	W	H	I	M				
				7	D	E	A	L			
		8	B	A	R	G	A	I	N		

2
1	off	4	up	7	back	10	back
2	around	5	to	8	out		
3	by	6	aside	9	into		

Grammar

1
1 I wish I **had studied** harder when I was at university.
2 If I **had** a million euros, I would buy a yacht and sail around the Mediterranean.
3 If it **rains** tomorrow, you'll need to take an umbrella.
4 *correct*
5 If my boss **hadn't left**, I would still be working for the company.
6 *correct*
7 If you **worked** in the shop, you would be able to buy watches, rings and jewellery at half price.

2
1 If the shop still has those nice earrings, I **will** buy them.
2 I would get the DVDs online if I **were** you. They're cheaper.
3 If I **had** known that you can only cook this dessert in a microwave, I wouldn't have bought it.

4 Customers can return products to the store **provided** that they are not damaged in any way.
5 I'll go to the shop as **long** as you do the washing up.
6 **Should** I see Eric, I'll ask him to call you.
7 Don't buy anything **unless** you really want to.

3 1 a 2 b 3 a 4 a 5 b 6 a

Spelling

1 1 h 2 k 3 e 4 m 5 c 6 i
7 b 8 g 9 f 10 d 11 l 12 a
13 j

Listening

1 1 B 2 B 3 A 4 C 5 A 6 A
7 C 8 A

Pronunciation

1 1 e 2 c 3 g 4 f 5 b 6 a
7 d

2 *The stress could be placed in six different places.*
WE don't want to watch the concert tomorrow.
We DON'T want to watch the concert tomorrow.
We don't WANT to watch the concert tomorrow.
We don't want to WATCH the concert tomorrow.
We don't want to watch the CONCERT tomorrow.
We don't want to watch the concert TOMORROW.

Reading and Use of English

1
1 wish I had helped
2 did the bank lend you
3 you mind if I tell / you mind if I told
4 wish I hadn't told / wish I had not told
5 unless you phone
6 if I were you
7 came up with
8 lend you my racket provided

1 1 A 2 D 3 C 4 B 5 D 6 B
7 C 8 C

Writing

1 1 d 2 f 3 a 4 b 5 c 6 e
2
1 Yes.
2 Formal.
3 If stores open every day, it will create more jobs.

Speaking

1/2 Picture 1: department store, a special deal, included in the price, a guarantee, special features, shop assistant
Picture 2: to try, spices, to taste, sacks, merchant, to haggle

3
1 What the pictures have **in common** is that they show customers talking to salesmen.
2 Both the **salesmen** seem to be very friendly.
3 These pictures show very **similar** situations.
4 One thing **that** is the same in the pictures is that the customers are really going to buy something.
5 We can see the same thing **happening**: the customers are asking questions.
6 In **each** picture the salesman looks very friendly.
7 There isn't a big **difference** here: we can see people thinking about buying something.
8 The pictures show **the** same sort of thing.

Unit 11

Reading and Use of English

1 1 D   2 D   3 A   4 C   5 B   6 C

Vocabulary

1
1 dreary   4 facing   7 pale
2 cluttered   5 strong   8 bare
3 terraced   6 cheerful

2
1 run   3 impersonal   5 suburban
2 cared   4 cosy

3
1 up   4 turned   7 out
2 doing   5 picked   8 brighten
3 up   6 let   9 go

Grammar

1
1 must have been   6 must have found
2 can't have been   7 must have run
3 might have made   8 can't have done
4 might have sent   9 must have been
5 must have happened

Note that you can use *couldn't have* instead of *can't have* in sentences 2 and 8.

2
1 You should read his email right away! It **could** be important – we don't know.
2 He **must** have been in a hurry because he ran out of the room.
3 I know she spoke French but she might **not** be from France because we also have students here from Quebec.
4 It may not **have** been the postman. We get a lot of people here delivering junk mail.
5 You **can't** have seen Diana at the station: she's in Lithuania at the moment!
6 He says he's a detective so he must **be** from the police.

3
1 A parcel has arrived for you. It's a **big brown cardboard** box.
2 We saw a **mysterious long pink** light in the sky.
3 Are you going to throw that **horrible old woollen** coat away?
4 I saw these **cool black leather** boots in the shops.
5 Can you pass me that **round green plastic** thing please? It's part of this toy.
6 We have just got a **cute little ginger** kitten.

Spelling

1
1 friend   4 review   7 chief
2 experience   5 perceive   8 inconceivable
3 receipt   6 deceive

2
1 neither   5 foreign   9 species
2 ancient   6 proficient   10 height
3 efficient   7 weird   11 science
4 neighbour   8 protein

Listening

1
1 amateur
2 computer science
3 neighbour
4 bed and breakfast
5 curtains
6 four friends / some friends
7 nothing (at all)
8 Your Weird Events
9 (their own) ghost stories
10 foreign countries

Reading and Use of English

1 1 B   2 A   3 A   4 C   5 B   6 D
7 B   8 C

2
1 neighbourhood   5 addition
2 homely   6 solution
3 environmentally   7 designer
4 rectangular   8 ambitious

Writing

1 You must describe your home and the neighbourhood, and you must also say whether you live in a house or flat.

2
1 hear   5 looks
2 asked   6 mentioned
3 There's   7 welcome
4 As   8 care

Speaking

1 Could you repeat the question please?

2
1 first one   7 the thing is
2 called   8 really
3 like   9 much
4 like that   10 lot more
5 The question   11 the two
6 certainly

3 certainly, really (boring), much (prefer), a lot more, definitely (the better)

Pronunciation

2
1 a Q b C   4 a C b Q
2 a Q b C   5 a Q b C
3 a C b Q   6 a C b Q

Unit 12

Reading and Use of English

1 1 C   2 E   3 A   4 G   5 F   6 D

2 1 c   2 e   3 g   4 a   5 b   6 h
7 f   8 d

Vocabulary

1
2 drought   6 volcanic eruption
3 earthquake   7 famine
4 flood   8 tidal wave
5 tornado

2

3
1 died   4 was killed
2 raised   5 was lost
3 rose   6 disappeared

Grammar

1
1. Despite the rain, we had a really good holiday in Britain.
2. He was wearing a winter coat, even though it was warm and sunny *or* Even though it was warm and sunny, he was wearing a winter coat.
3. Although there was a lot of drizzle, no one was carrying an umbrella.
4. The government says there is no danger of drought. Nevertheless, people are buying every bottle of water in the supermarket.
5. People are suffering from famine throughout the country. However, no help has arrived from the international community.
6. Despite living in Paris, I have never been up the Eiffel Tower.

2

1	a	4	Ø	7	Ø
2	The	5	the	8	the
3	a	6	the		

Spelling

1
- *-os*: radios, videos, studios
- *-oes*: potatoes, tomatoes, heroes
- *-os/-oes*: mangos/mangoes, dominos/dominoes, volcanos/volcanoes

Listening

1
1 B   2 A   3 B   4 C   5 C   6 A
7 B

Pronunciation

1
1. the answer /ði:/, the question /ðə/
2. the end /ði:/, the book /ðə/
3. the orange /ði:/, the banana /ðə/

2

1	/ði:/	3	/ðə/	5	/ði:/
2	/ðə/	4	/ðə/	6	/ðə/

Reading and Use of English

1
1. have
2. without
3. so
4. in
5. that *or* which
6. be
7. would
8. no

2
1 D   2 A   3 D   4 C   5 D   6 B
7 C   8 A

Writing

1

1	this problem	5	their
2	these places	6	even though
3	They	7	Instead
4	In this case	8	it

2
(correct spellings given)
paragraph 2: information, batteries, special
paragraph 3: elderly, heavy
paragraph 4: Finally, available, separated

Speaking

1

Extract 1 e	Extract 3 a
Extract 2 c	Extract 4 b

2
1. I don't think this is a good idea **at** all.
2. This doesn't work **for** me.
3. I don't see the point **of doing** this.
4. This is not **an** effective solution to the problem.
5. In this **case** I don't think this is the best option.
6. I don't think it's a bad idea, but I think some of the other **ones** are better.
7. Does this really work? I**'m not** sure.
8. **What** if nobody comes to the event?

Unit 13

Reading and Use of English

1
1 B   2 B   3 A   4 D   5 C   6 D

Vocabulary

1

			1 N	E	W	S		
		2 S	C	I	E	N	C	E
3 E	D	I	T	O	R	I	A	L
			4 S	P	O	R	T	
	5 H	E	A	L	T	H		
	6 B	U	S	I	N	E	S	S
7 C	R	O	S	S	W	O	R	D

2

1	obituary	4	politics	7	horoscopes
2	personal	5	listings		
3	classified	6	showbiz		

3

1	going	4	ahead	7	up
2	broke	5	up	8	leak
3	out	6	out		

Grammar

1
2. Rich said that he hadn't seen Tina.
3. Maria asked if I was going to buy a newspaper. *or* Maria asked if we were going to buy a newspaper.
4. The school teacher said that it would be a nice day tomorrow.
5. The policeman said that no one could go in the building.
6. Katy asked if Simon had heard the news.
7. Joe said that they had been asking him questions.

2
1. When we left, our parents warned **us** not to speak to people who seem too friendly.
2. Gemma advised me **to** compare prices on the Internet.
3. His sister reminded **him** to post the letter.
4. He didn't apologise **for** arriving late.
5. When the teacher spoke to Jim and me, he suggested **we** do an exam preparation course.
6. They criticised the people **who** didn't do the work.
7. I recommended **he** ask for some help from our teacher.

Spelling

1
1 a   2 a   3 b   4 b   5 b   6 a
7 a   8 b   9 a   10 a

2
- *-able*: advisable, believable, notable
- *-eable*: changeable, knowledgeable, manageable

Listening

1
1. prime minister
2. politics and news
3. college newspaper
4. nothing
5. office junior
6. editorials
7. the town name
8. a (famous) singer
9. hospital
10. a music magazine

Pronunciation

1
1 b	2 b	3 b	4 a	5 b	6 a
7 b	8 a	9 b	10 a	11 b	12 a

Reading and Use of English

1
1. by
2. as
3. own
4. more
5. of
6. to
7. who
8. which

2
1 B	2 A	3 C	4 A	5 C	6 A
7 D	8 B				

Writing

1
1. I think that's Gary's **wife's** car.
2. Eight **students'** answers were right.
3. Tina's **brothers** go to the same school as me.
4. *correct*
5. I couldn't find **Charles'/ Charles's** phone anywhere.
6. We were surprised by **people's** response to the questionnaire.
7. *correct*
8. **Everybody's** answer is wrong.

2 The text below shows a possible answer with the text in five suggested paragraphs. The six apostrophes have been corrected and appear in bold.

> ### Sports in Zagreb
>
> Zagreb**'s** sports facilities are the best in Croatia. There are plenty of opportunities for playing sports all over the city.
>
> One of the most popular facilities is the Mladost Sports Park. This contains two of the country**'s** largest swimming pools. The park is enormous and there are also clay courts for tennis. It is popular for with anyone because you can buy a visitor**'s** ticket to use in any part of the park.
>
> For people who like winter sports, there is the Sljeme ski resort. This is incredibly popular because it is only a twenty-minute drive from the city centre. The resort**'s** pistes are enormous and several thousand people can ski there at the same time. There are also children**'s** slopes and areas for beginners.
>
> When the weather is hotter, many people like to go to the Jarun Sports Centre. The lakes at the centre are a great place to go sailing. It is also a lovely place to go running and cycling, because there are no cars and there are lots of green spaces.
>
> Zagreb is a sports city and you can play almost any sport here. The probably explains our national teams**'s** success in several sports like football, handball and basketball.

Speaking: topic discussion

1 1 f 2 b 3 a 4 e 5 d 6 c

3
a. It really depends.
b. I have to think about this one.
c. Personally
d. I absolutely love it.
e. I've not really thought about this before.
f. That's an interesting question.

Unit 14

Reading and Use of English

1 1 B 2 A 3 D 4 C 5 C 6 A

Vocabulary

1

		1	F	A	D	E			
			2 C	R	A	Z	E		
			3 C	O	O	L			
	4 T	R	E	N	D	Y			
	5 F	A	D	S					
	6 C	L	A	S	H				
7 R	E	T	R	O					
8 F	L	A	I	R					
	9 S	T	Y	L	I	S	H		

2
1. wardrobe
2. classic
3. designer
4. into
5. logos
6. brand
7. comeback
8. scruffy
9. suit

3
1. put
2. turn
3. try
4. do
5. take
6. let
7. dress
8. take

Grammar

1
1. had their heads shaved
2. had her windows cleaned
3. has her shopping delivered
4. are having the walls painted *or* are going to have the walls painted
5. had it repaired
6. is having his eyes tested

2
1. The city **was destroyed** by a volcanic eruption.
2. I couldn't believe that he was being **questioned** by the police.
3. *correct*
4. Many synthetic fibres, like nylon and polyester, are **used** in clothes manufacture.
5. *The Name of the Rose* was written **by** Umberto Eco.
6. The window had been opened **with** a screwdriver.
7. The washing machine **has ruined** my new shirt!

3
1. made
2. allowed
3. let
4. made
5. allow
6. let
7. made
8. make
9. allowed
10. allow

Listening

1
1 C	2 C	3 B	4 A	5 C	6 A
7 B	8 A				

Speaking

1 They disagree because Claudio thinks it is not a problem to spend too much money on clothes because you need to buy brand names to get good quality. Eleni thinks that there are better things to spend money on when you are young.

2
1	don't you think		5	suppose not
2	After all		6	the same
3	I mean is		7	suppose
4	but we're			

3 b

Reading and Use of English

1
1 made him wear
2 let me leave
3 allow us to wear
4 need to be watered *or* need watering
5 has to be given *or* must be given
6 am having mine repaired *or* am having my car repaired
7 has his house cleaned
8 were being designed by

2
	a		b
1	hunger		anger
2	fashionable		miserable
3	trendy		handy
4	width		depth
5	exploitation		imagination

Writing

1
1 horror
2 science fiction

2 Appearance: fashionable, young, ugly, plump, beautiful
Personality: wordly, cruel, fun, lively, determined

3
2 wrinkles
3 skinny
4 lively *or* sociable
5 freckles
6 messy
7 dyed
8 determined

Pronunciation

1 1 c 2 b 3 b 4 a 5 c

Unit 15

Reading and Use of English

1 1 D 2 A 3 C 4 F 5 B 6 G
2 1 g 2 d 3 a 4 f 5 b 6 h
       7 e 8 c

Vocabulary

1

```
C E R E M O N Y
U       E
S       M
T     P O R T R A I T
O   F   R             M
M   E   I         S   U
    S   A   L A N D S C A P E
    T           I   T   U
    I           T   U   M
    V           E   E
    A
G A L L E R I E S
```

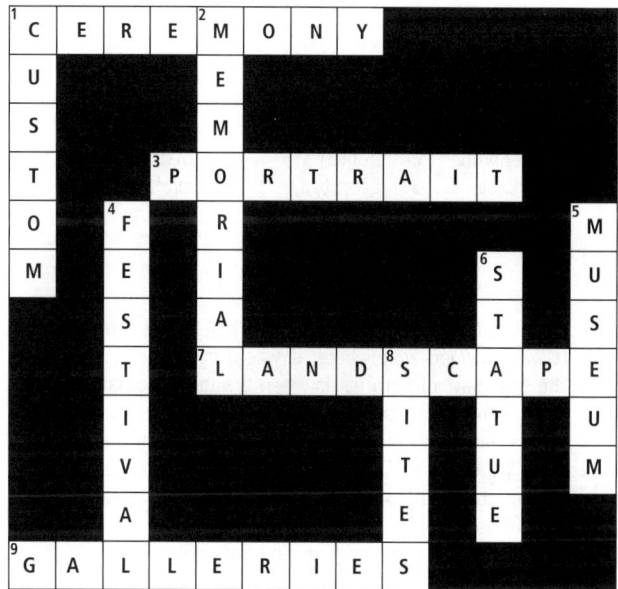

2
1	priceless	4	invaluable	7	heritage	10	infamous
2	worthless	5	heirloom	8	exhibition		
3	historical	6	Ancient	9	notorious		

3
1	out	4	up	7	through	10	down
2	off	5	out	8	off		
3	after	6	out	9	in		

Grammar

1
1	such	4	such	7	enough
2	too	5	so	8	so
3	enough	6	too		

2 1 e 2 a 3 d 4 f 5 b 6 c

Listening

1 1 D 2 H 3 A 4 F 5 C

Pronunciation

1
1	Unfortunately		6	Amazingly
2	Basically		7	Nevertheless
3	Surprisingly		8	Anyway
4	Actually		9	interestingly
5	however			

2 They pause after the sentence adverb in sentences 1, 2, 3, 4, 6, 7 and 8. They pause before the sentence adverb in sentence 5. They pause both before and after the sentence adverb in sentence 9.

3
2 He didn't tell anyone the bad news, | surprisingly.
3 They did not ask the cost of the painting, | however, | because they weren't interested in buying it.
4 This is a very dangerous expedition. Nevertheless, | I want to be involved in it.
5 Basically, | they weren't really interested in art.
6 Actually, | I have a degree in History of Art.

Reading and Use of English

1
1. don't mind if / do not mind if
2. make up your mind / make your mind up
3. you mind working
4. took me in
5. going through
6. take part in

2
1 relationship	4 unlikely	7 historical
2 remarkable	5 recently	8 explanation
3 infamous	6 building	

Writing

1
1. 1 b   2 e   3 c   4 f   5 a   6 d

2
1. We all put on fancy **dress**: I was dressed as a pirate.
2. **It** was crowded everywhere: it was difficult to move.
3. The best part of Carnival is when a huge **procession** walks though the main street of the city.
4. Several people have been invited **to** our party tomorrow.
5. It's a **tradition** in Carnival that women can cut off men's ties. *or* It's **traditional** in Carnival that women can cut off men's ties.
6. The whole city **goes** crazy during Carnival.

Speaking

1   Student 1 c   Student 2 a

2
1 let	4 while
2 foreground, background	5 both
3 Regarding	6 going

Practice Test

PAPER 1: READING AND USE OF ENGLISH

Part 1
1 C   2 D   3 A   4 D   5 B   6 A
7 B   8 C

Part 2
9	a	13	more
10	because	14	where
11	to	15	have/need/ought
12	than	16	your

Part 3
17	musician	21	ability
18	wealthy	22	deafness
19	independent	23	historical
20	loss	24	(in)valuable

Part 4
(|| *shows where the answer is split into two parts for marking purposes*)
25 delivered the package || on/in **time**
26 was interviewed || **by** the detective
27 (that) he || didn't/did not **need**
28 are || **hardly** any
29 **must** be || turned/switched off
30 **unless** it || starts to rain/starts raining

Part 5
31 C   32 A   33 B   34 D   35 B   36 A

Part 6
37 B   38 D   39 A   40 G   41 F   42 C

Part 7
43 B   44 D   45 C   46 A   47 C   48 B
49 D   50 A   51 B   52 C

PAPER 2: WRITING

Sample answers

Part 1

1

Should all school and college students wear a uniform? It's certainly an interesting question. In my opinion, there are more advantages to wearing a uniform than disadvantages. Although people have to pay to buy the uniform, this is usually cheaper than buying many different outfits, despite needing several shirts and a sports kit, for example.

Regarding style, I don't think uniforms are particularly stylish, but they do make students look smart. Some students try to bend the rules and be creative with their uniforms to make them trendier, though I don't think this is necessarily a negative thing.

Another reason why uniforms are a positive choice for a school or college is that everyone looks the same when they're wearing them. This means that no one needs to worry about whether they have the latest gear, or feel left out if they are unable to afford the coolest brands.

In conclusion, I believe that uniforms are a positive thing and should be worn in schools and colleges.

Part 2

2

Hi Jo!

Thanks for your email. An open day sounds like a really good idea. It will give potential students an idea of what it's like to study at the college.

I think the idea of displaying students' work is great. It means visitors will be able to see the kind of work you do, and that will help them to decide whether they want to take the course. I think it would be good to display creative writing if you've done something like that because it will be interesting for people to read.

I'm sure visitors would enjoy some refreshments. Why don't some of the current students serve them and then visitors can chat to them and ask questions about the college?

Let me know how the open day goes. I might suggest the idea to my own teachers.

Good luck!

Kim

3

Lawton Castle

I live in a town called Lawton, which has a spectacular castle for such a small place. That's what makes it so interesting to visit. It is set high on a hill overlooking the town and it is a major tourist attraction in the region.

You can take a guided tour of the castle. People sometimes avoid doing things like this because they think it's boring, but this tour is a really special one. You find out a lot about the history of the castle and the town, but you also get to look inside a courtroom! Many people don't realise that the castle holds a restored courtroom and also cells where prisoners were held during their trial.

There's also an art gallery, a museum and a café at the castle and they hold events during the year to celebrate special occasions, such as a fireworks display for the summer festival.

Visiting Lawton Castle is a great day out for the whole family, and I'd definitely recommend it to people of all ages. It's open all year round and there are some great views from the tower!

4

Review of *Add it!* Maths website

Add it! is a website which helps students to understand maths better. It's especially useful for me because maths is one of my weaker subjects at school.

The website's really user-friendly. You can find what you're looking for straight away, which saves a lot of time and frustration. There are some excellent explanations of different maths topics and everything's really clear and easy to read. It has some extremely good animations, too, which help to get the message across.

There are plenty of practice questions for you to do on each theme, and you can submit them so that they will be marked. The really great thing about this is that they're marked by actual teachers, so you get feedback on what you've done wrong.

I think anyone studying maths at any level will find the site useful because it covers so many areas of the subject.

PAPER 3: LISTENING

Part 1

1	B	2	B	3	A	4	A	5	C	6	C
7	A	8	C								

Part 2

9	retirement	14	transport
10	intelligent	15	carer
11	volunteers	16	calm
12	city	17	composition
13	ride	18	phone

Part 3

19	F	20	C	21	G	22	A	23	D

Part 4

24	A	25	B	26	C	27	B	28	B	29	C
30	A										

Notes